THE ECONOMICS OF LIFE

THE ECONOMICS OF LIFE

*From Baseball to Affirmative Action to Immigration,
How Real-World Issues Affect Our Everyday Life*

GARY S. BECKER

GUITY NASHAT BECKER

McGraw-Hill

New York   San Francisco   Washington, D.C.   Auckland   Bogotá
Caracas   Lisbon   London   Madrid   Mexico City   Milan
Montreal   New Delhi   San Juan   Singapore
Sydney   Tokyo   Toronto

Library of Congress Cataloging-in-Publication Data

Becker, Gary Stanley.
  The economics of life / Gary S. Becker, Guity Nashat Becker.
      p.   cm.
  Includes index.
  ISBN 0-07-005943-8
  1. Economic history—1990— 2. Social history—1970— I. Nashat,
Guity.   II. Title.
HC59.15.B44   1996
306.3—dc20   96-24445
                                                                CIP

McGraw-Hill

A Division of The McGraw-Hill Companies

1 2 3 4 5 6 7 8 9 0   BKP/BKP   9 0 1 0 9 8 7 6

ISBN 0-07-005943-8

The sponsoring editor for this book was Susan Barry, the editing supervisor was Patricia V. Amoroso, and the production supervisor was Suzanne Rapcavage. It was set in Cochin by Terry Leaden of McGraw-Hill's Professional Book Group composition unit.

Printed and bound by Quebecor/Book Press

The articles in this book were all previously published in *Business Week* between 1985 and 1996.

This publication is designed to provide accurate and authoritative information in regard to the subject matter covered. It is sold with the understanding that the publisher is not engaged in rendering legal, accounting, or other professional service. If legal advice or other expert assistance is required, the services of a competent professional person should be sought.

> —*From a declaration of principles jointly adopted by a committee*
> *of the American Bar Association and a committee of publishers.*

This book is printed on recycled, acid-free paper containing a minimum of 50% recycled, de-inked fiber.

To the memories of Marvin Becker and Amir Nashat,
wonderful brothers who were taken much too early.

CONTENTS

PART 14.   ECONOMISTS   305

ACKNOWLEDGMENTS

Once again, Myrna Hieke did a fine job of helping in many ways to get the manuscript ready for the publishers. Jamie Johnson prepared the index and provided other assistance. Our good friend, Richard Stern, gave us excellent suggestions for changes in the introductory essay.

We received fine cooperation and assistance from McGraw-Hill, especially from Susan Barry, Pattie Amoroso, and Danielle Munley.

THE ECONOMICS OF LIFE

PART 1

From the Ivory Tower to Columnist

How It All Started

Long acknowledged as a leading academic, Gary's career took a decidedly different path when he began his new calling as a "journalist" more than 10 years ago. Gary received a phone call from Seymour Zucker, an editor for *Business Week*, early in 1985 to inquire whether he was interested in writing regularly for that magazine. We were very surprised by the invitation because he had never before written a single word for newspapers or other mass circulation periodicals. His books and articles were full of mathematical jargon and were directed to a professional audience.

The *Business Week* proposal was for Gary to write a column every four weeks, rotating with three other writers who had already agreed: Alan Blinder, Robert Kuttner, and Paul Craig Roberts. Kuttner and Roberts were considered on the political left and right, respectively, while Blinder and Gary were supposedly more academic and centrist, with Blinder left-of-center and Gary right-of-center.

Gary's instinct was to decline the invitation, even though he knew many economists would jump at the opportunity. He felt that writing for a popular audience would take a lot of time, especially given his inexperience, and that he would be diverted from a considerable research program he was involved in.

At that time almost everyone who wrote regularly about economics for newspapers and magazines was interested in macroeconomic issues: whether business activity would continue to improve or would worsen into a recession, how unemployment and interest rates would evolve during the next few months, and similar questions. These were not Gary's professional interests, partly because he believed economics contributed little to forecasting short-term changes in economic activity (see the discussion in Part 14).

These doubts fed the most powerful reason for Gary's reluctance: fear that he

1

would fail. What made the possibility of failure greater was that the columns had to cover a single *Business Week* page, no more and no less. Many fine writers have noted that it is much harder to write short than long. Blaise Pascal in 1656 apologized that "I have made this letter longer than usual because I lack the time to make it short." And academics are among the worst at abusing space—George Stigler once said that it takes a typical professor five pages just to clear his throat! Having come to maturity in this academic tradition, Gary did not believe that he could express himself clearly in the 800-odd words allotted to each column.

Gary consulted three mentors and friends: Milton Friedman, Ted Schultz, and George Stigler—all Nobel prize winners in economics. He had expected Friedman to be encouraging since for many years Friedman had written a remarkably successful column for *Newsweek*. However, Gary was surprised that both Stigler, one of his close friends, and Schultz believed he should accept, although George cautioned that he might run out of good topics after two or three years.

Of course, Gary also consulted his wife Guity—an associate professor of history at the University of Illinois at Chicago—and she had the greatest influence on his decision. She believed the columns would provide an excellent vehicle for influencing government policy as well as for communicating his ideas to a much wider audience. And to ease Gary's fears, Guity promised that she would read drafts of the columns and offer suggestions to help make them more effective.

Guity has in fact read several drafts of every column, and she has been his severest critic. She has also proposed many topics, especially those dealing with contemporary issues of public policy. She has earned her co-authorship of this book. Although the columns were published under Gary's name, they would likely not have been written without Guity's encouragement, criticism, and suggestions, and the results would have been vastly inferior.

In May of 1985 Gary accepted Zucker's offer on a trial basis. Zucker indicated that *Business Week* also looked upon this as an experiment that might fail. The editor, Stephen Shepard, sent a contract that could be cancelled by either side on one month's notice. This was a wake-up call to the real world, very different from the sheltered indefinite academic tenure that protects university professors.

THE FIRST STEPS

Gary and Guity came to their interest in public policy through different routes. Gary's desire to "do something for society" was the reason he chose to major in economics as well as mathematics when an undergraduate at Princeton. The interest in economics developed at Princeton, and after graduating he went to the University of Chicago for graduate studies under the guidance of Milton Friedman and other eminent economists who were teaching there.

Chicago economists were doing the most innovative research anywhere by applying basic economic theory to important contemporary problems. As a young graduate student Gary absorbed this atmosphere, and he came to believe that economics could unlock the mysteries of economic and social life. His doctoral dissertation dealt with discrimination against Blacks and other minorities, a subject that economists had neglected. After publishing a book based on this dissertation, Gary continued to work on questions that extended the frontiers of economics, including investments in education and other forms of human capital, behavior of families, determinants of crime, and competition for political power among special interest groups.

This work was not well received by most economists, who believed these subjects should be left to specialists in sociology, political science, and other fields. Controversy over his work followed Gary throughout his career, and was not put to rest until he received the Nobel prize in economics in 1992. The Nobel Committee cited his work on discrimination, human capital, and crime, but even they said that his research on the family continued to be "controversial."

Gary could weather the many years of sometimes very nasty attack because of the support and encouragement from Guity, and from his colleagues—first at Columbia and then at Chicago. The Chicago connection was especially important since so many economists there were doing original research that was at odds with most of the profession. The vitality of the economics research at Chicago explains why it has been so successful in redefining different fields within economics, and why it won more Nobel prizes over the past two decades than any department in the history of the Nobel awards.

Guity is a native Iranian with family and cultural roots in other Middle Eastern countries. Her interest in politics and current events began when she attended the American University at Cairo and decided to major in journalism. In her brief stay there, she worked as correspondent for *Ettela'at*, the largest daily newspaper in Iran at that time. She also began the Persian language program at the Egyptian Broadcasting Service.

She came to Barnard College in her junior year and majored in English literature in order to understand Western culture. After graduating from Barnard she went on to Columbia School of Journalism to further her journalistic aspirations. During a five-year stay in London, she worked as a freelance journalist for the Persian language program of the BBC and other media.

Political oppression in the Middle East discouraged her from returning to Iran, so she returned to the United States. She decided to study history because the political upheavals in the Middle East convinced her that the many problems that beset the region had deep historical roots. After receiving a Ph.D. from the University of Chicago, where she also met and married Gary, she began to teach Middle Eastern history at the University of Illinois at Chicago. Her scholarly work is based on the belief that many serious problems today, including the treatment of women in various parts of the world, can be better understood only by appreciating how they evolved over time.

LINKING ECONOMICS AND PUBLIC POLICY

It was clear that the columns should be built around economic analysis so that they would amount to more than the expression of personal opinions. Moreover, the numerous ways economic markets and public policies affect behavior is not sufficiently appreciated by most economists, let alone by others.

Economics analyzes how markets, public policies, and other events affect the behavior of individuals and organizations that try as best they can to improve their situations by competing against each other for incomes, jobs, customers, and even prestige and power. Markets and prices help reconcile the unbounded desires of individuals and organizations to make themselves better off and the very finite resources available to satisfy these desires.

In this approach, behavior crucially depends on incentives. For example, families consume less goods and utilize fewer services when they become more expensive, or companies produce more when they receive higher prices for their products. The fact that behavior responds to incentives in this way is consistent, in most situations, with common sense. Unfortunately, common sense is thrown out the window when the effects of public policies are discussed. How often have we heard the claim that crime cannot be deterred by apprehension and punishment, or that subsidies to hospitals and physicians through Medicaid and Medicare have not contributed in a major way to the explosive growth in medical expenses?

The term "market" usually connotes a formal way to trade goods or assets and establish explicit prices, as in financial markets for common stocks and bonds, or the world markets for oil and wheat. But we consider markets as informal structured arrangements for allocating resources. These informal markets may use implicit, rather than explicit, prices to guide resources to different claimants. Gary did not start the columns with any statement of purpose, but practically all of them have in fact emphasized this link between incentives and public policies and other events. Our experience indicates that while readers have short memories about the content of individual columns, they appreciate the general thrust of a series of columns with a common theme.

Gary's professional work has been distinctive because it shows the importance of purposive choices and markets not only in the economic sphere, but also in social and political life. We wanted the columns to reflect this broad approach to behavior. Indeed, the very first one (published in May, 1985 [Part 6]), analyzed the economic and social influences on the occupations and earnings of women in the United States that began in the late 1970s. The next to last one in the book (Part 2) considers the effects that competition among religions has had on religious beliefs. Other columns discuss marriage and divorce, birth rates, discrimination against minorities, education, drunk driving, crime, the appointment of Supreme Court Justices, the religious right, term limits for politicians, and the role of special interest groups in political decisions.

ARE WE LIBERALS OR CONSERVATIVES?

Reacting against particular columns, many people have sent irate letters that accuse Gary of being conservative and reactionary. Does the confidence that we have in the importance of incentives and markets lead to conservative positions on economic, social, and political issues? We do support the case for individual freedom and private enterprise economies made by Adam Smith, David Hume, and other eighteenth and nineteenth century thinkers. They preferred a system where individuals have the freedom to make the vast majority of decisions that affect them. This preference does not assume that people are always rational and seldom make mistakes, but only that the great majority of people are more rational and make fewer mistakes in promoting their own interests than even well-intentioned government officials. Such a view of the world is more relevant now than in earlier times because of the huge expansion during the past century of taxes, government regulations, and bureaucratic powers.

Therefore, we are liberals in this classical or European sense, and we prefer a decentralized economic, political, and social milieu that allows freedom of choice as long as one person's freedom does not impose clear and sizable harm on others. Such liberals are not conservative in the traditional meaning of wanting to preserve the status quo. Although classical liberals recognize that what has survived is often functional and contributes to social welfare, they also realize that some hallowed customs and traditions in law, politics, and the economy have survived because of the influence of powerful interest groups that orient public policy in their own favor. This is why the columns do not hesitate to advocate changes in the status quo to improve efficiency or to raise opportunities for the poor. Some of these recommendations have appeared to some readers as being too liberal rather than too conservative.

We do not closeley identify with any political party in the United States since none takes a consistent position on whether individuals respond to incentives and know their own interests better than politicians and bureaucrats. Of course, most political leaders acknowledge the importance of incentives when this supports their positions. However, they tend to ignore incentives when that would lead to behavior that is incompatible with their views. For example, some conservatives conveniently forget about their arguments in favor of competition when they oppose free trade among nations. Many libertarians also fail to acknowledge that the modern welfare state artificially stimulates migration to wealthy nations that offer social security, medical care, and other entitlements. Many conservatives' commitment to free movement of people leads them to downplay the response of migrants to these benefits.

Similarly, liberals remember that incentives matter a lot when advocating higher cigarette taxes to cut down smoking, or when supporting little or no tuition at public universities in order to encourage students from modest backgrounds. But liberals more frequently than conservatives ignore the importance of incentives when that helps their arguments—as in considering whether welfare breaks up marriages and encourages dependency, or whether high income tax rates reduce work and investments.

Despite his classical liberalism, Gary wanted the columns to follow his research and avoid taking positions on policy issues. The first few did refrain from doing this, but he soon realized that readers want columnists to indicate where they stand on contemporary issues.

George Stigler's experience confirmed this conclusion. A few years after Gary started writing for *Business Week*, a competing business magazine asked George to write a monthly column. George Stigler was not only an outstanding economist but one of the finest economic writers. George's columns were witty, incisive, and well-written, but they concentrated on analysis and offered few policy recommendations. After a year he quit writing them because he felt that he was writing only for himself since he received essentially no feedback from readers. This was mainly because he did not take a strong stand on policy questions.

Gary soon decided to recommend ways to improve the problems highlighted by the columns. But the foundation would still be the analysis of incentives and choices over a broad class of behavior. He would try to show how policy recommendations naturally emerge from this approach to behavior.

As a result, the columns collected in this book contain recommendations on important and controversial issues. They are unambiguously opposed to big government and central planning, illegal immigration, employment quotas and set-asides for minorities, union exemption from antitrust laws, highly subsidized tuition for middle-class and rich students at state universities, the NCAA restrictions on pay to college athletes, term limits for members of Congress, ESOPs and other subsidies to employee ownership of companies, and tariffs and quotas—even when other nations impose them.

But the columns are not only "against" certain issues. Among other things, they advocate selling the right to immigrate legally, extensive privatization of public enterprises, introduction of school vouchers primarily to poor children, legalizing many drugs, substituting an individual-account system for pay-as-you-go social security, moving to fully voluntary armed forces, cracking down on fathers who fail to pay child support, enforcing marriage contracts and prenuptial agreements, encouraging free competition among religious sects and denominations, amending the Constitution so that federal judges would serve renewable terms rather than for life, instituting strong punishment for serious crimes, especially when committed with guns, and changing welfare to concentrate on helping children rather than mothers and social workers.

HAVE WE HAD ANY EFFECT ON PUBLIC POLICY?

Have the ideas and analyses in these columns had much effect on public policy and the views of readers? We believe they *have* had an impact, although it is often delayed and roundabout. If we believed there was no effect, we would not be interested in writing on contemporary issues, and would have little incentive to propose reforms in economic and social policies.

Intellectuals like to exaggerate the influence of ideas since the quality and originality of their ideas determine the reputation of intellectuals. In a well-known passage, John Maynard Keynes claimed that "Practical men, who believe themselves to be quite exempt from any intellectual influences, are usually the slaves of some defunct economists.... It is ideas, not vested interests, which are dangerous for good or evil."

Some intellectuals even expect politicians, voters, and readers to quickly accept cogent analysis that is stated clearly and forcefully. In our judgment, this claim is a very mistaken view of the impact of ideas on policies and beliefs. Political decisions are not mainly determined by a dispassionate evaluation of ideas and analysis, but by a pragmatic balancing of power among competing special and general purpose pressure groups. Ideas are often impotent when arrayed against powerful interests.

International trade policies provide a clear illustration of the victory of interests over ideas. Economists have generally been vocal and unambiguous advocates of free trade ever since Adam Smith and David Ricardo analyzed specialization and the comparative advantage of nations two centuries ago. Yet most states impose sizable tariffs and quotas to discourage imports that compete against domestic producers. The intellectual case for free trade has been too weak to overcome the political power of domestic industries that fear competition from foreign producers.

Still, ideas can have a large impact on policies and beliefs *in the long run*, even when they are overwhelmed by interests in the short run. Particular ideas may be adopted by groups who recognize that these ideas are helpful in promoting their interests. Political groups cannot admit publicly that the chief aim of the policies they advocate is to benefit themselves at the expense of others. Samuel Gompers, the powerful leader of the AFL, could bluntly state that unions simply wanted "more" in their *private* negotiations with industrialists, but such an admission would be a death blow to the ambitions of groups that want political favors. They must surround their arguments with ideas that suggest that helping them is good for the country.

So industries never state openly that they seek tariffs and quotas on imports because foreign producers are more efficient. Instead, they try to persuade voters with claims that foreign producers compete unfairly, or that imports will reduce employment. Witness Perot's "great sucking sound" that appealed to his supporters because they feared, completely erroneously, that NAFTA would cause many American jobs to migrate to Mexico.

Groups that become influential after a significant shift in the political balance of power may discover that ideas scribbled by an intellectual years earlier bolster their claims for public support. They then package and promote them as ideas whose time has come. Although the ideas may play an important part in obtaining general political support, they would no more be the fundamental cause of the shift in the balance of power than expert witnesses in a courtroom cause the litigation between plaintiffs and defendants.

The long-term importance of ideas is the motivation behind the sometimes new and frequently "unrealistic" proposals advocated in this book. We do not believe that sharp alterations in the direction of policies are adopted quickly or easily, even if the case for change is strong. But political power and intellectual fashion could change and the time become ripe for radical alternatives to present policies.

We take the same long-run perspective about the adoption of other proposals in this book. We are under no illusion that the time has come for legalization of drugs, a Constitutional amendment to abolish lifetime tenure for federal judges, the inclusion of unions under antitrust laws, sharp reductions in the scale of governments, or the end of NCAA restrictions on pay to college athletes. But we do expect that some of these suggestions will be accepted in the future as the harm from continuing present policies becomes increasingly apparent.

A LOOK INTO THE PAST

Newspaper and magazine columns deal with contemporary issues that are usually quickly forgotten. We agreed to reprint the columns collected in this book only because we believe they have a more enduring interest, even when discussing questions that are no longer remembered. The analysis developed in these columns will help students, executives, entrepreneurs, and other readers understand much better the economic, social, and political questions of any day.

Students have unnecessary difficulties learning economics because textbooks generally do not have enough good examples of real-world applications of the economic principles being taught, even though the study of applications is absolutely essential to mastering the principles. The numerous examples of economic thinking in this book, such as what is involved in deciding whether sports stadiums should be privately or publicly owned, or whether government loans to students should have a fixed rate of interest rather than rates that depend on subsequent earnings, can be an invaluable supplement to textbooks that develop the basic analysis.

Executives and other businesspeople can especially profit from the discussion of public policies and business practices that affect the performance and behavior of companies. These include an analysis of the effects of golden parachutes on the incentives of top executives, the impact of higher minimum wages on employment and profits, and the costs imposed on business by The Americans with Disabilities Act and other regulations.

We believe these columns contain much of interest to general readers who want a better understanding of the causes of changes in the economy and in social life, such as the growth over time in both the labor force participation of married women and in divorce rates, or the dismal economic performance of nations with little economic freedom. These columns also help prepare readers to analyze controversial public policy issues, such as whether religions should be protected by the state or forced to compete for private funds and members, whether an "industrial policy" is desirable, or whether many immigrants should be allowed to enter the United States and other popular nations.

How Accurate Have Our Predictions Been?

To aid readers in judging how many "insights" are provided by this economic approach to understanding behavior, let us consider how well our analysis of public policies and economic and social changes have withstood the test of time. One early column (1985) predicted a further narrowing of the gap in the United States between the earnings of men and women; another claimed that the Japanese stock market is not "rigged" (1990); still others argued that "industrial policy" is dreadful (1985, 1992, and 1993); that Supreme Court Justices should have renewable term appointments (1990); that Blacks in the United States were greatly improving their relative economic circumstances (1986); that the voluntary army is a great success (1988); and that term limits is a bad idea (1990).

On international issues, we claimed that Sweden was in serious economic trouble, and that its policies should not be copied by the Eastern European nations that had recently thrown out the communists (1990); that apartheid in South Africa did not result from capitalism but from the political influence of white unions and other groups that feared competition from Black workers (1990); that low-priced oil is good for the western world (1986); that the harmful consequences of any "greenhouse effect" are greatly exaggerated (1991 and 1992); that world population growth is not leading to catastrophe (1986 and 1994); and that many nations with mixed ethnic populations—such as Yugoslavia or Czechoslovakia—would break up because small nations could now compete in the world economy (1990 and 1994).

The verdict is still out on some of these conclusions and analyses, but they do appear to our prejudiced eyes to have a high batting average. Women's earnings in the United States have continued to advance; despite strenuous efforts, the Japanese government was unable to manipulate its stock market to produce recovery; the Mandela government has been following rather procapitalistic policies; contrary to the claims of fear-mongers, doubling of the world's population since the 1950s has been associated with a rise, not a fall, in world per capita incomes; and few countries still take industrial policy seriously.

Of course, not all predictions have worked out so well. Although Black women have continued their economic progress, Black men have not done as well because the earnings of all men with fewer skills declined sharply during the 1980s. We expected Japan to recover more quickly from its serious economic recession than it has, perhaps because we did not expect the strong deflationary pressure from its Central Bank. Concern about the greenhouse effect continues to grow despite far-less-than-conclusive evidence. We still believe that the Americans with Disabilities Act imposes an enormous cost on business and consumers, but this is not easy to document.

Even a high batting average for the analysis in these columns does not mean we can foretell the future. Rather, it is testimony that the economic way of thinking, with its recognition that choices are sensitive to the costs and benefits of different actions, offers many insights into economic, social, and political behavior. These insights are overlooked by persons who look at behavior from purely political, social, or psychological perspectives.

To assist readers in locating specific topics, we have grouped the columns under broad categories, including regulation, investments in human capital, international trade, immigration, education, women, crime, the environment, drugs and other addictions, capitalism, labor markets, family behavior, politics and government, stock markets and management, and the elderly and social security.

WHAT THE COLUMNS HAVE MEANT TO US

We are very happy *Business Week* asked Gary to do the columns and that he accepted. More than 130 columns were published during this past decade, and we immensely enjoyed the process involved in writing them. However, we have not been pleased about the commitment when a column is due and Gary is overseas, or when an idea for a column does not work out. But we have not yet run out of steam because changes in the world continue to raise new and exciting issues to write about.

Contact with readers has been one of the unexpected pleasures from writing these columns. This usually comes in the form of letters to the editor that either approve or, more frequently, criticize particular arguments. Some readers are ill-tempered and nasty, but most are polite. We sometimes wish a letter had arrived before a column was written so that its analysis could have been incorporated. Gary tries to answer all the letters since readers who take time to write deserve the courtesy of a reply. Moreover, sometimes even better ones come back, and a valuable correspondence may develop.

We are surprised by how frequently Gary runs into people who read and appear to like the columns. A few even claim to subscribe to *Business Week* in order to read them. We feel he is not writing in vain, and that an audience looks forward each month to the next column. This interaction with people outside of academia is something most academics do not get, and we are lucky to have it.

From the beginning Gary received considerable assistance from the copy desk and other writers and editors at *Business Week*. During the first few years Jack Patterson handled the columns, and during subsequent years Jack Pluenneke did, although occasionally others pinch hit, and Bruce Nussbaum has recently taken over this responsibility. The two Jacks and others provided excellent suggestions, and gave Gary valuable lessons on how to write more effectively for a popular audience. We are greatly indebted for their help and for their invariable courtesy.

We also want to thank the editor of *Business Week* Stephen Shepard, for general encouragement, and for the magazine's policy that provides Gary with freedom to write about anything that interests him. No effort was ever made to slant his opinions, even when they were controversial or differed substantially from those expressed in editorials and other *Business Week* commentary. It has been a pleasure to be a small part of such a magazine.

PART 2

Regulation and Privatization

The essays in this part consider the effects of government regulations that distort the incentives of companies, consumers, and employees. Among the examples discussed are the pervasive inefficiencies of government-run postal systems, and the increased number of auto accidents caused by extensive government restrictions on the ability to raise the cost of premiums to drivers who tend to have accidents.

Another essay calls for essentially complete deregulation of the telecommunications industry because rapid technological advances, including the Internet and fiber optic cables, enormously increased the potential for competition and further innovation in this industry. Some companies in the industry recognized that government regulations were inhibiting their response to these fundamental changes, and concluded that they could do better in a freer environment. They joined the movement for extensive deregulation of this industry. That pressure forced the worldwide trend toward deregulation and increased competition, including legislation that deregulates telecommunications in the United States.

We strongly criticize the way New England regulates fishing in the waters off Cape Cod and elsewhere to prevent overfishing of striped bass and other kinds of fish. Aggregate quotas on the total catch, the present method used to reduce fishing for striped bass, encourage intensive efforts to catch stripers early in the summer season before competitors do. As a result, the quota is exhausted during most of the peak summer season. We are concerned personally because we summer on Cape Cod, and like to eat fish almost every day. To make fish available to consumers when they want it, and also to improve the financial situation of commercial fishers, we propose that taxes on the catch of individual fishers replace the present quota system.

This proposal elicited many letters, especially from government officials, journalists, and economists in Iceland, where fishing is the number one industry.

Iceland apparently is in the midst of an extensive and rather bitter debate over whether it is better to regulate overfishing by giving quotas to each fishing boat, or by taxing the catch of each boat. Despite some good arguments advanced in this correspondence by quota advocates, we continue to believe taxes are better, especially if the additional government revenue generated by these taxes leads to a reduction in other taxes.

REGULATION

Religions Thrive in a Free Market, Too

Many people are disturbed by the rising appeal of the religious right. But I don't believe there is reason to be concerned—so long as religions must compete for followers and no religion receives special treatment from the government.

In a competitive environment, born-again Christians, Orthodox Jews, fundamentalist Moslems, and other groups attract members only if they meet spiritual and moral needs better than mainline religions. Most people believe individuals have the power to determine their lifestyles even when they grow up under difficult circumstances. They expect religious preaching to reaffirm their need to take responsibility for their behavior. With mainline religions failing to stress the need for people to exercise self-control and responsibility, they are losing members to fundamentalist groups with more traditional teachings. Fundamentalists also have been in the forefront of attacking the breakdown of the family, pornography, and disrespect for authority.

Some nations, such as the U.S., have an open "market" for religion. Different denominations and sects compete for members through spiritual guidance and other appeals. Competition is good for religion, as it is for ordinary commodities, because religious groups are forced to learn how better to satisfy members' needs than they do when they have a monopoly position.

ON THEIR TOES. The importance of competition to the behavior of religious organizations was recognized 200 years ago by Adam Smith in a neglected chapter of his *Wealth of Nations*. He presented considerable evidence that the Church of England had become unresponsive to the needs of the British because the government gave it a privileged position. Smith argued forcefully that the only way to end church leaders' sloth and indifference was to remove these privileges and make the Church of England compete for members against the newer religions.

Thomas Jefferson and other founders of the U.S. understood that church and state should be separate in the new nation. The First Amendment states that "Congress shall make no law respecting an establishment of religion, or prohibiting the free exercise thereof." One reason for the separation of church and state is to force religions to remain on their toes as they compete for congregants.

Lawrence Iannoccone of Santa Clara University tested the Smith-Jefferson doctrine with evidence on the degree of religiosity among the Protestant nations of Europe and North America. He found that religion—measured by the number of regular churchgoers and the strength of religious beliefs—was more important to people in societies with many competing churches, compared with countries that have a single church. For instance, only a small percentage of the population in Scandinavian countries is interested in religion, in large part because the Lutheran Church has a privileged position and receives most of its financing from governments (though church and state are starting to separate in Sweden). By contrast, religion thrives in the U.S. because different sects and denominations compete fiercely for members.

COMMUNIST SUPPRESSION.   The Catholic Church is losing its powerful monopoly position in South America, and fundamentalist Protestant sects are growing rapidly in its place, because too many priests have ignored spiritual needs while focusing on political goals. And prior to World War II, Japan's government subsidized Shintoism and discriminated against other religions. The protected position of Shintoism was abolished after the war, and hundreds of new groups are flourishing now in Japan. These groups have appealed to spiritual needs that apparently were not being satisfied by Shintoism.

No modern example shows the competitive appeal of religion better than what is happening in the onetime communist nations of Eastern Europe and the former Soviet Union. For almost 75 years, the Soviet Union tried to reduce opposition to communism by closing churches and imprisoning religious leaders. In essence, communism tried to establish a secular monopoly. Yet religion has been booming since the collapse of communism. More than 22% of Russians interviewed say they used to be atheists, but they now believe in God. More than 6,000 Russian Orthodox churches and monasteries have reopened, and many other religious organizations have begun to recruit members there.

These examples indicate that both liberal and strict religious groups are more dynamic when they have to compete for members on a level playing field. Healthy competition requires open markets for religious beliefs, where no religious organization receives special protection or privileges from the state.

HOW TO SCUTTLE OVERFISHING?
TAX THE CATCH

As a summer resident of Cape Cod, the Massachusetts seashore, I realize that the importance of fishing for food, livelihood, and sport may be a bit out of proportion there. But the local debate on controls over the striped bass — called stripers, a delectable white fish and longtime staple of gastronomes on the Cape — is a concrete example of the general issue of obstacles to intelligent regulation.

In the 1970s, the stock of striped bass in ocean waters offshore from Maine to Maryland became seriously depleted because of a combination of droughts, pollution in breeding grounds, and overfishing. In response, Massachusetts and other states in the region established strict quotas for commercial and recreational fishing. Overfishing may not have been the main reason for the dwindling supply, but environmentalists made a persuasive case that restrictions on fishing could help restore the stock.

Massachusetts placed a ceiling on the aggregate catch of stripers by commercial fishers. Unfortunately, this is a very poor way to control fishing, because it encourages each fishing boat to catch as much as it can early in the season, before other boats bring in enough fish to reach the aggregate quota that applies to all of them.

"FISHLESS WEEKS." This is precisely what happened last year, when the Massachusetts commercial quota of 200,000 pounds was already reached by the end of July, well before the normal finish to the fishing season in September. The rush to catch stripers early sharply lowered the wholesale price while fishermen had a lot to sell. The price then increased steeply, after the quota was exhausted and not much striper was on the market. The perverse incentives provided by the quota added to the difficulties of making a living from fishing in this region.

The number of striped bass in the waters off the coast has grown rapidly in recent years — perhaps because the controls over fishing helped in the breeding of additional stock — so Massachusetts increased the commercial allowance to 750,000 pounds in 1995, nearly four times the 1994 level. Because even this larger quota was expected to be reached early, the state tried to spread out the catch over the season by prohibiting commercial fishing for stripers during "fishless weeks" for stripers. As a result, fresh striper has been both expensive and scarce during these weeks.

A much better way to regulate fishing than quotas and fishless weeks — and one that should appeal to consumers, fishermen, sportsmen, and taxpayers alike—is for the states to tax the amount of fish caught. The tax would vary by weight and size, so that catching excessively small and young fish could be penalized severely. The present rules require stripers below a minimum size to be thrown back.

ONE A DAY. The size of the tax would control the total catch, because fishing for stripers would decrease when the tax rate is higher. This approach eliminates the incentive under the present system to catch fish early in the season, since fishermen who are taxed on their catch have no reason to attempt to bring in stripers before competitors do. Instead, they would spread their fishing over the season and try to catch more fish when prices are higher.

Recreational fishermen may be responsible for more than half the total stripers caught, which is why they too are regulated. Massachusetts presently allows each person fishing to catch one striper per day. The same tax rate should apply to both commercial and recreational fishing, since the effect on the stock of stripers in the sea is no different when fish are caught by one group or the other.

A system of taxes on fish caught by commercial and for-hire recreational fishing boats is no harder to implement than monitoring the catch, as required by the present quota system. A tax has the further advantage of providing additional state revenues, which could be used to fund research on the causes of the large and disturbing fluctuations in the stock of striped bass and other fish and to find ways of improving the marine environment.

It is not easy to enact sensible controls even in a small-scale industry such as fishing for striped bass, where the case for regulation is rather strong. One must wonder about what happens in the larger political arena when the advantages of regulation are questionable, especially in large national industries with lots of media attention. This may be particularly pertinent to current disputes over general environmental regulations and deregulation with regard to health and safety issues. This is the main lesson about regulation from the big fish story on the Cape.

CONGRESS, SET THE PHONE COMPANIES FREE

In 1982, after a lengthy court battle, AT&T agreed to divest itself of the 22 Bell companies that operated its local exchange networks. The presiding judge, Harold H. Greene, gave the seven surviving regional Baby Bells a monopoly on local telephone service in their territories. AT&T was limited mainly to long distance and, as a carrot, entry into the computer business.

Rapid changes in the telecommunications industry have since rendered these and other restrictions obsolete. Unfortunately, the judge kept the power to deny—subject to appeal to higher courts—any proposed changes by telephone companies in their activities. But because Greene is a judge, not a businessman, it isn't surprising that he has been slow in recognizing the radical transformation of telecommunications. As a consequence, he has been an obstacle to efficient organization of the industry.

His 1982 judgment was based on the belief that the local exchange was a "natural monopoly," since many telephone calls could be handled cheaply by a single company that strung wires in a town. Indeed, the lawsuit arose because AT&T was alleged to have used this monopoly power to block competition in long-distance calls. The judge justified his imposition of line-of-business restrictions on the Baby Bells as being necessary to prevent them from leveraging their monopoly power in local exchanges to compete unfairly in other markets.

Among other things, Judge Greene blocked the Baby Bells from selling phone services and many products outside the regions where they operated local exchanges. Yet the potential abuse of monopoly power in local service could hardly apply to activities lying entirely outside the Baby Bells' own markets. There, they would simply be new entrants who would compete against established companies in supplying telephone services and products.

WONDER WIRE.   When AT&T was broken up, the potential abuse of monopoly power may have justified some control over telephone pricing. But most other curbs on phone companies made little sense even then, and the revolutionary changes in telecommunications have destroyed the case even for price controls.

That's because cable-TV-wire systems and cellular phones have the potential to override any local monopoly power the Baby Bells have. About 90% of American houses have access to cable, and cable wiring can be fitted to provide two-way telephone communication. But regulations have kept cable companies from providing phone service and limit video programming offered by phone companies. Competition would increase if these companies were allowed to pool their knowledge—and offer both local and long-distance phone services along with video and TV services.

YANKEE RAIDERS.   Several months ago, Judge Greene finally approved the merger of AT&T and McCaw Cellular Communications Inc., the nation's largest cellular-phone company. Other mergers are rapidly taking place among telephone, cellular, and cable companies—partly to position them for the upcoming auction of additional radio-frequency licenses, for providing cellular-phone, paging, E-mail, and many other services.

Competition in long-distance phone calls and video programming has been vigorous in the U.S. But America is falling behind Britain and New Zealand, for example, in other services. Britain now lets cable companies offer both phone and TV services through their wires. Cable outfits are competing for local customers against British Telecom PLC, the dominant phone supplier. The paradox is that the competition is coming from U.S. cable companies and Baby Bells, which are doing overseas what they cannot do at home: freely offer both cable-TV and telephone service.

New York, California, and several other states have begun to allow much greater intrastate competition in local phone and cable-TV services. But federal legislation to overhaul telecommunications got bogged down during the current congressional term in conflicts between Republican- and Democratic-sponsored bills. In the Congress soon to end, Bob Dole (R-Kan.) took the lead in the Senate in calling for substantial deregulation of the telecommunications industry. That's a good reason to believe the new Republican-dominated Congress will move quickly to scrap the regulations on prices and on what lines of business the phone, cellular, video, and cable companies may offer. As a result, consumers will be able to get full benefit of new technology.

No judge—and no lawmaker, regulator, or economist—can foresee the future in an industry changing as fast as telecommunications. That is why competition, rather than officials and bureaucrats, should determine its evolution.

How the Disabilities Act Will Cripple Business

One of the most far-reaching pieces of labor legislation in years took effect in late July. Unfortunately, the Americans with Disabilities Act is more a make-work project for lawyers than an effective way to help the disabled.

The act covers not only people with hearing, sight, or mobility impairments but also those with emotional illness, dyslexia, AIDS, and past drug or alcohol addictions. This is why some of the act's supporters claim that it will help more than 40 million Americans. But it is a distortion of the meaning of "disability" to pass a law that may include almost 40% of the labor force.

It is no longer legal for the more than 2 million businesses with 25 or more employees to ask job candidates or their references about disabilities. This is broadly defined to include questions about medical history, past absenteeism because of illness, and past treatment for alcoholism. Employers must also make "reasonable" efforts to accommodate the disabled, and, if a disability is revealed as a result of a medical exam, an employer cannot withdraw a job offer unless the action is justified as a business necessity.

The new law defines disability so ambiguously that whether or not a person has been excluded from a job unfairly will often be impossible to determine with any confidence. Are people handicapped—and hence entitled to special consideration—simply because they cannot work under stressful conditions or because they object to any criticism of their work that may mean a return to alcohol or drug dependency? Lawsuits arguing these and many other strange positions are possible under the new law. Civil rights legislation has plenty of weaknesses, but ambiguity about who is included isn't one of them. Discrimination is banned on the basis of characteristics that are usually easily determined, such as race, gender, or religion.

SHOTGUN APPROACH. Under the 1991 Civil Rights Act, the disabled gained the right to sue for compensatory and punitive damages. So the additional provisions of the Disabilities Act can be expected to be a boon to litigation. A disturbingly large number of lawsuits already clogs the U.S. judicial system. It is senseless to have another poorly drafted act with a very broad sweep.

Those members of Congress and others who sincerely want to help the disabled could support such a shotgun approach only if they believed U.S. business was incapable of determining the employment qualifications of persons with minor hearing impairments, emotional problems, or a history of alcoholism or drug abuse. Yet this is highly unlikely under present conditions, when companies are hard-pressed by international as well as domestic competition to cut costs and fill jobs with the best available candidates. And it is particularly ludicrous to believe that juries and judges are better qualified than competitive pressures from the marketplace to determine whether someone measures up to a job.

The U.S. is surely rich enough to help those who have serious disabilities, innate or contracted. And since gainful employment fosters self-respect, the help should include assistance at finding useful, satisfying work. But the new law illustrates the disturbing recent tendency by Congress to impose the cost of its actions on business rather than on taxpayers. Obviously, this allows Congress to hide the costs of compliance and doesn't add to the budget deficit.

MEAN-SPIRITED. The world competition confronting American business makes it ill-prepared to bear higher costs without losing markets and cutting employment. Most of the cost will be passed on to workers, consumers, and, eventually, the disabled themselves. Walter Y. Oi, a distinguished economist at the University of Rochester, blind since youth, believes that many companies will seek loopholes to avoid taking on handicapped applicants, because they fear costly litigation. Anyone who questions legislation to help the disabled risks being branded as mean-spirited or too miserly to spend a little to help those hit by misfortune. This is why the new act sailed through Congress with the full support of the President. But it is still a bad law that is likely to do more harm than good — which is why a very different approach is needed.

I believe disability coverage should be limited to the perhaps 3 or 4 million people estimated to be seriously handicapped in vision, hearing, or movement, as outlined by objective definitions of these impairments. Instead of shifting the responsibilities to business and the courts, Congress should offer employers who hire disabled workers a generous payroll subsidy that increases with the severity of the handicap. This approach would place the burden directly on taxpayers and would concentrate help on the truly handicapped.

The total cost of such a program would be manageable. For example, an average subsidy of $3 per hour—which may be much larger than necessary—for 3 million disabled workers who average 1,200 hours of work per year adds up to about $11 billion per annum. That is not a negligible addition to government spending, but it is far smaller than the likely total cost of the vague present law.

UNCLE SAM SHOULD KEEP HIS MITTS OFF OIL PRICES

With oil selling at close to $40 a barrel, the U.S. and other industrialized countries are under enormous pressure to do something, anything, to stabilize prices. But what governments are being asked to do will hurt rather than help their economies. Here are a few dos and don'ts for a sound oil policy.

The most important step is to avoid interfering with the market for oil and other sources of energy so that supply and demand can determine prices. If oil continues to be expensive because of anticipated cutbacks in supply, businesses and households worried about their budgets will discover many ways to reduce energy use, including smaller cars, greater reliance on nuclear energy, and more insulation in homes. After all, the threefold jump in the world price of oil from the early 1970s to 1980 caused the amount of oil used per real dollar of gross national product to fall in all industrialized countries.

Japan's oil consumption changed hardly at all since 1970, while its industrial output grew enormously. Even though Japan imports all of its oil, it adjusted much faster than the U.S. to the first crunch partly because Tokyo permitted domestic oil prices to rise to world levels, whereas Washington cushioned the impact with controls and rationing.

PAINFUL MEMORIES.   Governments should resist the strong temptation to ration and allocate oil and natural gas. Rationing was the most blatant of many misguided U.S. reactions to the price rise of the '70s. Voters' painful memories of long gasoline lines should help Washington avoid repeating that mistake.

It is also unwise to control specific uses of oil, such as setting tougher fuel-economy standards for cars. Indeed, I still believe that Congress should abolish the corporate average fuel economy (CAFE) standards altogether. These require that the new fleet of each manufacturer average at least 27.5 miles per gallon. When gasoline prices are high, car owners choose between the economy of more fuel-efficient cars and the safer, smoother, roomier rides of larger, heavier cars that guzzle more fuel.

A federal tax on gasoline is another attempt to control a specific use of oil. Thus, though it may be a good way to help reduce the budget deficit, it is a bad way to cut down the demand for oil because it artificially reduces one type of oil use rather than all uses. This distorts the allocation of oil among gasoline and other petroleum products.

A general tax on oil imports encourages a shift to domestic oil. This is undesirable because it would encourage U.S. oil reserves to be used up faster, and in the long run, would increase rather than reduce U.S. dependence on imported oil. What makes more sense is a selective tax on oil imported from the Middle East. Such a tax would shift some import demand toward Venezuela, Mexico, Indonesia, and other, safer sources. This tax would also have the advantage of raising funds from Middle Eastern states to help defray the cost of their defense in the current gulf crisis and at other times.

BUSH'S MISTAKE. Governments should avoid using "moral suasion" to jawbone oil companies into holding the prices of gasoline and other petroleum-using products below market-clearing levels. Artificially low prices create shortages: They stimulate excessive demand for these products while taking away any incentive refiners would have to increase supplies and search for new oil fields.

The U.S. surely does not need another "excess" profits tax on oil companies. Such a tax discourages investments toward discovering new reserves and getting more output from producing wells. High profits when supplies are scarce and prices are high help offset oil companies' low profits when oil supplies are plentiful and prices are low.

President Bush made a mistake in yielding to pressure to sell oil from the Strategic Petroleum Reserve, even though he is only selling a small amount. The U.S. and other governments have no more business trying to stabilize the price of oil than they have trying to stabilize copper, platinum, plastics, or other commodity prices that fluctuate widely. Profit-seeking private companies are much better positioned than federal bureaucrats to determine how much oil inventory to hold in light of expectations about price fluctuations. But rational private-inventory policies require clear signals about what a government will do with its oil reserves. Government strategic-oil reserves should be used only for military purposes during a war, boycott, or other periods of severe oil shortage.

The newly emerging market economies of Eastern Europe may be in for a difficult period since world oil prices have risen just as the Soviet Union stopped selling them oil at subsidized prices. But even at $40 a barrel, oil will not have a devastating economic effect on most other countries unless it generates silly policies such as those introduced during the '70s' crunch. If governments can resist the formidable political pressures to intervene in the markets for oil and other energy sources, it is possible to ride out the present crisis with only modest damage to the world economy.

NOT EVERYONE DESERVES
AFFORDABLE AUTO INSURANCE

Bitter complaints about high auto insurance rates have resulted in tighter regulations during the past few years. The effect has been that many states have capitulated to political pressure to subsidize certain groups through price and other regulations.

Prior to 1966, all states except California regulated car insurance rates, but 15 states deregulated in the 1970s. In 1988, California voters did a U-turn and easily passed a referendum that proposed to end their free market in the setting of auto insurance rates and to force insurance companies to cut many rates. In California, where some companies have decided to stop writing car insurance policies, the Supreme Court recently overruled that state's insurance commissioner and held that companies can abandon the state without first finding other insurers to take over their customers.

In the early 1980s, New Jersey set up an insurer-of-last-resort for drivers unable to obtain insurance at regulated rates in the voluntary market. New York has barred the use of sex, marital status, and other characteristics in the setting of rates. Several other states either resumed or tightened their regulation of auto insurance.

FETTERED COMPETITION.   Regulation has not lowered car insurance rates to most car owners, despite complaints about high rates in unregulated markets. A still-valuable study conducted a decade ago by economist Richard A. Ippolito, now of Pension Benefit Guaranty Corp., found no significant difference between average rate levels in regulated and unregulated states.

He found instead that regulation impeded competition among insurance companies, increased the cost to drivers with good records, lowered rates for high-risk drivers, and raised the number of cars covered under subsidized plans for drivers unable to obtain insurance in the voluntary market. For example, in the early 1970s, 12% of high-risk New Jersey drivers were assigned to various insurers. After the state "reformed" its regulation of automobile insurance and tightened controls over rates in 1983, almost half of its more than 4 million cars became part of the subsidized pool.

Therefore, it is not surprising that the insurer-of-last-resort has run up a large deficit—in excess of $3 billion—even though cars not in the pool in the Garden State are assessed some of the highest rates in the nation. Governor James J. Florio recently proposed to eliminate this insurer, force rates down in the voluntary market, and require other auto insurance companies to help pay the deficit. Whatever New Jersey decides, I do not believe that rates to safer drivers can be cut without the state freeing rates for most of the riskier drivers.

In unregulated markets, people who are more likely to get into auto accidents must pay above-average rates to cover the greater expected damage to persons and property from their driving. They may try to get around stiff costs by not insuring their cars, but compulsory car insurance, found in a growing number of states, can help prevent this.

Higher rates discourage accident-prone persons from owning and driving cars, and thereby reduce the number of auto accidents. The serious harm to life and property by having more high-risk drivers on the road when rates are kept artificially low may have a large social cost.

A common criticism of unregulated rates is that some good drivers then have to pay high premiums only because they are placed in rating groups that have a large number of accident-prone members. Even careful drivers in the inner city usually pay a lot in unregulated markets because accidents and auto theft are common there.

SAFELY STORED. But free competition among insurance companies does give good drivers some protection against high rates, for companies make more profits if they can separate out and charge lower rates to the less accident-prone members of a group. This is why females, married males, and those who have completed a drivers' education course often receive lower rates than young unmarried males. Living in a part of Chicago where car theft is common, I receive a discount on the rate for my area because I keep my car in a garage. However, since companies lack information about relevant characteristics of drivers, some careful drivers pay big premiums in free markets because they are classified in high-risk groups.

Even if the political decision is made that riskier categories of drivers are to be helped, the necessary subsidies should be paid from tax revenues rather than through higher rates to careful drivers and car owners in areas with a low incidence of accidents and auto theft. Higher rates to low-risk drivers in exchange for lower rates for high-risk drivers through rate regulation illustrates the growing tendency to economize on public spending by mandating higher private spending—in this case from certain groups of car owners.

The experience with auto insurance has important lessons for proposals to restore extensive federal regulation of airlines and other industries. Just as regulation reduces the efficiency of the market for auto insurance, it will also lower efficiency in these industries.

THE RESULTS ARE IN:
OVERREGULATION KILLS GROWTH

Why do some countries grow much faster than average and others much slower? Although the causes of growth are not fully understood, clearly private enterprise and open competition help stimulate it. Conversely, growth is slowed when special-interest groups use their influence to obtain extensive political favors, such as large subsidies for exports or big quotas and tariffs on competing imports. When government regulation and control go too far, the engine of growth first sputters and then stops working altogether.

A good example is the newly independent African nations that emerged after World War II. Their leaders admired socialism and brought an interventionist mentality to the task of running their countries. As a result, their economies did badly. In an important study for the World Bank, Professors Robert Summers and Alan W. Heston of the University of Pennsylvania analyzed more than 70 countries, comparing their growth in per capita income from 1950 to 1980 to their per capita income in 1950. The average rate of growth of the African economies studied was less than 1.5% per year, well under the mean for other countries. By contrast, the free-market tigers of Asia—Hong Kong, Japan, South Korea, Singapore, and Taiwan—had high rates of growth. According to Summers and Heston, for example, the annual rate of growth in per capita income from 1950 to 1980 was 7% for Japan and 5.5% for Taiwan.

MEDIOCRE PERFORMERS.   True, the centrally planned economies in Summers and Heston's sample of Communist countries did better than average. But the authors could not lower the income estimates for these countries to reflect shoddy consumer goods and other distortions in their economies. Also, several mediocre performers—including China, North Korea, Albania, and Cuba—are not included because satisfactory data were unavailable.

China has privatized its huge farm sector, and it is promoting private initiative in industrial production, while Russia under Mikhail S. Gorbachev is trying to shake up a stagnating economy by following China's example. These actions amount to a confession that Communist economies cannot continue to grow without a large reduction in centralized planning and an expansion in private production and initiative.

It is often alleged that the economies of Japan and other newly industrialized countries grew faster than those of the U.S. and Europe during the past few decades because the West is too old and rich to compete effectively against their young and hungry economies. Analogies between the aging of people and economies are seductive, but, fortunately, they are not supported by the evidence.

Age and wealth have not slowed the growth of the U.S. economy. Studies by Professor Paul Romer of the University of Rochester and others show that per capita income in America probably grew more rapidly, not more slowly, as its economy grew older and richer. Per capita income, for example, increased faster from 1950 to 1970 than during most decades of the 19th and early 20th centuries. Growth did slow from 1973 to 1983, but a decade of slow growth is not unusual: Remember the dismal record of the 1930s.

GOLDEN YEARS.   Nor does the evidence indicate that richer countries grow more slowly than poorer ones. Growth rates differ greatly even among countries with similar incomes. The average rate of growth for the countries in the Summers and Heston study during 1950 through 1980 is about 2.8% per year, which is much higher for the great majority of countries than their past rates of growth. The most reasonable conclusion from their data is that wealth was not a hindrance to growth—richer countries in 1950 grew just about as rapidly as poorer ones did.

Per capita income in the U.S., by far the richest country in 1950, grew at 2% per year from 1950 to 1980. This is as fast as America grew in the past, but it is slower than the average for all countries. Although this may appear to indicate that rich countries do not grow as easily as poorer ones, other wealthy countries in 1950 grew faster than the U.S. The average rate of growth for the 10 richest countries exceeded 2.3%, not much below the mean for all countries.

Such evidence clearly shows that wealth does not condemn a country to a mediocre economic future, nor does poverty guarantee eventual prosperity. Poorer countries that try to catch up do have certain advantages, such as relatively easy access to the capital and technologies of the front-runners. The latter, however, also have advantages that are conducive to continued growth. Indeed, rich countries appear to have as many advantages as handicaps. Especially important is the highly skilled labor force usually found in a rich country. Skilled labor is necessary to develop new products and cost-reducing methods of production.

Rich countries that do not perform well should blame policies and behavior— not age and wealth. Their rate of growth will not slow if they avoid complacency and the perennial temptation to overregulate and control economic life.

FUEL-EFFICIENCY STANDARDS:
AN IDEA WHOSE TIME HAS PASSED

"No profit is made save at a loss to someone else." So claimed Michel de Montaigne 400 years ago, and people continue to believe that, in modern parlance, business and its customers are engaged in a zero-sum game. This belief surely explains some of the opposition to General Motors' and Ford Motor's success in persuading the Transportation Secretary to relax the Corporate Average Fuel Economy (CAFE) standards. Yet the country's interests, as well as those of the auto companies', are served by relaxing the standards. Indeed, the country would benefit if these standards were completely abolished.

At the height of public concern over the energy crisis in 1975, Congress mandated that carmakers must meet specified fuel-economy standards that grew more stringent until 1985, when the new cars of each manufacturer were to average at least 27½ mpg. These standards may have been justified at that time because price controls distorted the choices of car buyers.

The real price of gasoline almost doubled from 1973 to 1981, and consumers faced limits on gasoline purchases during some years. To economize, car buyers shifted toward more fuel-efficient cars, especially smaller Japanese models. Up to 1982, American car manufacturers readily met CAFE standards because they had to increase production of smaller and more fuel-efficient cars to satisfy consumer demand.

SAFETY AND PRESTIGE.   Then after 1981, the real cost of gasoline fell by more than 30% when the world price of oil declined and when price controls were eliminated. This increased the demand for larger, less fuel-efficient cars that some consumers found more comfortable, safer, and prestigious. In order to raise the average fuel efficiency of their cars during 1983–85, GM and Ford discouraged the demand for larger cars by increasing prices of these cars relative to those of smaller cars and by offering other incentives to purchase smaller cars. Still, GM and Ford did not meet CAFE standards in 1983–85 because they are oriented to produce larger cars. It is clear that CAFE standards are now affecting consumer choices by reducing the availability of cars that are less fuel-efficient.

Should not consumers be allowed to satisfy their demand for such cars without the constraint of fuel-economy standards? Some people say "no" because car buyers are not fully considering the greater pollution and other environmental damage done by less fuel-efficient cars. But fuel-economy standards neglect the damage done by older cars and do not distinguish between persons who drive a lot and those who drive a little. The best way to force drivers to pay for environmental damage from driving is to impose a tax on gasoline equal to the social cost of the damage. The federal tax is now 9¢ a gal., and state taxes average about 12¢ a gal. Maybe federal and state taxes should be raised, but 21¢ a gal. is not a negligible allowance for pollution and other driving damage.

SUPPLY CRISIS?   *The New York Times* editorially supports CAFE standards to reduce the demand for oil and lower "the risk of a supply crisis." But the capacity of OPEC or any other small number of countries to withhold supplies and generate an oil crisis weakened during the past decade as the world market for oil became more integrated and less concentrated. OPEC's share of world oil production was almost cut in half, from about 60% in 1973 to about 30% in 1984. If OPEC again boycotted the U.S., this country could buy oil on the world market from other producers. Moreover, improved fuel economy in the U.S. cannot substantially lower world oil prices because gasoline consumption here is less than 20% of world consumption. Furthermore, fuel-economy standards are a poor way to prepare for a "crisis." Public and private inventories of oil and gasoline are much more effective.

A 1979 report titled *Energy in Transition, 1985–2010,* by the prestigious National Academy of Sciences, supported standards for fuel and other uses of energy by alleging that consumers are "more influenced by first cost than by prospective operating costs." In particular, the report alleges that car buyers do not fully consider the higher gasoline operating cost of less fuel-efficient cars. The available evidence does not support this allegation. For example, research by Professor Zvi Griliches of Harvard University and Professor Makoto Ohta of Japan's Tsukuba University suggests that buyers of used cars fully took into account prospective operating costs when they reduced the demand for less fuel-efficient cars after gasoline prices rose in the 1970s.

The energy scare after 1973 encouraged many unwise energy policies: CAFE standards, price controls on oil, entitlements, various tax favors, and a wind-fall-profits tax on oil companies. Some of these policies have been rescinded, and most of the others should be. The country would be better off if CAFE standards were abolished because fuel-economy standards restrict consumer choice and cannot be justified. That GM and Ford would also benefit, at least from relaxed standards, only proves that what is good for business is sometimes good for the country.

PRIVATIZATION

NEITHER RAIN NOR SLEET NOR GOOD IDEA
SHALL SHAKE UP THE POSTAL SYSTEM

It is far easier to create bad public programs than to eliminate them once they have been around for a while. This old but frequently ignored law of political science has been called "the tyranny of the status quo," and it helps explain why even downright perverse government policies stubbornly survive and sometimes even expand.

The political status quo is important because groups with a lot to gain from particular programs fiercely defend their continuation, regardless of harmful consequences to others. At the same time, opposition often is weak and fragmented because the damage, in the form of high taxes or bad service, may be spread over so many groups that no single one has a strong enough incentive to protest vigorously. Sometimes, the harm becomes apparent only after a policy is changed, as when privatization reveals how inefficient a state enterprise had been or when drastically reduced tariffs and quotas on imports encourage imports of attractive foreign products.

Government monopoly over mail delivery provides an excellent example of the influence of the status quo. In the past, most nations gave government enterprises sole responsibility for the delivery of letters. The U.S. Constitution does not stipulate a government monopoly, but it does give Congress the power "to establish post offices and post roads."

DEAD LETTERS.   Yet after the experience of the past 50 years, few rational people anywhere would advocate a government monopoly to collect and distribute mail. The quality of service in different countries ranges from barely adequate to atrocious: In Canada, Italy, Israel, Argentina, and most Third World countries, no one expects letters to be delivered within a reasonable time. The U.S. postal system is better run than average, but dissatisfaction is widespread. In my home, Chicago, a recent scandal revealed that tons of mail had either been burned, discarded, or left undelivered for years.

The monopoly enjoyed by postal systems has made them sluggish and unimaginative. Successful overnight delivery of mail and small packages was pioneered by Federal Express Corp. despite obstacles erected to prevent regular private-mail service. United Parcel Service Inc. and other companies have taken over most of the market for larger packages by offering speedier, more reliable, more convenient, and sometimes less expensive service. Postal systems played no part in developing fax transmission, computer-based electronic mail, and interactive TV, though a less-regulated system would have tried to branch out into these newer forms of message delivery.

But except in a few nations, it hasn't been possible to get more than cosmetic changes in postal monopolies. Privatizing mail delivery and other reforms are strongly resisted politically by postal workers who fear, correctly, that many of them would lose their jobs. In the U.S., politics is an integral part of the system because postmasters are often political appointees. Postal managers also oppose radical change, since they expect to be replaced by more efficient managers from the private sector, while regulators expect their power to be reduced if competition replaces government controls. Businesses and households that benefit from subsidies to third-class mail and delivery in rural areas often oppose reform because they expect the cost of their mail service to rise.

MOMENTUM.   Fortunately, the status quo can be undermined when the harm becomes sufficiently large and transparent. Dynamic political leaders, such as Margaret Thatcher, may come to power calling for widespread privatization and other cutbacks in government programs and regulations. Other politicians, such as President Carlos Menem of Argentina, change their views after being in office for a while, because they see the opportunity for political gain by catering to the interests of those hurt by bad government policies.

The trend during the past 15 years toward privatizing badly run government enterprises has gained worldwide momentum. Many nations have sold off telephone companies, oil refineries, airlines, and government enterprises in various other sectors. Even state-owned postal systems have not been immune to pressures toward privatization. The Netherlands announced in April that it will shortly begin to sell a majority interest in its post and telephone monopoly. Although Britain has one of the more efficient postal systems, it recently proposed a public equity offering that will place a majority of the shares in private hands. Sweden is letting private companies compete with the state-run system in delivering mail in Stockholm. I expect other countries to follow Sweden's example and allow private competition against the state postal system.

If the tyranny of the status quo ever becomes generally recognized as a reliable law of politics, there will be increased opposition to bad proposals, even those framed on a small scale or characterized as temporary. And it may become a little easier to eliminate existing policies that have clearly done far more harm than good.

WHY PUBLIC ENTERPRISES
BELONG IN PRIVATE HANDS

When I was in college, the Tennessee Valley Authority was widely regarded as a showcase for how electric power should be produced and distributed. So I was greatly surprised recently to learn of proposals to sell TVA to the private sector, mainly to increase its efficiency. Conrail may be sold, and pressure is also mounting to sell other federal government enterprises, including Amtrak, the postal service, public housing, and even much of America's vast public lands.

Some people dismiss proposals to sell publicly owned enterprises as desperate attempts to help reduce budget deficits. These ideas, however, are not fully explained by pressure to reduce the size of the government sector. Ronald Reagan and Margaret Thatcher, for example, are strong advocates of privatization, yet total public spending has grown appreciably under them both.

Privatization is actually a world-wide movement. It is best known for what has happened in Britain, where Thatcher's government has sold hundreds of thousands of public housing units as well as major publicly owned companies in aerospace, automobiles, and telecommunications. It is planning also to sell British Airways, Rolls-Royce, British Gas, and many other public enterprises.

Socialist and Third World governments have climbed aboard the privatization bandwagon. Spain's Socialist government, elected in 1982, immediately nationalized a major private company. Since then, however, it has returned most of the company to the private sector and sold several other state companies. In France, the Socialist government of François Mitterrand nationalized banks and several other industries soon after it came to power in 1981. But the tide in France is now running strongly toward privatization and deregulation. Mexico, Brazil, India, and other Third World countries have sold some public enterprises and plan to sell others.

BOLD SWITCH. China has taken the most decisive steps toward privatizing its economy. In the 1950s, China herded its huge farm population into communes and other forms of collective production. But when per capita grain production failed to increase from 1955 to 1977, the leaders who succeeded Mao Zedong boldly decided to dismantle communes and return most land to private ownership. China is now also privatizing a portion of its service and manufacturing sectors, and it is generally reducing the degree of central control over the economy.

Government enterprises are widely perceived to be sluggish and inefficient. Perhaps the most persuasive evidence is the rapid expansion of food production in China once farming was privatized. During the same period, production from the collective agriculture of the Soviet Union has remained rather stagnant. Because few careful studies have been done that compare the performance of private and public enterprises, most of the evidence is circumstantial. Still, I am convinced that the intrusion of politics into economic decisions greatly handicaps public enterprises.

Consider Britain: After six years of privatization under Thatcher, state-run steel, coal, and rail industries still received more than $5 billion in subsidies during 1984–85, compared with less than $3 billion during 1979–80. The U.S. Postal Service lost $250 million in 1985 after racking up cumulative losses of more than $2 billion during the previous four years. Obviously, private companies sometimes lose money, too. In recent years most U.S. steel companies have not been profitable. But private companies that continue to lose money usually either go bankrupt, as McLouth Steel did, or are absorbed by other companies, as Republic Steel was by LTV. And some sell assets, as International Harvester and Pan Am have done.

SUSCEPTIBLE TO PRESSURE.   Political considerations also have a major impact on the employment and pricing policies of public enterprises. Political opposition to "scandalous" salaries means that the top managers of publicly owned enterprises receive substantially lower incomes than executives in private companies. For example, the Postmaster General receives only $86,000 a year, a fraction of the combined salary, bonus, and stock options of the chief executive of almost any equally large private company. How many able business people choose careers in public management when they can earn so much more in the private sector?

At the same time, public enterprises cannot easily lay off workers. They also tend to yield to union demands for generous wage settlements and to consumer pressure for low prices. No wonder that unions and subsidized consumers are strong opponents of privatization and deregulation.

The sale of government enterprises to the private sector can—and should—be carried much further. Publicly owned enterprises apparently are less efficient and less flexible than competitive private companies because they are unable to separate economic choices from political considerations. In a subsequent column, I will elaborate on this general case for selling government enterprises by considering proposals to privatize education.

PART 3

Labor Markets and Immigration

This part deals with minimum wages, social security and other labor taxes, employee ownership of companies, immigration, and other aspects of the market for labor. Economists have debated for more than six decades how minimum wages affect employment, profits, and poverty. But pressures to raise the minimum level continue to affect conservatives as well as liberal politicians. A conservative French government increased the minimum wage during the summer of 1995 to the equivalent of over $7 (or 36 French francs) an hour, even though French unemployment exceeded 11 percent. At this time, the United States is debating whether to increase the federal minimum from $4.25 an hour, where it has been for several years. The chances for about a $1 increase look good during this election year since Republicans in Congress do not want to buttress the impression they are opposed to the poor.

The momentum for increasing minimum wages in Europe and the United States has been spurred by a few recent American studies claiming that small increases in the minimum do not lower, and may actually raise, employment. These studies have been severely, and we believe fatally, criticized for containing flawed evidence. One of the essays discusses the criticism and the fundamental economic arguments against raising the minimum wage.

The most contoversial essay on immigration advocates that governments auction off the right to immigrate into their countries. This proposal was initially criticized by persons appalled at the seeming "heartlessness" of selling rights to citizenship. However, support for this approach has been growing over time — even an immigration commission established by President Clinton partly adopted this approach when it proposed to give employers the right to buy visas for foreign skilled workers.

Immigration has become a major political issue in the United States and Western Europe as the number of persons from poorer countries who want to emigrate to improve their economic circumstances has escalated. Rich countries have had contradictory criteria for determining who they accept from the large pool of potential immigrants.

Selling admissions puts reason and order into the selection process, for it favors young and skilled immigrants who are willing to bid a lot because they greatly gain economically from working in rich countries. It also blunts the criticism that immigrants unfairly collect generous welfare and other benefits, since immigrants who pay to enter would, in effect, have paid also for the right to collect some benefits.

LABOR MARKETS

IT'S SIMPLE: HIKE THE MINIMUM WAGE, AND YOU PUT PEOPLE OUT OF WORK

Higher labor costs reduce employment. That is why President Clinton's proposal to raise the federal minimum wage should be rejected. A higher minimum will further reduce the employment opportunities of workers with few skills.

Teenagers, high school dropouts, immigrants, and other low-skilled workers frequently earn less than $5.15 per hour, the proposed new minimum. They find employment in small establishments, especially in fast-food chains and other retail sectors. Increasing the minimum, as the President wants, would put some of them out of work since their productivity is not high enough to justify the cost to employers.

During the past several decades, many studies found that raising the minimum wage does reduce the employment of teenagers and others with low skills. But minimum-wage laws have remained popular among trade unionists and many politicians. And periodically, some economists have contested the prevailing wisdom about harmful effects.

SERIOUS FLAWS. A recent and widely cited challenge of this kind has come from several studies by two Princeton University economists, David Card and Alan B. Krueger—the latter now Robert B. Reich's chief economist at the Labor Dept. One study finds that the change in employment after a minimum-wage hike is generally not bigger in states with a larger fraction of low-wage workers—the group that should be most affected by higher minimums.

Another study is frequently mentioned by Reich and others in the Administration to bolster the argument that a higher minimum does not lower employment. That study compares employment changes in fast-food restaurants in New Jersey and Pennsylvania after New Jersey raised its own minimum in 1992. Card and Krueger argue that because employment fell in Pennsylvania as much as it did in New Jersey, the drop in both states must have been due to other causes than the raise in the minimum.

There are some, and I am one of them, who believe that these studies have serious defects. Several of these were spelled out by Donald R. Deere and Finis R. Welch of Texas A&M University and Kevin M. Murphy of the University of Chicago in research they reported at the January meetings of the American Economic Assn.

For example, the higher federal minimum in 1990 and 1991 caused a much larger drop in New Jersey's teenage employment than Pennsylvania's, which could explain why employment did not fall more in New Jersey when that state increased its own minimum in 1992. New Jersey employers presumably anticipated the increase in their state's minimum when they sharply cut employment in responding to the earlier wage hike.

DUELING STUDIES.   The Card-Krueger studies are flawed and cannot justify going against the accumulated evidence from the many past and present studies that find sizable negative effects of higher minimums on employment. The Deere, Murphy, and Welch study shows that the two-stepped increase in the federal minimum from $3.35 to $4.25 in 1990 and 1991 reduced employment of teenagers, high school dropouts, and other groups with low earnings.

The magnitude of these reductions sounds about right, particularly after the authors take into account the economic recession of that time. After the 27% increase in the minimum wage, employment of male and female teenagers lowered by 12% and 18%, respectively, while employment of high school dropouts shrank by about 6%. If Congress raises the rate by 18%, to $5.15 an hour, these results imply that employment of workers with few skills will fall by over 5%.

President Clinton justified the need for a higher rate of pay by noting that a family cannot live decently on minimum wage earnings. However, even Card and Krueger do not find that raising the minimum is an effective way to reduce poverty, since poor families typically get only a small fraction of their income from members whose wages are near the minimum.

The President also wants to increase current subsidization of the job training of less skilled workers, but these subsidies might be unnecessary if Clinton did not also advocate raising federal minimum wages. Higher minimums discourage on-the-job training of workers with few skills since they spend their time learning rather than producing.

Even a wizard would have a great deal of difficulty repealing the economic law that higher minimum wages reduce employment. Since politicians are not wizards, they should not try.

DOWN AND OUT ALL OVER EUROPE:
A LESSON FOR AMERICA

Many intellectuals in the U.S. and Asia believe that European social welfare policies should be a blueprint for action in their own countries. But those policies are financed by high taxes and mandates on business that are at least partly responsible for a spectacular increase in European unemployment during the 1980s and 1990s.

In the early 1980s, unemployment was less than 4% in France, Germany, and most other Western European nations. It now averages more than 10%, and the rate for those under 25 is close to 20%. By contrast, unemployment in the U.S. has not increased much during the past 15 years and is still less than 7%, while Japan's rate has risen only slowly and is still below 3%.

The U.S. and Japanese experience shows that the growth in European unemployment is not due simply to greater competition from the less developed world or to other forces that have affected all countries equally. The rapid growth of labor costs throughout Europe appears to have had much to do with the explosion in unemployment.

About half of Germany's average labor cost of $27 an hour results from social security, health, unemployment compensation, disability, and other taxes. And in France, Italy, Spain, and Sweden, the portion of total labor costs attributable to the government is nearly as large. By contrast, this fraction is less than 25% in Japan and the U.S., and even lower in Korea and Taiwan.

Regulations that restrict layoffs and mandate numerous vacation days and other paid leaves raise Europe's cost of labor far above the already high level of wages and taxes on labor. Generous leaves for sickness and other reasons increase Sweden's absenteeism rate to 10% and Germany's to 9%, compared with 2% to 3% in Japan and the U.S.

UNDERGROUND ECONOMY. To reduce costs, many European companies increasingly resort to temporary workers, because they are easy to dismiss and do not qualify for fringe benefits and taxes. In Spain, where it is almost impossible to fire workers on the regular payroll, about one-third of employees are temporary. Even in France and Germany, more than 10% of workers are temps.

Europe's underground economy has also grown enormously, in part because it provides a way to escape government-imposed employee costs. Although no reliable figures on this sector exist, crude estimates suggest perhaps 25% of all Italian and Spanish workers work underground at least part of the time, as do 10% of those in Belgium, France, Germany, and Sweden.

When labor is expensive and when firing employees is difficult, companies replace departing workers only slowly—and are reluctant to expand even when the economy picks up. This is why it now takes much longer than it did a decade ago to find a job in Europe if you are a first-time job seeker, a mother returning to work after childbirth, or an immigrant. It also explains why the youth unemployment rate is so high and why those out of work for over a year have grown to more than one-third of the unemployed. During the past two decades, private employment in the European Community has barely increased: The public sector has accounted for almost all the growth in employment. Japan and the U.S. have had the opposite experience: Private employment has surged, while government employment has grown little.

THE HARD WAY.   The long-term unemployed, youths, temporary employees, and underground workers—none of these groups have any opportunity to invest in job skills and training. The sharp growth in these categories means that fewer workers are being trained to work in modern economies, which demand high levels of skill and knowledge. The inadequate training that workers receive makes it still harder for them to find satisfactory long-term jobs.

Fortunately, a reaction seems to be setting in. Sweden's conservative government has tightened up its rules for paid sick leave—although they are still generous to a fault. Theo Waigel, Germany's Finance Minister, wants to cut unemployment pay and social-security handouts and scrap maternity pay and payments to construction workers who are temporarily laid off. The French government has frozen social-security benefits and increased the number of years of work needed to be eligible for pensions. In the Netherlands, the Christian Democrats want to shelve the minimum-wage law. A Socialist Spanish government is trying to make it easier for companies to fire employees.

Unfortunately, President Clinton's proposed health tax on employers is just the latest example of a trend in the U.S. to mandate business spending. Others include excessive Social Security and Medicare taxes, difficult-to-meet requirements to employ disabled job applicants, and compulsory leaves for employees to bear children. The European experience should be a lesson to the U.S. and other countries: Employment is much more buoyant when governments interfere less in labor market affairs. Let's hope that this lesson doesn't have to be learned the hard way—through higher unemployment.

MAKE FAMILIES COUGH UP
FOR MEDICAL COVERAGE

Tightness in federal and state budgets was the driving force behind the 1980s' trend toward government mandates of many business actions, including child care facilities at work and employment of particular groups. Putting obligations on companies, however, does not create resources. It merely shifts the burden to employers and employees and saddles companies with activities they may not be good at.

A bill sponsored by Senator Edward M. Kennedy (D-Mass.) would force companies to provide health insurance for their employees. Comprehensive health insurance is desirable, but I believe families, not businesses, should be required to buy it.

If the objective is to protect as many citizens as possible against major medical expenses, requiring companies to provide health insurance just won't do the trick. The unemployed, the retired, and others without jobs would have to find coverage elsewhere. It would raise the cost of labor, especially that of low-wage workers, for companies that would not voluntarily offer insurance.

Although group health insurance helps spread the risk of major illness, many companies are not big enough to provide much protection. A big claim by even one employee of a small company often leads to a large increase in insurance premiums or, in some cases, to cancellation of the insurance. This is why employers are reluctant to hire people who are likely to have large medical expenses.

FREE RIDERS. Corporate employers are the most important provider of health insurance in the U.S., but that's only because the Internal Revenue Service doesn't treat the expense as part of employees' taxable income. This is a subsidy. Taxing company health benefits would increase federal and state revenues by perhaps $60 billion annually and remove a tax incentive for companies to overinsure. If their company health benefits were taxed, many more employed persons would get their insurance from unions, churches, professional associations, and clubs that would be able to compete effectively against smaller companies and offer cheaper coverage.

People in rich countries who suffer illnesses that require long hospital stays and a lot of doctor's care are usually not allowed to go untreated, even when they do not have insurance or the resources to cover the costs. To eliminate the resulting temptation to take a free ride on the insurance and taxes of others, a federal mandate should require all families that can afford it to buy a basic package that covers major medical expenses and perhaps some preventive care also. Any family could, of course, opt to buy more extensive coverage.

Families that could not afford to buy protection would have their insurance premiums covered by the federal government. Eligibility would be determined by family income and the cost of obtaining private coverage. People with a history of serious illness who are not in a reasonably priced group health plan would be disproportionately included in the public program, because they would have to pay a lot to get private insurance.

MORE REVENUE. Some 34 million Americans are presently not covered by any type of health insurance. They would either be required to buy their own or would qualify for public assistance. But the uncovered population is not as serious a problem as the aggregate numbers might suggest. According to the National Center for Health Statistics (NCHS), most are employed people between the ages of 15 and 40 with a low incidence of serious medical problems. They could be included in the proposed system with a modest increase in public and private spending on health insurance.

The uninsured tend to work at small businesses that have been priced out of the health care market and by state-government mandates to include unnecessary medical services such as chiropractors and acupuncturists in all insurance plans. It is often said that the insurance companies' practice of denying coverage to the most vulnerable is to blame for the large uninsured population. The NCHS statistics suggest that charge is exaggerated.

The well-off elderly should also be required to buy private coverage against major illness. Over three-fourths of those over 65 already have some private insurance as well as medicare. Although many of the elderly would need public support—since private catastrophic health coverage would be very expensive for them—the growth of group plans unrelated to employment should reduce the cost.

If the federal government covered 60% of older people, the families presently under medicaid, and half of those currently without private insurance, it would be subsidizing the health insurance of about 20% of the population. This is the same fraction now covered under medicaid and medicare, so federal spending on health care would not increase. And federal revenues would expand if employee health insurance were taxed.

The health insurance approach I am advocating does not increase the federal government's role. The problem with the present system is not too little government intervention but the wrong type of intervention. The federal role should be to ensure that all families are protected against major illness.

THE LONG-TERM UNEMPLOYED NEED LONG-TERM HELP

The present U.S. unemployment insurance system fails to protect workers against the risk of long-term joblessness. The segment of the unemployed without jobs for longer than 26 weeks has more than doubled since the late 1960s. This explosion in long-term unemployment helps explain why so many of the unemployed now do not qualify for benefits. In 1988, over one-fourth of those unemployed had been without work for more than half a year.

Under present laws, benefits begin one week after a worker becomes unemployed. Eligible unemployed people then receive payments for up to 26 weeks, usually collecting a little less than half of what they had been earning. But benefits then cease unless the number of insured unemployed in the state is higher than about 5% of total employment. That's not likely, and only a few states have extended benefits during the present mild recession, since the national unemployment rate has so far remained under 7%.

Many people who are unemployed for short periods of time manage to scrape by without undue hardship by drawing down savings, borrowing from relatives and friends, or delaying mortgage payments and other bills. Those who are seasonally unemployed or on temporary layoffs often are expecting to return to their old jobs.

Common sense suggests that the long-term unemployed are less able to cope because they exhaust their savings and their credit with others. They don't have the means to pay for basic needs, let alone anything else.

TAX HIKE OPPOSITION.   Clearly, the present system is not doing what it should do: protect the unemployed who need it most. A step in the right direction would be to lengthen the period of eligibility from 26 weeks to perhaps a year. Those unemployed for much longer than that are unlikely to find regular jobs again, and they should be helped in other ways, such as through the welfare system.

Unemployment compensation is presently financed from a trust fund in each state built up by a payroll tax on the first $7,000 of wages earned in the state. Some members of Congress are calling for higher tax rates or large increases in the wage base beyond $7,000 to finance an extension of the eligibility period beyond 26 weeks. But there is also much opposition in the Senate and House to higher taxes on payrolls.

The present system, however, could generate the revenue needed to cover the long-term unemployed without imposing new taxes, if some of the short-term unemployed were made ineligible for benefits. Since those out of work for only a few weeks usually cope fairly well, the money would be better spent on those in greater need of assistance.

If the waiting period to receive benefits were extended to five weeks from the present one, the tax revenue released would be sufficient to allow an increase in coverage to a full year from the present half year. If the unemployed were not eligible before six to eight weeks, the trust would have sufficient funds to bring into the system some others who are not eligible. The fraction of the unemployed who collect benefits is now much lower than the 60% who were covered during recessionary times in the early 1970s. Many of those not eligible now are low-skilled workers who have been unemployed for several months and have trouble making ends meet.

WHERE TO START.   The fact that eligibility begins after just one week tends to encourage abuse of the system. Some companies more readily lay off workers who will be recalled in a few weeks because they know the trust fund is there to bear the burden. Seasonal employment is also lent a bogus attractiveness because the system covers regular spells of unemployment. These abuses of the system would be greatly curtailed if eligibility for benefits did not begin until after several weeks of unemployment. Although extending benefits to a full year would encourage some of the long-term unemployed to stop looking for work, the vast majority want to find jobs soon to prevent further erosion of their skills.

Other government safety-net programs are also too generous early on, but not generous enough at later, much more difficult stages of adversity. The welfare system should have a longer waiting period before a family becomes eligible, providing instead greater benefits to the long-term poor who have few prospects of improving their circumstances. The aim of Social Security and medicare is to protect the elderly against long-term illnesses and other serious risks of old age. In contrast, we give too much to the well-off elderly and to those with short-term illnesses, and we are too stingy with the sick and poor.

Tax and budgetary pressures are forcing a reexamination of all government programs in the search for more effective policies. A good start can be made with the unemployment-compensation system by removing the short-term unemployed from coverage and extending assistance to those out of work for a long time. An unemployment insurance fund should mitigate the economic hardships of workers who are facing the prospect of protracted, even permanent, privation through no fault of their own.

ESOPs Aren't the Magic Key to Anything

Almost everyone loves the concept of employee ownership. Social democrats who are disillusioned with state-owned enterprise yet doubtful whether capitalism protects workers' rights, relish the idea. And conservatives who want to spread "people's capitalism" favor it. But wishful thinking has outrun hard analysis. The advantages of employee ownership have been oversold, and its disadvantages have been overlooked.

The number of employee-owned companies increased rapidly during the past decade in Western Europe, Yugoslavia, and China. The number in the U.S. grew from a handful in 1974 to more than 5,000 now because of tax advantages introduced during this period. A company that borrows money to create an employee stock ownership plan (ESOP) has a tax-subsidized, low-cost way to provide employee benefits.

A common argument for the tax breaks is that employees work harder and are more conscientious when they own stock in the company. It's possible that ownership does indirectly motivate employees, but the direct incentive is weak: Almost all the additional profit created when an employee works harder goes to fellow employees and other owners of stock.

GREATER RISK. Nor is it clear that shares of stock motivate workers better than profit-sharing and other incentive-pay plans, which probably do a better job of tailoring additional pay to contributions by particular employees. Some companies have partly replaced or supplemented older profit-sharing plans with ESOPs only because of the tax benefits and other privileges.

Employee stock ownership increases workers' exposure to risk from fluctuations in the fortunes of their companies. Even without equity ownership, the wealth of most workers is poorly diversified because it's largely in the form of human capital tied to the success of their employers. The risk is bad enough for those still working, but it's even worse for retirees, since the income from and value of pension-fund assets also depends on how well the company does. On the other hand, profit-sharing plans can motivate workers without linking their retirement income or assets to the company's stock.

ESOPs often become a management tool to fend off unfriendly takeovers and other efforts to oust current managers. For example, the pilot-led, $6.7 billion ESOP bid at United Airlines Inc. countered an outside offer by Marvin Davis. So, too, were many other large ESOPs created after takeover bids. Employee-owned stock often aligns with management to turn down bids that benefit stockholders but may replace management and restructure operations. Surely, Congress didn't give ESOPs tax advantages that significantly reduce government revenue just to further entrench inefficient management.

The best study of whether employee ownership improves a company's performance was published in October, 1987, by the General Accounting Office. It found that profits and productivity remained about the same after companies introduced ESOPs. Michael Conte at the University of Baltimore and Jan Svejnar at the University of Pittsburgh reached similar conclusions in their recent survey of many studies on employee ownership in different countries.

LOST REVENUES. The GAO estimates that ESOP tax breaks cost the federal government more than $12 billion in revenue from 1977 to 1983. Reforms in 1984 and 1986 replaced most of the existing tax advantages with new ones. Companies can deduct the principal as well as interest on the amount borrowed to create an ESOP, and lenders pay taxes on only 50% of their income from ESOP loans. Dividend payments on stock held by an ESOP are also tax-deductible, unlike dividends paid to other holders of stock. These new tax benefits have reduced federal revenues by billions of dollars since 1983, a period of large budget deficits.

Employees can participate in some decisions even when they don't own stock or set policy. Spurred on by the success of Japanese companies with their problem-solving committees, called quality circles, many more businesses in the U.S. and Western Europe are seeking employee input on production methods, grievances, product development, and other matters. The GAO study and others found that productivity is greater when employees are involved in company decision-making.

During a meeting in Warsaw last June, I urged Solidarity advocates of employee ownership not to stack the deck in its favor when privatizing the woefully inadequate Polish economy. The only way to tell whether employee-owned companies benefit workers and improve productivity is to force them to compete fairly against profit-sharing plans, privately held companies, and companies with publicly traded stock.

Based on the available evidence, I believe that employee-owned companies have too many shortcomings to win a large number of fair contests. To guarantee judicious competition, the U.S. and European countries should eliminate the tax breaks and other privileges that artificially encourage employee ownership.

LET'S PUT DEREGULATION TO WORK IN LABOR

The dramatic deregulation of airlines, trucking, telephone communications, and banking during the past decade has created the erroneous impression that a deregulation movement is under way in the U.S. Just as fast as these sectors have been deregulated, others have become more regulated. An important example is the rapidly growing legislative, executive, and judicial involvement in labor markets.

The common-law tradition advanced the principle of "at-will" labor contracts, under which workers could quit and employers could hire and fire without having to justify their actions. In the U.S., this principle was altered in the 1930s to require collective bargaining with certified labor unions. More recently, major modifications of this principle have taken place. Now, government regulations rather than workers and employers often determine conditions of employment. For example, hiring is not permitted if it is judged to violate affirmative action and antidiscrimination goals, and companies are not allowed to solicit certain information from prospective employees about their criminal records and drug use. Moreover, firings may require proof of "just cause." Some localities insist on no-smoking areas at work, and companies are required to maintain health insurance for former employees for up to 18 months.

Some regulation clearly is needed in access to jobs and the terms of employment. But we are going too far and forgetting the lessons of deregulation. Consider the gathering momentum behind recent proposals in the U.S. to mandate paid leaves to men and women after a child is born or adopted and to require companies to provide child-care facilities at work. Most companies in the U.S. do not guarantee that employees will be able to return to their jobs after they take leave to care for their children. Moreover, a recent Conference Board study suggests that few companies operate child-care facilities or provide substantial other assistance to employees with young children.

SHIFTING THE BURDEN. Supporters of regulations requiring business to provide such benefits point out that most European countries already have mandatory paid leaves. In Sweden, leaves are paid for a full year after a child is born, and the right to return to the previous employer is guaranteed for 18 months. Supporters argue that mandatory paid leaves and child-care facilities at work would remove the disadvantage that mothers with young children have when competing for jobs. Such laws, supporters say, also would make it easier for working women to have children and would raise the amount of care provided young children with working mothers.

The advocates of legislated leaves and child-care facilities, in effect, want to shift some of the burden of child-rearing from working parents to employers and taxpayers. Because such legislation raises the total cost of employing women with young children, however, employers would become reluctant to hire women with small children and younger women who are likely to have children. The results would be lower earnings and greater unemployment for younger women. Thus the burden of paying for leaves and child-care facilities would be partly transferred to all younger women, a consequence that surely is contrary to the intent of these proposals.

Some might think this conclusion is the product of ivory-tower economic thinking. But consider that unemployment rates in Britain, West Germany, France, and many other European countries rose during the past decade from much below unemployment rates in the U.S. to well above them. Europe also increased its regulation of earnings and conditions of employment more rapidly than did the U.S. A recent study, "Unemployment in Britain," by Professor Richard Layard of the London School of Economics and Professor Stephen Nickell of Oxford University, concludes that the growth in employment-protection legislation in Britain was responsible for much of the rise in the male unemployment rate from 5.5% in 1975 to more than 15% in 1984.

A FAIRER WAY. It is by no means obvious that we should shift more of the burden of raising children from working parents to others. If we want to do so, however, it would be more efficient and fairer to shift the burden to taxpayers and divorced fathers rather than to young working women through regulation of labor contracts. For example, the tax credit for expenditures on child care can be raised. Working women would be helped by the higher tax credits for earned income in the Senate Finance Committee's tax reform bill. One important step would be to curb the disturbingly high delinquency rate of child-support payments from divorced and separated fathers. Adequate child-support payments would let divorced women provide better care for their children.

One need not advocate laissez-faire in labor markets to be concerned about the trend toward increased regulation of wages and conditions of employment. The plain truth, borne out by the benefits deregulation has brought to some industries, is that a plethora of government regulations in labor markets does more harm than good.

IMMIGRATION

Prop 187 Is Fine
—Now Rewrite Federal Law, Too

There was bitter controversy during the recent midterm elections over the state referendum in California on Proposition 187, which would disqualify illegal aliens from education and health benefits. The case for greatly reducing the number of illegal entrants is overwhelming, but the criteria used in determining who can enter legally need changing.

Stiff quotas on the number of legal immigrants were put into place during the 1920s. But the number of illegal aliens did not grow rapidly until the past couple of decades, when travel became cheaper and the desire to immigrate exploded, partly because of the benefits provided by the welfare state. Still, remarkably little is being done to discourage illegal entry.

FEW TEETH. Anyone caught is flown or bussed back to where he or she came from, most often Mexico. Many of these simply turn around and enter the country again—some have been caught more than a dozen times. Such token punishment encourages aliens to enter illegally, since it usually takes years to receive a legal permit.

The 1986 Immigration Control & Reform Act attempted to put some teeth into the distinction between legal and illegal entrants by requiring companies to check whether a job applicant had the right to be in the country. Any employer who knowingly hires illegal aliens is subject to sizable fines or jail terms. But an apparently thriving market in bogus immigration documents has undermined these sanctions.

To address this point, the drafters of Prop 187 added lengthy jail terms or fines to the California penal code for persons convicted of either using or selling false documents concerning resident-alien status to obtain a job or for any other purpose.

Most of the controversy over Proposition 187 continues to center on other sections that deny illegal immigrants access to publicly funded schooling and nonemergency health care—illegal aliens would still receive emergency care—and require school and health officials to check whether patients and students have the right to be in the country. These sections make good sense to me. Why is it more objectionable to require of school officials and health-care administrators what already is demanded of employers? And why should individuals who are ineligible for these benefits because they live in another country gain eligibility by entering the U.S. illegally?

Proposition 187 received more than 60% of the vote in California, despite the opposition of most of the major newspapers in the state. Some opponents consider it a smoke screen for efforts to cut back on Mexican immigration. On a recent trip to Mexico, I was asked about this law more than about the North American Free Trade Agreement or other issues concerning relations with the U.S. To help allay fears of a cutback and possibly reduce the incentives to enter this country illegally, the U.S. could give special priority to Mexican applicants at the same time that it forcefully restricts illegal entry from there and other nations.

But the overwhelming case for tougher policies toward illegal aliens doesn't justify calls for a cutback on all immigration. Newcomers have added enormously to the culture and vitality of the U.S. and many other nations in the Western hemisphere. And immigration can hardly be seen as posing a threat to American culture when the foreign-born are a much smaller fraction of the population than they were 50 or 100 years ago.

TOO MODEST.   However, the criteria for entry should be changed to favor those who would contribute most to the economy and would not require subsidies from taxpayers. One way to do this is to assign greater priority to young, skilled immigrants—the 1990 Immigration Act's steps in this direction are much too modest. Younger skilled workers also are less likely to become a burden by being unemployed, going on welfare, getting sick, or receiving old age support.

A radical change in admission policies now being pushed by some House Republicans would introduce a waiting period of several years before any immigrant is eligible for medicaid, welfare, or other government programs. But if radical departures from current policy are feasible, a better approach would be to follow a suggestion I made in this space long ago (BW—Mar. 2, 1987): to auction off many immigration slots to the highest bidders. Such a policy would automatically give priority to skilled applicants, since they would tend to bid the most for the right to immigrate.

The U.S. will benefit from even larger numbers of immigrants if illegal entry is curtailed and if young, skilled applicants either directly or indirectly receive top priority.

ILLEGAL IMMIGRATION:
HOW TO TURN THE TIDE

The uproar over White House nominees for Attorney General who had employed illegal aliens has focused attention once again on unlawful entry of workers from poor countries. This is a perplexing issue not only for the U.S. but also for France, Germany, Italy, Japan, and other prosperous, democratic countries. I believe such immigration can be effectively discouraged by sizably increasing the number of legal immigrants and at the same time punishing more severely the illegal entrants or those who hire them.

Given the yawning gap between the incomes of rich and poor countries, the issue will not simply go away—as long as it remains so easy to enter prosperous countries illegally or on tourist visas. Workers are attracted to rich countries because the jobs available there are much better-paying than anything they can find in their homelands. And that's true even though they are usually employed as low-paid, unskilled labor in restaurants, households, agriculture, or, in a few cases, manufacturing industry.

Since illegal aliens mainly take jobs shunned by native workers, some economists oppose punishing them. Instead, they advocate what amounts to "benign neglect"—especially if the immigrants are not eligible for tax-supported benefits. But democracies find it politically impossible to deny them health care, education for their children, and other benefits paid for by the taxpayer. And when the number of illegals in a country gets large, political pressure often mounts to grant them amnesty, as happened in the 1980s in the U.S. I am troubled, too, by the morality of a policy that encourages violations of the law by employers and illegal immigrants, while entry is denied to millions who stoically wait their turn for the right to enter legally.

SELDOM PENALIZED.   This is why democratic countries must take stronger steps than simply shipping illegal entrants who get caught back to where they came from. Entry cannot be reduced without effective punishment of either illegal aliens or their companies. Employers will not stop hiring illegal aliens on their own, because they do not believe they are doing anything wrong. The 1986 U.S. Immigration Control & Reform Act includes penalties for companies that hire illegal aliens, but households and very small businesses have seldom been penalized. Even though domestic help is believed to account for a considerable fraction of all off-the-books workers, Zoë Baird's household appears to be the first one fined.

The reasons I have given for greater restrictions on illegal entrants should be distinguished from erroneous claims that they take jobs from native workers or that they are often exploited. Research has found that the employment prospects of native workers are only slightly reduced when immigrants enter a local labor market. And although some illegal workers are afraid to complain about bad treatment—because they may be deported—there isn't room for extensive exploitation in the highly competitive labor markets where most illegals find jobs. For example, those households and small companies that do not pay Social Security and unemployment-compensation taxes for illegal employees are forced by the competition for labor to pay higher wages than if these taxes were paid. In a study of apprehended illegal workers, economist Barry R. Chiswick of the University of Illinois at Chicago found that their average pay was in fact well above the minimum wage.

SANE ASYLUM.   I am not advocating the erection of a wall against immigration. Instead, a more generous immigration policy should go hand in hand with greater punishment of illegal entrants, including fines and possibly jail terms. Greater legal immigration is not only desirable in its own right but would also reduce the number who seek to enter illegally. Not surprisingly, illegal entry generally expands when a country contracts the number of immigrants accepted.

France, Germany, and other countries are mistaken if they believe that they can reduce their immigration problem by cutting back on the right to political asylum or other legal means of entry. When legal immigration is curtailed, the number who sneak in or seek work after entering on a tourist visa will expand— unless a country is willing to punish effectively either the illegal entrants or the households and small companies that hire them.

I suggested in an earlier column that the most rational approach would be to sell the right to immigrate, but a less radical method of improving present policy and combating illegal immigration would be to allow a larger number of skilled and young people to enter legally. To prevent immigrants from taking advantage of government handouts, however, they should not be eligible for welfare, food stamps, government-financed health care, or certain other benefits until they become naturalized citizens. Politicians on both sides of the debate might well support this requirement, because it would not permanently exclude legal immigrants from taxpayer-financed benefits. Meanwhile, it would give them an incentive to become citizens as soon as they could.

BARBARIANS AT THE GATE
—OR AN ECONOMIC BOON?

The specter that haunts Western Europe is no longer communism, as Karl Marx asserted in the *Communist Manifesto*, but immigration from North Africa and the collapsed states of Eastern Europe and the Soviet Union.

Germany, France, Italy, and other European Community countries are sure that they will be the first stop if hordes begin to pour out of the East. And the number seeking entry into the West to improve their economic situation will climb even more if the Soviet republics throw open their borders.

Although all countries still strictly limit access to citizenship, the trend toward open borders, the facility of travel between Eastern and Western Europe, and the easy passage into Italy and France from North Africa make it difficult to control entry into more affluent countries. Berlin is already filled not only with East Germans but also with Turks, Poles, Hungarians, and others from Eastern Europe. The difficulty of keeping tabs on immigrants extends to the U.S., where many of the 11 million or so visitors who entered the U.S. during 1990—mainly on tourist visas—worked illegally. An additional million or so were apprehended trying to come in illegally.

Illegal immigrants and many who enter these countries legally as tourists come to get jobs. The number of immigrants working illegally in the U.S. is surely in the millions, although no one knows exactly how many. Construction projects, domestic work, restaurants, and some factories in Berlin are becoming dependent on Turks and other immigrants, many there illegally.

More illegal immigrants might be prevented from entering Germany and other countries of Western Europe if they beefed up their border patrols and severely punished the companies that employ illegal workers as well as the workers who are apprehended. But even such draconian measures may not be successful given the immense economic advantages of working in Western Europe and the strength of the underground economy.

It would be wiser to maintain a tolerant attitude toward illegals who work at unpopular jobs. However, there is no reason to provide gratuitous incentives to enter. Illegal aliens should be excluded from welfare and other subsidized social benefits, and they should not be allowed to gain legal status from periodic amnesty programs. And with the dramatic changes in Eastern Europe, the number of political refugees accepted can be sharply scaled back.

Denying illegal entrants social benefits and refusing to legitimize their status may appear cruel and exploitative. But would they be better off if they were prevented from coming, or were sought out and sent back in much larger numbers? That is the likely alternative to the approach I am advocating, for many Western Europeans resent not only their alien cultures but also their access to benefits paid for by taxpayers. No matter what is done, without a miraculous economic boom in the East, immigration will grow as a political issue in Western Europe. Extremists such as Jean-Marie Le Pen of France and neo-Nazi groups in Germany will appeal to many voters with their calls to seal borders and deport foreigners.

Part of the extremists' appeal stems from misunderstandings about the effects of immigration on natives. Despite the widespread perception that unskilled immigrants mainly take work from natives and lower their wages, the evidence shows that they generally accept jobs not wanted by indigenous workers.

University of San Diego economist George Borjas' summary of several studies in his 1990 book, *Friends or Strangers,* shows that immigrants to the U.S. have not had much of an effect either on the earnings or the employment of citizens.

BENIGN NEGLECT.   Also fallacious is the perception that illegal immigrants are especially exploited by employers and others. Evidence from apprehended illegal workers in the U.S. indicates that they earn considerably above the minimum wage and have low unemployment rates. They put up with the difficult conditions involved in coming to a strange country only because they do so much better economically than they would back home in Mexico, the Caribbean, Latin America, or Asia. They return home when they become unemployed for an extended period or accumulate a nest egg to buy a house or start a business.

A liberal policy toward skilled immigrants and benign neglect of illegal entrants would enable Europe to cope well with the pressure of large-scale immigration. West European nations could take advantage of their ready access to a pool of talent from the East by allowing generous numbers of younger skilled workers to enter. Younger immigrants not only become highly productive but also adjust relatively well to foreign cultures. And when they become citizens, they make fewer claims on Social Security, unemployment compensation, welfare, medical care, and other social benefits.

The opening up of Eastern Europe and the Soviet Union can be a boon to the West as well as to the peoples of these countries if demagogues in the West do not erect their own iron curtain.

OPENING THE GOLDEN DOOR WIDER—
TO NEWCOMERS WITH KNOWHOW

The 1986 law punishing employers who hire illegal immigrants has failed to stem the flow. But the U.S. can take effective steps to reduce illegal crossings. At the same time, we should greatly raise the number of skilled workers admitted legally.

The Immigration & Naturalization Service estimates that more than 750,000 illegal entrants are apprehended each year. Most are caught by border patrols and are simply sent back across the border. Those discovered at work or in other places are sent home as well. But many enter illegally again.

Illegal immigration can be cut without identity cards and unwarranted intrusions on privacy by punishing those who are apprehended before sending them back. They should be fined, if they have any money, and sometimes forced to spend time in jail. Punishment can be lighter for first offenders, but it should become severe for repeated illegal entry. This would deter many who have entered illegally in search of higher wages.

The present law has failed in part because employers often accept the poorly forged documents that illegal entrants acquire on the thriving black market. Although a study by the General Accounting Office shows that some companies play it safe by turning away workers with foreign accents, apparently enough employers either don't look at papers or don't ask many questions about those they accept. If illegal immigrants were the ones subject to punishment, companies would have no reason to shy away from hiring Hispanic workers and others with foreign accents. The onus of violating the law would be on illegal workers.

FALSE RECORDS. The American tradition of welcoming immigrants may appear to be jeopardized by a proposal to punish illegal entrants. Defenders of this tradition question the wisdom of punishing men and women who find jobs and draw little from welfare and other government programs. But such objections confuse the value of immigrants with encouragement of illegal entrants.

Immigration has surely benefited the U.S. enormously, but the present system discriminates against law-abiding persons who wait years for one of the several hundred thousand green cards issued each year for legal entry.

The amnesty provisions of the 1986 law worsened discrimination by rewarding many people who had entered illegally. Those who got in early enough can remain under the law, while others manage to win amnesty by submitting false records of when they entered.

Punishment of illegal entrants should be part of a new immigration policy that also admits many more younger, skilled workers. Such newcomers can help alleviate shortages in engineering, nursing, computer programming, and many other fields. Since they would have above-average incomes, they would pay above-average taxes and make few demands on welfare, medicaid, and other transfer programs. And it would be many years before such young immigrants would qualify for Social Security benefits—during which time they would be contributing to the system.

The economy can use many more well-trained workers, yet almost all current immigrants have few skills. They're either unskilled illegal entrants or beneficiaries of the preferential treatment given to parents, children, and other close relatives of current residents. In 1988, fewer than 4% of the 640,000 legal immigrants were admitted on the basis of their skills.

It is bizarre to have a policy that one way or another gives preference to unskilled entrants. Australia and Canada admit much larger fractions of their immigrants under special priorities for skilled workers. A bipartisan Senate bill sponsored by Edward M. Kennedy (D-Mass.) and Alan K. Simpson (R-Wyo.) takes a step in the right direction by expanding to 150,000 the number of skilled workers admitted each year. But even more skilled immigrants should be accepted.

Unfortunately, the House bill sponsored by Democrat Bruce A. Morrison of Connecticut is a big step in the wrong direction. It would strengthen rather than weaken the preference given to family members. And while it would take skills into account, the bureaucracy of the Labor Dept. would have to determine how many can be admitted in particular regions or industries.

DISGRACEFUL. Millions of workers all over the world are eager to come to America. To me, it is disgraceful that the U.S. hasn't accepted the hundreds of thousands of skilled Hong Kong residents who want to leave before China takes over in 1997. And close to a million Jews and other Soviet citizens—many of whom are quite skilled—have requested exit visas. Yet the U.S. has revoked their political-refugee status and is sharply limiting the number accepted. Countless other skilled workers from Eastern Europe, Ireland, South America, Africa, and elsewhere would jump at the opportunity to move here.

The U.S. should use punishment to discourage illegal entry, and it should admit many more skilled workers. These steps would go a long way toward providing a sensible immigration policy that would greatly benefit the economy.

HONG KONG'S BEST AND BRIGHTEST: OURS FOR THE ASKING

Uncertainty has pervaded Hong Kong since China signed an agreement with Britain in 1983 that guarantees the island's free market for 50 years after Beijing's takeover in 1997. The slogan is "one country, two systems," yet natives' behavior reveals considerable skepticism about whether China will adhere to its agreement. It may seem paradoxical that property values have remained high while emigration abroad is rising rapidly. But this simply reflects the different risks that China's takeover presents to financial and to human capital.

Property values did fall sharply after Britain agreed to cede all of Hong Kong—only the New Territories had been leased from China. But values recovered and now exceed their 1983 levels, making land in Hong Kong among the most expensive real estate in the world. The recovery might give the impression that after the initial shock, Hong Kong residents decided China will keep its side of the bargain. Much evidence contradicts that, however. All the local businessmen I met on a recent visit are diversifying their assets out of Hong Kong. Some are also taking foreign companies as partners, while others are seeking protection from China's government by entering into joint ventures with local authorities and other groups on the mainland.

STILL BOOMING. Commercial property in Hong Kong remains so expensive because large foreign investments have offset the loss of local capital. Chinese as well as Japanese, American, and other foreign companies are buying land, renting space, and engaging in construction and manufacturing. These companies expect Hong Kong to become an even more important port connecting China with the rest of the world. Trade between Hong Kong and China has already increased rapidly in the past five years and is expected to continue growing. Since China is expanding its world role, foreign companies also believe their governments will have the leverage to protect them against expropriation and other harassments by China.

Some Hong Kong economists disagree and argue that property values remain high because future income in Hong Kong is usually discounted with high interest rates that reflect the large uncertainties about returns on investment found there. With such high interest rates the nine years remaining until 1997 are a long time, from an economic point of view. But high rates cannot explain the huge amount of long-term construction under way that will yield income only for a few years prior to 1997.

Nor can such rates explain the sharp rise in emigration out of Hong Kong, from only 11,000 people in 1985 to more than 25,000 in 1987—with a much higher number expected for 1988. Many local residents have invested heavily in education, skills, and training. Such investments are what make up human capital. Since such capital must go where people go, emigration is the only way people can reduce the risks to their human capital from China's takeover—they cannot diversify by investing only part of their human capital abroad.

GREEN-CARD BLUES. Although emigration is still small compared with the more than 2 million members of the Hong Kong labor force, it's concentrated among people with marketable skills. Severe shortages have already developed among computer programmers, engineers, English teachers, researchers, middle managers, and a number of other occupations. Many more would be leaving if other countries, especially English-speaking ones, would take them.

Hong Kong residents may be the world's greatest experts on the minutiae of other countries' immigration policies. The U.S. is typically their first choice, but it's also the hardest to enter and requires a five-year waiting period for citizenship. Australia is considered less desirable, but skilled people can enter relatively easily and need wait only two years for citizenship. Canada has a three-year waiting period, however foreigners can buy citizenship there—and many Hong Kong residents are doing that—by investing sufficiently in certain types of activities. In a previous issue of BUSINESS WEEK, I suggested that we sell the right to emigrate to America.

The waiting period is relevant because some of those who are leaving plan to return after gaining citizenship elsewhere. That enables them to protect their human capital in case China abandons its one-country, two-system policy. Their children would also have a refuge should life under China's rule become unbearable.

American immigration policy gives priority to relatives of citizens, and this severely limits immigration of skilled Hong Kong residents to the U.S. In recent years, less than 4% of the legal immigrants were accepted on the basis of their skills—even though America is said to be suffering from a shortage of engineers, computer experts, and other skilled workers. An easy way to help alleviate this problem is to raise sharply the number of skilled immigrants accepted from Hong Kong and elsewhere. In this way America can take advantage of the uncertain outlook in Hong Kong to gain many ambitious and hardworking immigrants with needed skills.

WHY NOT LET IMMIGRANTS PAY FOR SPEEDY ENTRY?

In a market economy, the way to deal with excess demand for a product or service is to raise the price. This reduces the demand and stimulates the supply. I suggest that the U.S. adopt a similar approach to help solve its immigration problems. Under my proposal, anyone willing to pay a specified price could enter the U.S. immediately.

The U.S. now severely rations the number of legal immigrants—close to 500,000—that it accepts each year. Most would-be immigrants must wait many years, or give up hope, or enter illegally. Under the new immigration law, 10,000 special entry permits are to be awarded on an arbitrary, first-come basis. More than 1 million applications have been received for these few permits, clear evidence of the enormous demand for entry to the U.S. Selling rather than giving away the right to come to this country would provide some of the many persons who cannot get in through regular channels the opportunity to enter without delay.

LESS RESENTMENT. Under my program, each year the Immigration & Naturalization Service would set the price for a permit to reside permanently in the U.S. Anyone who paid this price and did not have some bar to entry—such as having a criminal record or carrying an infectious disease—would have the right to enter. Potential immigrants who could or would not buy their residence permits could still wait their turn through regular immigration channels.

Of course, many details would have to be worked out. Should there be a special price for families with children? Should immigrants who returned home after a short period in this country receive refunds? Experience would determine a reasonable price for the right to enter, but assume it to be $50,000. Perhaps 40,000 people annually would be willing to pay this fee, which is less than 10% of the number who have been legally admitted each year. Although the main purpose of this proposal is to improve the immigration process, a few extra billion dollars of annual revenue would be welcome, especially in the light of the large federal budget deficit.

Selling residence permits has several additional advantages over the present system. The U.S. is reluctant to admit large numbers of immigrants partly because they become eligible for welfare, medical payments, and other assistance. Immigrants who can pay to enter are not likely to require help from the government. Even when they do, because such immigrants have already paid to enter, they arouse less resentment than newcomers who seem to be taking a free ride at the taxpayer's expense.

Ambitious, energetic, and highly skilled persons generally gain the most when they join the open and competitive U.S. economy. And the U.S. benefits from their presence. Yet such people find it difficult to enter, since more than three-fifths of legal entrants are parents or other relatives of citizens. Immigrants willing to pay for immediate entry would include many of the most desirable newcomers, because they could expect to recoup even a large entry payment with a few years of good earnings.

One objection to selling the right of entry is summarized in the phrase: "Citizenship should not be for sale." This objection ignores the fact that most previous immigrants to these shores endured enormous burdens. The fare for crossing the Atlantic in the early 19th century equaled about one year's annual earnings in the colonies. While transportation costs declined sharply relative to wages in the late 19th and early 20th centuries, immigrants still had a long and arduous trip. Beyond that, they were likely never to see their families and friends again. The growth of quick and cheap air travel in the middle of this century greatly reduced the cost and psychological burden of immigrating, but people wanting to come to this country now must wait in long lines. In one way or another, then, immigrants usually have paid a lot for the right to enter. The proposed system of charging fees for immediate entry would be different only in that the immigrants' burdens would also make a contribution to tax revenue.

RADICAL SURGERY. The U.S. has benefited enormously from its millions of poor and ambitious immigrants. Fortunately, selling the right to immigrate would not keep out poor people. Some persons of modest means would save or borrow from friends and relatives to raise the funds to enter immediately. Others might borrow from U.S. companies that wanted to hire them. Commercial lenders might help finance reliable and able immigrants. The federal government could lend part of the fee to needy immigrants, as it now lends to needy college students. Government loans might stipulate that the borrower could not become a citizen until the loan is repaid. Poor people could still come in the usual way by waiting in line for their green cards.

A program to sell immigration rights may not seem politically feasible. But Canada has begun to do it. The present system of legal immigration to the U.S. is badly flawed and needs radical surgery. Selling immigration rights would harness the advantages of the price system to improve substantially the market for immigration to this country.

A Missed Chance
for True Immigration Reform

One must admire the political skills Congress displayed in passing an immigration bill. Passage came after repeated failures and in the face of vocal opposition from the U.S. Chamber of Commerce, Mexican-Americans, and other groups. Many people welcomed the new law because U.S. immigration policy is defective and needs drastic overhaul. Nevertheless, the law is badly flawed and likely to worsen not improve immigration policy.

Millions of people from other countries are attracted to the U.S. by its high wage scales, the opportunities for advancement it offers those from poor backgrounds, and its economic and political freedom. Yet the U.S. severely rations the number of people who can enter legally. So far during the 1980s, a little more than half a million immigrants have been admitted each year, and of these more than 40% were related to U.S. citizens. The large numbers of potential immigrants who are not accepted must either give up trying to enter, wait many years in immigration queues, or attempt to enter illegally.

Potential immigrants, therefore, are tempted to enter illegally not only because of the attractive working and living conditions in the U.S. but also because they face severe constraints in entering legally. Yet the principal shortcoming of the new law is its silence on legal immigration. It does not consider alleviating the problem of illegal entry by raising the number of people admitted legally and by changing the criteria for selecting legal immigrants.

VIRTUE UNREWARDED. The act does offer many illegal aliens amnesty. All illegal aliens who can "prove" they have resided here continuously since 1982 and most illegal aliens who worked in agriculture during the past year would become legal residents. They are granted this amnesty despite the millions of potential immigrants who have obeyed U.S. laws by waiting patiently in immigration queues—or by giving up trying to enter. While large numbers of illegal aliens receive amnesty, many students and other immigrants who have been here legally will be forced to leave because they do not qualify for legal immigration status.

Unfortunately, amnesty programs tend to encourage the very behavior they pardon. If political considerations produce amnesty now, surely a rational person contemplating illegal entry will expect future amnesties. Many potential illegal immigrants have feared the disruption of being deported after having lived and worked in the U.S. for a while. Once deported they have to start over in their native country or reenter the U.S. illegally and begin again without the benefit of the seniority they had built up previously. The expectation of future amnesty reduces that fear.

To cope with illegal immigration in the future, the new law establishes fines and prison sentences for employers convicted of hiring illegal aliens. Unlike some critics of the law, I see nothing wrong in principle with these employer sanctions. But they are an inefficient way to try to control illegal immigration.

BLAMING THE VICTIM. Employer sanctions in this case violate the Anglo-Saxon principle of law that the burden of avoiding an illegal action should be placed on the people best able to do so. Criminals should be punished, for example, rather than victims who might have taken greater care to avoid becoming victimized. Under the act, employers must distinguish illegal foreign-born workers from legal residents. The already thriving business in counterfeit identity cards—passports, birth certificates, driver's licenses, and the like—will expand much further. As a result, many employers will become reluctant to hire workers with foreign accents, including legal residents.

The most efficient way to discourage illegal entry is to catch and punish illegal entrants. After all, who knows better than immigrants whether they are in the U.S. illegally? Punishing illegal aliens would be far more effective in deterring illegal immigration than any system of employer sanctions. Yet the U.S. has followed the policy of simply returning apprehended illegal aliens to their countries of origin without imposing fines or imprisonment. Those caught along the Mexican border—where most apprehensions occur—can simply turn around and try to enter again.

The immigration law has many less-important provisions that are also undesirable. Its special treatment of seasonal agricultural workers has no justification but the political clout of farmers in California and other states. It stipulates that illegal aliens who receive amnesty will be eligible immediately for medicaid and will become eligible in five years for welfare, food stamps, and other federal benefits. The law raises the likelihood of national identity cards and greater government surveillance of residents.

But the main defects are its emphasis on employer sanctions rather than sanctions on illegal aliens, its granting blanket amnesty, and especially its failure to deal with policies to raise the number of legal immigrants and to change the criteria for legal entry. For these reasons, I view the law as a missed opportunity for sensible immigration. It will probably do more harm than good.

PART 4

Human Capital and Schools

Sizable investments in education and other forms of human capital are essential to economic growth. Since governments are responsible for financing most of the spending on education, the essays in this part concentrate on government policies toward education in developed and undeveloped countries.

The returns from higher education have been increasing in the United States and some European countries primarily because modern economies are organized around the effective utilization of knowledge, and hence they reward persons who command extensive knowledge. Yet government educational policies in most countries are designed to favor the well-to-do since they are more likely than the poor to attend public colleges and universities with highly subsidized tuitions. This is a perverse form of income redistribution since the state subsidizes students who come from richer families and will generally earn incomes that are well above average. We discuss replacing government subsidies with government-financed student loans, and contrast the effects on efficiency of loans with fixed interest rates and those with rates that depend on earnings.

Several essays consider how to increase competition among primary and secondary schools in order to improve the responsiveness of schools to the educational needs of students, particularly those from disadvantaged backgrounds. We claim that the best way to foster competition is to give vouchers to families that help them pay for the education of their children at schools of their choice — either public or private, and including religious-denominated as well as secular schools. Unfortunately voucher proposals have met powerful, and so far successful, political opposition from teachers unions who fear correctly that vouchers will reduce union control over educational policy.

INVESTMENTS IN HUMAN CAPITAL

MAYBE THE EARNINGS GAP
ISN'T SUCH A BAD THING

Income inequality grew substantially during the Reagan and Bush Presidencies, yet the midterm elections suggest voters did not hold this against the Republican Party. The reason may be because they realize that the increase in inequality is related to economic growth. When greater inequality is due to higher rates of return on human capital and other investments in knowledge, it can be an engine that drives an economy toward more rapid economic growth.

Ever since Jean-Jacques Rousseau's *Discourse on the Origin and Foundations of Inequality* (1755), the emphasis has been almost exclusively on the negative aspects of income inequality. But in modern economies, growth requires an educated and trained labor force, since production of computers, other electronics, and most manufactured goods and services needs knowledgeable workers. An economy grows faster when rates of return on investments in human capital increase, or when the amount invested expands.

The increased earnings gap during the past two decades in the U.S. is mainly the result of higher returns on education, training, and experience. This didn't happen because of Presidential or congressional policies but because companies competing for skilled workers bid up their pay compared with the wages of less-skilled workers.

GRADUATION GIFT. Starting in the 1970s and continuing unabated until the end of the '80s, the gap between the weekly earnings of college and high school graduates rose from about 40% to 70%, while the premium on completing high school pushed up to over 30%. Similar trends raised the compensation of older and more experienced employees compared with that of younger and newer workers. These trends toward higher benefits from knowledge slowed during the past few years, but they have not reversed direction.

Most Western European countries experienced related trends in earnings differences by education and job skills. Labor markets are not as flexible there, so the gap in weekly earnings between more and less knowledgeable employees rose less in Europe, while unemployment rates of younger and other less trained workers increased much more than in America.

The widening inequality in earnings and the buoyant demand for skilled workers also indirectly encourages greater growth in the economy by increasing the incentives for young people to invest in themselves. That's one reason why government data shows high school graduation rates of blacks in the U.S. have risen substantially since the late 1970s to the point that they are now close to the very high rates of whites.

HIGHER ENROLLMENTS.   And despite the rapid increase in college tuition since 1980, the fraction of male high school graduates who continued their education grew by several percentage points, while college enrollment rates of women expanded even more rapidly. Students from poorer families were hurt by cutbacks during the 1980s in federal grants to college students, but a study by Thomas J. Kane of Harvard University shows that college enrollment rates of blacks rose sharply during the latter part of the 1980s after falling earlier in the decade.

Unfortunately, the higher returns on human capital have been associated with deteriorating earnings for persons at the bottom of the economic ladder. Real earnings of high school dropouts and others with few skills not only declined relative to more educated and trained employees but also fell by a lot in absolute terms. This explains why the labor-force participation rates of unskilled groups have dropped noticeably since the latter part of the 1970s while the number of jobs have expanded dramatically.

This makes it even more essential to help young persons from poorer families overcome any artificial obstacles to improving their education and training. State, local, and federal governments can help with policies that do not require greatly increased public spending. States can improve the quality of high schools in low-income neighborhoods by raising the competition among schools for students. I believe the best way to accomplish this is by offering tuition vouchers to students from poor families that they can use at private as well as public schools.

The federal government has a limited but valuable role to play in raising skills. Its loan program to college students should be expanded. At the same time, however, strenuous efforts are needed to reduce the embarrassingly high delinquency rate on past loans to students.

Everyone, from government to the intellectuals, must rethink the pluses and minuses of income disparities.

WHY THE THIRD WORLD
SHOULD STRESS THE THREE R's

The rebellion in the poverty-stricken Mexican state of Chiapas has dramatized the inequality in living standards in a country trying to promote rapid economic development. Third World nations that neglect the education, training, and health of the poor perpetuate divisions that may tear apart their social fabric.

At a recent education conference in Brazil, I argued that economic development cannot be sustained when a nation neglects elementary education for a sizable part of its population. Education lets young persons from poor backgrounds acquire the skills to rise in the world, and it reduces the tendency for inequalities in wealth to be perpetuated from one generation to the next. The example of the so-called Asian tigers—Hong Kong, Korea, Singapore, and Taiwan—is instructive: Early in their development, they largely eliminated illiteracy and raised the schooling of the bottom stratum to decent levels.

According to statistics compiled by Robert J. Barro of Harvard University, more than two-thirds of Brazilians over the age of 25 have less than four years of schooling, and a further one-fourth have none at all. The situation in Mexico is almost as bad. Education of the poor in both nations has greatly improved over the past two decades, yet even now fewer than one-third of teenage Brazilians are in school. The slums scattered throughout Rio de Janiero are filled with children who spend their time not in school but on the streets, terrorizing residents and visitors with burglaries and robberies.

The social problems from unequal education are often compounded by racial differences: In Brazil, Mexico, and many other nations, wealth, education, and occupation are polarized along racial lines. The poor in Mexico are mainly Indians, while in Brazil they are primarily descendants of slaves brought from Africa.

SQUARE MEALS.   Children from homes with poor, illiterate parents need schooling that addresses their special needs. My wife and I spent a day as the guests of Governor Leonel Brizola of the state of Rio de Janiero at one of several hundred schools in the state that were created during the past decade for poor children. Students in these schools get three meals and almost 10 hours of instruction and recreational activity a day, and they do their preparation in the classroom rather than at home. But since such schools are expensive to build—$1 million per school—as well as to operate, they are not the solution for poor children.

A better way to help poor families in the Third World (as well as elsewhere) would be through a tuition voucher system. Low-income parents would receive vouchers that help pay the tuition at any approved school that accepts their children. Participating schools could be required to provide nutritious meals and health checkups. Such vouchers would stimulate competition among public and private schools to improve the education and health of children who most need to be helped. Middle- and upper-income families have less need for tuition vouchers, for they often manage wherever they are to get decent schooling for their children.

Poor mothers and fathers usually want a better life for their children than they have had themselves, and many of them would choose schools wisely. Even some of those who care very much about their families, however, often force children to leave school early so that they can help contribute toward the meager household resources, even when that violates child-labor and minimum-schooling laws.

WASTE NOT.   One way to provide incentives for poor parents to look out for their children's interests is to give them a bonus that offsets the income loss from keeping children out of the labor force. The bonus could be larger when the children attend school regularly, and it could even rise when the children receive good grades.

Apologists for the status quo claim that poor countries do not have the resources to raise the education of all their citizens to decent levels, and they believe international organizations such as the World Bank should finance the education of their poor. But governments in these countries usually spend a quarter or more of gross domestic product on financing deficits in inefficient state enterprises, on excessively expensive universities, and in many other wasteful ways.

The real obstacle to greater government spending by Third World countries on basic education, combating crime, and other important public activities is not their limited resources but the diversion of these governments from what should be their major priorities. They are too busy doing things that either should not be done at all—or that should be left to the private sector.

Countries such as Brazil and Mexico have enormous human energy and economic potential. But they will further delay their entry into the First World if they continue to pay insufficient attention to the schooling and health of their poor.

CLINTON'S STUDENT-LOAN PLAN
DESERVES AN "F"

President Clinton has proposed changes in the way the federal government subsidizes the education of college students. He wants to eliminate banks from the lending process, compensate students who perform what is deemed community service, and give students another option on how to pay back their debt. These ideas are misguided in every major respect.

To cut out middlemen expenses, the President would bypass banks by having the federal government make loans directly to students. The House Education & Labor Committee has already approved this part of the package. But if governments are better at lending than the banking sector, they should take over lending to companies for investments and to families for housing and cars. Despite many well-publicized failures of private banks, government agencies do a much worse job of lending money, which is why the worldwide movement toward privatization highlights banking and other financial activities. I do not know of one federal lending program—including those to small businesses and farmers—that gets high marks for its efficiency.

Banks can provide a valuable service in screening student borrowers and monitoring repayments. But under the present system of student loans, banks have no incentive to perform these functions, since the federal government covers all bank losses on student loans. This explains why the default rate is a disturbingly high 10% and why many more borrowers are in arrears. The savings and loan scandal has shown what happens when banks are relieved by government guarantees of their responsibility for unwise lending decisions. Thus encouraged to make extremely risky loans, they reap all the gains from profitable ones while taxpayers foot the bill for the mistakes.

YOUNG BEGINNERS.   The solution is not to eliminate banks and their experience but to require them to bear a larger share of the cost of their bad student loans. Banks covet the student loan business. When the default rate on a bank's student loans increases, it should have to pay a higher insurance premium.

In return for two years of community service after students finish their education, Clinton wants to forgive up to $10,000 in loans that help pay for college or vocational training. Qualifying jobs are to be selected by state governors and other officials from the categories of education, the environment, public safety, and human services. To be sure, these four categories all have problems, but they are not going to be solved by giving politically determined jobs to young beginners who are trying to qualify for tuition grants. And why these categories? What about other charitable activities and private employment in profit-making companies?

The President's plan sends a dubious message to young people. It rests upon the proposition that it is more beneficial to spend time helping to build housing for the homeless—one frequently mentioned example of community service—than to contribute to the productivity of the U.S. economy by becoming better engineers, computer programmers, architects, etc. This is a dangerous message for the economy at any time, but especially when the U.S.'s capacity to compete in world markets is being severely tested.

Student borrowers from the federal government now pay fixed interest rates on their debt after completing their education. The President would keep this as an option, but he wants to offer students another one whereby those who earn more pay higher rates.

FIXED OR VARIABLE.   The new option is designed to balance larger payments by high earners against smaller ones by low earners so that the average
earner would pay about the same interest rate as under the present system. But
the desirable objective of insuring repayment on student debt against uncertainties about future earnings isn't likely to be attained because of a phenomenon
that economists term self-selection. Students who expect to go into law, business,
and other well-paying fields will tend to choose the fixed-interest-rate option,
under which they pay a lower rate. Those who expect jobs that pay little will
select the option whereby people with low earnings pay back less—the variable-
rate option. Since much of the borrowing is by professionals and graduate students, many loan applicants know whether they are preparing for fields that pay
well or poorly.

Either fixed or variable repayment rates are manageable, but not both. On the
whole, the existing approach is probably better because the many students who
know they are in fields that pay a lot will not participate when rates are tied to
earnings. When Yale University in the 1970s made repayments depend on earnings, it found that students going into law, business, and medicine generally
chose not to borrow from Yale.

The President's proposed reform of the student-loan program may be good
politics with its call for community service, saving middlemen expenses, and an
option that allows borrowers who earn less to pay back less. But from the stand-
point of the nation as a whole, it won't be as good a way to reform federal assistance to students.

THE HUMAN-CAPITAL DEBATE:
ADVANTAGE, BUSH

To raise the productivity of the U.S. economy and its competitiveness in world
markets, President Bush and Governor Clinton are offering rival plans to invest
more in the skills, training, and other human capital of American workers. Who
has the better plan?

Both candidates pay considerable attention to education reform. They recognize that many public elementary and high schools are awful and fail to educate
their students, but they propose very different remedies. Governor Clinton supports greater competition only among public schools, whereas the President is
advocating a government-funded voucher system of choice that would include
private schools as well.

Bush's approach to school reform seems to be far superior, since the absence of
effective competition from the private sector is the biggest defect in the present
education system. Greater competition only among public schools probably will

improve their efficiency, but the effect will be small compared to the impact on innovation and school productivity of harnessing the forces unleashed by private initiative. Comparisons of the performance on standardized tests of students in public and private schools—especially studies of Catholic high schools by sociologist James Coleman of the University of Chicago and others—clearly indicate that private schools tend to provide a better education for less money.

GROWING GAP. More than 20% of all students who enter high school fail to graduate, and the inadequate preparation of most dropouts for work highlights a major failure of the public school system. I advocate subsidies to improve the job skills of dropouts as part of my "G. I. Bill" for ghetto youth (BW—June 22). The President calls for "a G. I. Bill for children" that includes an apprenticeship program with both academic instruction and on-the-job training for all persons who do not go on to college.

The governor has similar plans for training and apprenticeships. But he would also require companies to spend no less than 1.5% of payrolls on worker education and training. Clinton is making a major mistake by proposing additional government mandates for business spending, including health insurance. The growth in such mandates during the past decade is one of the most pernicious developments in federal legislation. His training mandate reflects Clinton's desire in several fields to extend the influence of the federal government over business decisions.

Both candidates favor more generous grants to college students and expanded student loans. But neither candidate makes a good case for greater subsidies. The gap in earnings between the typical American college graduate and high school graduate is now about 60%, the largest in the past half century. With all the concern about growing income inequality, it is unseemly to propose additional subsidies to a high-income group that is doing better than ever.

FAMILY AFFAIR. It would be easier to understand the concern about helping college students if the fraction of U.S. high school graduates who continue their education was falling or lagging behind the percentages of other countries. However, the U.S. sends more than half of its high school graduates on to college, which is the largest percentage in the world. And the fraction of high school graduates who go to college increased significantly from the mid-1970s to the 1990s; even the racial gap in college attendance narrowed a little during this period.

The human capital of the working population is determined not only by schools and job training but also by parental efforts to improve the health, habits, values, and skills of their children. Most parents may do a reasonably good job, but a few of them are failing badly, especially those who are drug addicts, alcoholics, have too many children, or just don't care. Both candidates address the issue of family responsibilities partly by supporting welfare reform that places greater emphasis on workfare and puts limits on how long families can stay on welfare.

It is desirable to get families off welfare, but the most urgently needed reform is a change that rewards parents whose children invest in their own human capital. We should change the present welfare system to make benefits depend not mainly on the number of children but on what parents do for each child. Benefits should rise when children attend school regularly or when they are taken for health checkups, and they should fall when parents are on drugs or when children do poorly in school. These are not ivory-tower suggestions, because several states, including Wisconsin and Connecticut, have already proposed reforms along these lines, and it is a shame that neither Presidential candidate is supporting such an approach.

However, both candidates deserve credit for their emphasis on the skills, training, health, and values of the American population. Although the proposals of both have good and bad features, I believe the President's schooling and training proposals are clearly better because they more consistently support voluntary private choice rather than compulsion.

TUNING IN TO THE NEEDS
OF HIGH SCHOOL DROPOUTS

Since the early 1970s, real wage rates of young high school dropouts have fallen by more than 30%, probably the largest decline during this century for any education group. The fraction of students who drop out of high school remained fixed at about 15% during the '70s and '80s. But the overall dropout rate for inner-city black males is much higher—close to 25%.

Research by Professor Kevin M. Murphy at the University of Chicago also shows that during the past 15 years, earnings for the bottom quarter of young male high school graduates fell at almost the same rate as the dropouts' earnings did. By contrast, real wages of high school graduates rose over this period.

A number of explanations have been advanced for this trend. For one, methods of production and the goods and services appropriate to a modern economy strongly favor educated and skilled workers. Second, the fierce competition from goods produced abroad has hurt less-trained workers in the U.S.

Pressure to reform high school education in America, especially in the inner cities, reflects concern over the dismal statistics. Although teaching in many urban areas can be greatly improved, a well-funded federal-state program that combines training with on-the-job experience would be even more important.

USEFUL MODEL.   It's widely recognized that the bottom quarter of U.S. high school students aren't well prepared for employment. An extensive training and employment program designed for high school dropouts could greatly improve their economic prospects. Ideally, each dropout would get as much as two or three years of training and employment at a craft or other practical skill. Taxpayers would pick up the cost of training and might also subsidize companies that employ participants, especially in the early stages of the program.

Such a plan would partly supplement several current programs, especially the Job Training Partnership Act. This has apparently been rather successful at placing participants in useful jobs, but it has served only a fraction of young dropouts.

The West German system provides a useful model. Almost three-fourths of young Germans get classroom instruction in one of more than 400 trades, plus on-the-job experience. Training usually begins at age 15 or 16, typically when U.S. teens drop out, and continues for upwards of three years. State governments pay for classroom instruction, which comes to about a day a week, while employers pay wages, which average more than $500 per month. This system is probably the reason that West Germany has one of the lowest youth unemployment rates of any country in the Organization for Economic Cooperation & Development.

A program for U.S. dropouts would enroll a much smaller fraction of young people than in Germany because a much larger percentage graduate from high school in America. But the German experience shows that an intensive training and job program can greatly improve the performance of high school dropouts in the labor market.

GREATER CHOICE. Such a project would add to public spending when budget deficits have created pressure to cut expenses. But surely it's neither fair nor efficient to spend approximately $4,000 annually on educating each high school junior and senior—and only a pittance on training high school dropouts. Moreover, high school education would become cheaper if less effort had to be devoted to keeping in school young people who would prefer a training-employment program that better suits their interests and talents.

Some of the bottom quarter of students who now finish high school would drop out to take advantage of such a training program. This is no cause for concern, since the evidence on earnings shows that these students currently don't benefit much from finishing high school. They're better off getting training and experience more closely oriented to productive employment. And their participation might not add to total public spending because of the money saved on the portion of their high school education that they skip.

Education Secretary Lauro F. Cavazos recently endorsed the principle of giving students a greater choice in the public schools they attend. The inner-city and minority youth who would constitute a large fraction of participants in a skill-acquisition program for dropouts currently cannot choose the high schools they attend. But they would be able to choose the private trade schools and companies where they could get their training and jobs. Though it is true that some trade schools have notoriously poor training standards, I believe competition would force these trade schools and companies to serve these students better than inner-city high schools have.

The U.S. needs to improve the quality of its work force to become more competitive in the international market. What we are talking about is an investment in this nation's human capital. The dismal prospects of young high school dropouts would be much brighter if they could get extensive training and employment experience in a useful trade.

WHY DON'T WE VALUE SCHOOLING AS MUCH AS THE ASIANS DO?

The rise of Japan, South Korea, Taiwan, Hong Kong, and Singapore surely ranks among the most significant economic events of the past 30 years. Hundreds of books and articles provide conflicting reasons for this ascent. I am convinced that one crucial factor is that these countries pay much closer attention than the U.S. does to education, training, work habits, and other ways of boosting workers' skills.

The U.S. has been neglecting its human capital, as witnessed by the quality of education provided by many elementary schools and high schools in urban areas. More than 14% of the students in U.S. high schools never graduate, compared with only 6% in Japanese high schools. The dropout rate of black males in large American cities exceeds 20%. Real wage rates of young high school graduates in the U.S. have declined more than 10% since 1975, and wages of dropouts have plummeted even more, indicating that not only dropouts but also many graduates are ill-prepared for work in modern economies.

LOW GRADES. Schools in Japan and the other successful Asian countries emphasize mathematical and other technical skills demanded by modern industry, agriculture, and many service businesses. Students in Asian countries also work much harder on homework and in the classroom than do students in the U.S. In light of this, it is not surprising that Japanese and Hong Kong students placed near the top and U.S. students were close to the bottom in uniform mathematics tests given in 1984 to 12th-graders in more than 20 countries.

Japanese parents supplement their children's schoolwork with *juku*, which is remedial and preparatory tutoring in mathematics, sciences, language, and other subjects. The number of profit-making *juku* enterprises has grown rapidly during the past decade, and now more than 35,000 compete for students. Parents rely on *juku* to help their children do better in school and give them an edge in the keen competition for limited places in the best colleges. Almost half of all ninth-grade pupils get extra tutoring, and expenditures on *juku* make up about 20% of private spending by families on education.

Unlike elementary and high schools, American colleges and universities are not inferior to those in Asia, and the best in America are clearly superior. That is why increasing numbers of Asian students are pursuing postgraduate studies in engineering, science, economics, and other technical subjects here. Indeed, so many are flooding into our institutions of higher learning that the National Academy of Sciences has voiced concern about the disproportionate number of PhDs in these fields awarded to Asians.

Although hard statistics are not available on the amount of on-the-job training in different countries, circumstantial evidence suggests that it is much more important in the Asian countries than in America. Most workers in Japan, Korea, and elsewhere in Asia remain with the same company for much of their lives, so companies are willing to invest time and money in their workers. I was impressed by the number of workers in classrooms on a recent tour of plants in Korea and Taiwan. By contrast, the level of job turnover in American companies is not conducive to as heavy an investment in workers.

PAYS TO STAY. Even Japanese plants in the U.S. choose workers much more carefully than American plants in the same industries, as shown in a recent study. Presumably, Japanese plants here, like those abroad, have selective hiring practices because they keep workers for a long time and plan to invest heavily in training them.

Earnings rise more rapidly with experience in Japan and Korea than in the U.S. The steepness of the rise in pay for experienced workers is one measure of the quantity of on-the-job training and learning. Younger workers receive lower wages, as they spend time and effort learning rather than producing. Older workers earn a lot more because they had invested much in themselves when they were younger.

Education and training are of little use without proper work habits and commitments to the job. That's where the successful Asian countries excel. Workers are usually enthusiastic about their jobs and loyal to their employers: Many Japanese workers even refuse to take vacations. Men work an annual average of well over 2,000 hours in Japan and other Asian countries, compared with about 1,800 in the U.S.

In poorer countries, work hours are generally longer, but Japan is richer than many European countries, and employees there still work much longer hours. As incomes rose rapidly in Japan over the past 10 years, work hours did not decline.

As China found out during the Great Leap Forward and the Cultural Revolution, investments in human capital are unproductive and the work ethic will wither without proper incentives. Unquestionably, private enterprise and many other factors contributed greatly to the remarkable performance of the

Asian countries. But these countries also recognized that human capital is the foundation of a modern economy.

WHY THE CANDIDATES ARE
MISSING THE POINT ON COLLEGE COSTS

Widespread alarm over rapidly rising tuition and other costs at most colleges is reflected in the concern of George Bush and Michael Dukakis. Yet the paradox to be explained is why college enrollments are booming as never before.

Since 1980, tuition and fees have indeed risen much faster than family incomes. To make matters worse, federal assistance to college students did not increase much in real terms, while tuition rose rapidly. Also, federal aid shifted away from direct grants toward greater reliance on student loans, and new laws lowered the maximum loans available to students from middle-income families.

CROWDED CAMPUSES.   In view of the attention to the rise in student costs, one might expect that college attendance declined. But the number of young white high school graduates with some college education rose by about 10%, to more than 56%, in the 1980s, after declining during the 1970s. This number also rose for blacks, to about 48%, although more slowly than it had for whites.

And while there are fewer 18-year-olds now than there were in 1980, enrollments are at record levels at many colleges and universities. Campuses are reporting crowded classrooms and a shortage of faculty this fall because enrollments are much higher than anticipated. Throughout the past 20 years, the number of young people of college age has been a surprisingly bad indicator of future enrollment.

The paradox of greater enrollments in the face of higher costs is easily explained by the increased benefits of a higher education. Monetary gains from a college degree declined during the 1970s to the lowest level on record, but they are now higher than at any time during the past 40 years. The gap between the average earnings of college graduates and high school graduates with 11 to 15 years of work experience increased from under 40% in 1980 to almost 60% in 1987. The earnings gap is wider for workers with more experience and smaller for younger workers.

FORGOTTEN FACTOR.   Moreover, the total cost of attending college grew much more slowly than tuition and fees. It may even have fallen. With all the attention focused on tuition, it is easy to forget that more than half the cost of college is the result of earnings foregone by not working full time. And those foregone earnings dropped during the 1980s because the market for high school graduates has been weak. Is it surprising that enrollments grew to unanticipated levels when the rise in benefits from a college education greatly exceeded the rise in total costs?

Looking at earnings and enrollments this way, Senator Ted Kennedy's Education Savings Bond plan or Vice-President Bush's similar proposal to subsidize savings by parents for their children's college education make little sense. Why add to the subsidies of college students when they eventually will earn much more than the average worker?

Instead of highlighting the need for larger subsidies, the rise in tuition costs means that deserving students should have greater access to loans. Larger loans can be made available under present federal programs to students from middle-class and poorer families. However, much greater effort is needed to monitor who is allowed to borrow and who is allowed to collect interest due on outstanding loans. More pressure could be put on colleges to help in collecting payments from their former students. Or a leaf could be taken out of Governor Dukakis' suggestion to use the IRS to collect such payments along with income taxes owed. It is disgraceful that little pressure is being put on defaulting borrowers when about 10% of student loans are now in default. The problem is greater at public than at private colleges and is especially severe at two-year colleges and proprietary trade schools, where default rates exceed 17%.

MISSING SKILLS. The high default rate by graduates of these institutions is scarcely surprising, as they earn little more than high school graduates. Students who anticipate modest earnings will be attracted to programs such as Dukakis' proposed Student Tuition & Repayment System (STARS), in which earnings determine how much is repaid on a loan. But students who expect to do well—such as business majors, engineers, premeds, and prelaws—would have to pay back a lot and are unlikely to want to participate in STARS.

The evidence on defaults convinces me that income-contingent loan programs will not be financially viable because they would be used mainly by students who expect to earn relatively little. Therefore, larger loans and other modifications to present programs are probably a better way to help deserving students finance their higher education.

The candidates are not alone in missing the point. The true learning crisis rests not in the country's colleges but in the education provided by many elementary schools and high schools. The fall in real wage rates of high school graduates and the even sharper decline in the wages of high school dropouts during the past decade indicate that less-educated younger workers do not have the vocational and other skills and knowledge required by a modern economy.

TAX-FREE BONDS FOR TUITION:
A STEP IN THE WRONG DIRECTION

The high cost of a college education has become an issue in the U.S. Presidential campaign. Vice-President George Bush, for example, promises tax-free bonds to help parents finance their children's education.

During the past decade tuition and fees have grown almost 10% per year — far more than the 6% average rate of inflation. In the U.S., these costs now average more than $1,500 per year at four-year public universities, $7,000 at private universities, and $10,000 at elite private schools. An even larger cost to most students is earnings forgone as a result of being in school rather than being full-time members of the labor force. Forfeited earnings plus tuition exceed $35,000 during four years at a typical public college and $60,000 at a typical private college.

But these enormous costs must be viewed in economic perspective: A college education offers large financial rewards. A recent study by Kevin M. Murphy of the University of Chicago and Finis Welch of the University of California at Los Angeles shows that the spread between the earnings of college and high school graduates grew rapidly after 1979 after having narrowed in the 1970s, and is now larger than it was 30 years ago. Murphy and Welch attribute the sharp rise in the payoff of going to college in the 1980s to a decrease in the relative number of college-educated people entering the labor force. They also cite the decline of heavy industry, where high school graduates do well.

After 11 to 15 years of work experience, the average college graduate earns almost 60% more than a high school graduate. Over their lifetimes, college graduates receive some $600,000 more than high school graduates, equivalent to more than a 10% rate of return on the average cost of higher education. Therefore, college remains a good investment even without factoring in cultural and other advantages. This explains why applications to colleges are booming despite the rapid rise in costs and the relatively small number of students who are reaching college age.

WEAK COLLATERAL. Americans may have been overeducated during the 1970s, when the financial benefits of a college education were low, as Harvard economist Richard B. Freeman argued in his 1976 book *The Overeducated American*. But "overeducated" is no longer apt in the 1980s. The problem with a college education is no longer that it is a bad financial investment. It is that the costs are paid up front, while the benefits are received slowly, over a lifetime.

Parental help and the generous scholarships and employment opportunities provided by colleges do not meet the needs of many prospective students, especially those from families with modest means who do not qualify for large scholarships. In business language, the problem is how to finance an expensive and durable investment by unproven investors who can offer commercial lending only weak collateral.

During the past 20 years, the federal government has helped students finance their educations with Pell grants, work-study programs, and direct loans, and by guaranteeing low-interest loans from banks. More than half of all entering college freshmen now receive some form of federal help. During the Reagan Administration, federal assistance has shifted away from grants to greater reliance on loans. Since I believe this trend ought to continue, George Bush's proposal to subsidize parents of college students would be a step in the wrong direction. Why should the average graduate, who is a member of the earnings elite, receive a subsidy from taxpayers in the form of a tax break?

SHIFT THE BURDEN. The states also subsidize college students heavily by setting tuition at state schools far below cost. Yet many students move to other states after graduation and do not even benefit the economies of the states that finance their educations. States should shift the burden away from taxpayers and on to the students. Tuition should be raised sharply to cover the cost of providing the education. State loans could supplement federal programs to help students finance higher tuition levels.

Even students who borrow more than $25,000 to finance a college education — far more than the current average debt of graduates — could in most cases readily repay both interest and principal out of subsequent earnings. After all, many young people do not hesitate to borrow $50,000 or more to finance the purchase of a house or apartment that produces no financial benefits other than possible capital gains. Obligations on student loans could be made to depend on subsequent earnings by requiring a given percent of earnings to be repaid for each $5,000 borrowed. Borrowers who were not successful or who entered occupations that paid badly would be obligated for much less than borrowers who attained high earnings.

Students should not be denied a college education because their parents cannot help financially. But neither should we subsidize students who will earn good returns on their college investments when they become engineers, businessmen, lawyers, doctors, computer analysts, or other professionals with better-than-average incomes.

WHY SHOULDN'T COLLEGE
BE A SMART INVESTMENT?

The beginning of a new school year reminds many families of the financial sacrifice required to send children through college. At elite private universities, tuition runs about $12,000 a year. Expenditures on room, board, and travel, as well as forgone earnings while in school, add at least $8,000 a year, raising the total cost of four years of education to more than $80,000.

Tuition averages only about $1,500 a year at public colleges and universities, but students at public schools, as well as private ones, must also settle for lower-paying and usually part-time jobs. And many public-school students also pay room and board. In addition, an increasing number of students have the added expense of postgraduate education at law, business, and other professional schools.

In the past, the cost of higher education was less a problem because mainly wealthy families sent their children to college. Nowadays, well over half of all high school graduates continue their education; blacks, Hispanics, and other minorities account for almost 20% of all college students. To add to the burden, college tuition and fees have almost doubled since 1980.

NO DOWNPAYMENTS.   Yet when placed in perspective, the cost of college education does not seem so daunting. Four years at an elite university are no more expensive than, say, buying a nice home. Most college graduates eventually own their own homes, and the median price of single-family dwellings purchased recently exceeds the $80,000 that a college education cost them. Moreover, owner-occupied housing does not yield financial returns, except sometimes a real capital gain, whereas higher education usually greatly raises lifetime earnings. The average financial rate of return on the cost of a typical investment in a four-year college education is 7% to 10%.

True, attending college is a risky investment. Yet if an elite higher education is no more expensive than good housing and if college is a profitable investment, why do individuals who must pay all or part of their own education have more difficulty in financing a college education than in financing the purchase of a house? One reason is that most college students are young and have not had much time to save for a downpayment on their investment in education. More important, housing can be used as collateral for a mortgage, but a college education cannot serve as a collateral for an education loan. If a mortgage holder defaults, a lender takes possession of the house. Obviously, a lender cannot take possession of a college education without somehow requiring the defaulter to engage in involuntary servitude, which would be illegal.

To help pay for their college education, many students work during the summer and part-time while in school. Further, most parents help out with gifts or loans, and all colleges provide scholarships and employment opportunities. In recent years, the federal government has taken an active role in financing college education with Pell grants, direct loans, guaranteed student loans, college work-study programs, and educational-opportunity grants. More than half of all freshmen entering college now receive some form of direct federal assistance.

IT'S A GIFT.   Since education is poor collateral for strictly commercial loans, I believe that the federal government should help students. But the present programs are badly flawed. They subsidize college students with taxpayers' money, even though most taxpayers earn less than the typical college-educated person. These subsidies take the forms of loans at below-market interest rates, outright gifts, and allowing borrowers to default even when they can easily afford to pay. The current default rate on guaranteed student loans exceeds 10%.

To eliminate the subsidy, effective interest rates on student loans should equal the rate of return on business investments with similar risks. Students who default should be energetically prosecuted so that student loans would no longer be a free ride at the taxpayers' expense.

With few exceptions, interest rates charged students have not been related to their eventual earnings. One way a loan program could take into account the uncertainty about financial returns from a college education would be to require student borrowers who were later financially successful to pay back more than unsuccessful borrowers. A pilot program might require borrowers to pay a fixed percentage of their income for a specified period of time. In effect, the government would share the risk of college investments by buying nonvoting common stock in student borrowers. Stocks are usually the appropriate way to finance risky investments like a college education. Low returns from loans to students who do not do well would be balanced by high returns from loans to students who end up earning a lot.

Federal assistance can help college students finance the large and rising cost of higher education without imposing the burden on taxpayers. Student loans with appropriate fixed interest rates and with paybacks contingent on the financial success of borrowers would achieve this worthwhile purpose.

VOUCHERS AND COMPETITION AMONG SCHOOLS

SCHOOL-FINANCE REFORM:
DON'T GIVE UP ON VOUCHERS

The California school-finance scheme known as Proposition 174 would have given vouchers worth $2,600 to all students to help them attend private schools if they chose. It was opposed by the two national teachers' unions, many politicians, and other groups—and soundly thrashed in a November referendum. Despite that rejection and rebuffs of related proposals in Oregon and the state of Washington, radical school-finance reform seems inevitable.

Although I supported Proposition 174 because it offered an improvement on the status quo, grave defects in voucher proposals must be remedied if they are to appeal to a strong majority of voters. The vouchers should be provided only to low-income families, since it is almost always their children who are saddled with inferior schools in the inner city. These families do not have the economic means to choose communities with good public schools, whereas middle- and upper-income families already exercise considerable choice among schools. They can move to the suburbs or city neighborhoods with good public schools, or—if they have the means—they can send their children to private schools.

Limiting the vouchers to poor families answers the valid objection that if all families are included, richer families will surely be the main users of the vouchers to send children to private school. Milwaukee has started an experimental program that gives a limited number of vouchers to children from the inner city for private-school attendance.

The present system of public-school finance is roundabout and inefficient, first taxing households to provide revenues for public schools and then indirectly returning taxes to families with children in public schools. The California voucher proposal would have directly given back some of the tax revenues to all families who chose private schools. A still better system would not only give vouchers to students from poorer families but would also require public schools to become partly self-supporting by charging all students tuition equal to the voucher level.

PRECEDENT.   For example, public-school tuition would equal $3,000 if that is the value of school vouchers. Taxes would have to cover only the excess of public-school expenditures over tuition income. There is precedent for tuition charges by public schools in the early history of common schools in the U.S. and in the sizable fees currently assessed by state-run colleges and universities.

Tuition income would help offset any reduction in government spending on public schools because of the public financing of tuition vouchers. Such income would also make it easier for public schools to finance a continuing growth in spending on students—which more than doubled during the past 25 years.

Some voters who are fed up with public schools opposed the California initiative because they feared it would add to the deficit in the state's budget. But if vouchers were limited to poor families and if public schools charged tuition, the financial demands on state budgets might be reduced rather than increased. It would then be financially much easier to do more for the poorer students who need help the most by raising the size of their vouchers above the California proposal of $2,600. This figure amounts to less than half of the national average cost of a student in public high school.

TAX CUT.   Poorer families who continue to send their children to public schools would be financially no worse off under the proposed system than at present, since their vouchers would cover the tuition charges of these schools. It might appear that middle-class families with children in public schools would become financially strapped, since they would have to pay both tuition and school taxes. But the taxes needed to finance public schools would be reduced because these schools would now have tuition revenue. For this reason, an initial reduction in school taxes should be mandated to recognize that schools also will get revenue from tuition.

The present public-school financing system has encouraged sharp segregation of students by income, race, and other characteristics. Vouchers limited to students from poorer families would reduce this segregation because some private schools with a mainly affluent clientele would be happy to accept more students from diverse backgrounds if they brought vouchers covering part of their tuition. Even at present, segregation by race, income, and family education is much lower in Roman Catholic private schools than in public high schools.

If public schools were to charge tuition, families would determine where to send their children by comparing differences in quality between private schools and available public schools to differences in tuition. This would increase the competition between the private sector and all public schools, not just those with students who are eligible for vouchers.

This competition for students would force public schools to become better. The system of higher education in the U.S. is the world's best mainly because competition between private colleges and tuition-charging public colleges has improved the performance of both.

A TICKET OUT OF THE INNER CITY

Many explanations of the Los Angeles riots have been proposed, and I am not going to add to the list. Whatever the underlying causes, the riots highlighted the need to integrate many more ghetto youths into the economic system. I believe the best way to do this would be through the equivalent of a "G. I. Bill" for ghetto youth, financed by state and local government.

Under such a plan, all young people from ages 14 to 19 in eligible families would receive vouchers from local and state governments. Until age 16, these could be spent only at high schools of the student's choice, as in many education-voucher plans. Parochial and other private high schools would be eligible to participate, since they provide better education than do public schools in the inner cities.

To limit the cost of the program, initially only children in poorer families would be allowed to participate. Middle-class children already receive reasonably good schooling and training since they have access to schools in suburbs and smaller towns and know more about how to get better jobs.

The usual education-voucher proposals would not help the many inner-city youths who get little out of high school, even if better schools become accessible to them. And they do not guarantee that students who finish high school will have useful skills to help integrate them into the workplace. For it is the limited skills of inner-city youths, much more than racial or other discrimination, that handicap them in the competition for jobs.

WAGE DIVE.   One need only cite the depressing statistics on trends in real earnings: The wages of high school dropouts and the bottom fourth of graduates have fallen by more than one-quarter since 1975. The decline in these categories applied as fully to whites as to blacks and other minorities, but a much larger percentage of blacks and Hispanics drop out of school or do poorly in high school even when they graduate. It is fashionable to blame the Reagan and Bush Administrations for this trend, but the decline began under President Carter. Less well-trained workers are also doing badly in several European countries.

Under the system I am proposing, participants who drop out of high school before finishing could use vouchers until age 19 to get on-the-job training in the private sector. Those who finish high school would have a year's worth of vouchers that could also be used for additional training, either on a job or at a trade school that teaches marketable skills, such as computer programming or carpentry. To prevent these schools from using exaggerated claims to attract students, their continued participation would be contingent on placing most of their graduates in jobs that pay above a specified amount per hour, or more than a certain percent above the minimum wage.

It is essential to include on-the-job training in the program, since on-line training is especially important for ghetto and other poor youngsters. Their economic problems are partly caused by difficulties in getting access to promising work situations. Eligible companies would have to provide details about their training programs, including information about the kinds of job ladders available to successful participants.

MORE BANG FOR THE BUCK. The average public school in the U.S. spends over $5,000 per student each year. Yet many parochial and other private schools provide better education with much smaller expenditures per student, and trade schools usually spend only a fraction of what public schools do. A generous voucher system could cost only half of what is spent by public schools — even less for those in on-the-job and trade-school training programs.

Housing & Urban Development Secretary Jack F. Kemp, Representative Charles B. Rangel (D-N.Y.), and others are advocating federally subsidized enterprise zones for inner cities. I believe these zones are a mistake, because the subsidies would become part of the political pork barrel and would not meet the main problems facing ghetto youngsters. Black males from the inner city generally lack the skills to qualify for well-paying jobs, even if these jobs were located in plants in their own neighborhoods. By contrast, Koreans and many other immigrants living in the inner city often do manage to get good jobs precisely because they have valuable skills and work habits.

A five-year voucher system for poor teenagers would put further pressure on state and local government budgets at a time when their finances are already in bad shape. However, government spending on students who use vouchers at private schools, at trade schools, and for on-the-job training instead of attending public schools would be greatly reduced. That's because the average cost of a voucher would be much less than per capita spending on public-school students.

Moreover, an extensive schooling and training program for poor youth is well worth undertaking even if it adds to the strain on local government budgets, for it gets to the heart of the economic difficulties faced by young people. No one program can solve all the problems of inner cities, but this one will improve employment prospects among those who most desperately need better job skills.

PUBLIC FUNDS FOR RELIGIOUS SCHOOLS WOULD BE NO SIN

President Bush has proposed giving private schools the opportunity to compete against public schools for taxpayers' dollars. Although some cities and states already have programs that provide limited funds to private schools, there is considerable disagreement over whether schools supported by religious organizations should be allowed to compete for public funds, whatever the plan.

Many people believe that including parochial schools would violate the separation of church and state embedded in the First Amendment to the Constitution, which begins: "Congress shall make no law respecting an establishment of religion, or prohibiting the free exercise thereof...." But I believe that public funds should be available to religious-supported schools, provided that they are available on equal terms to all private schools.

Constitutional specialists differ over exactly what James Madison and the other proponents of the First Amendment meant, although they clearly wanted to guarantee freedom of worship. I am no constitutional expert, but I take the view that the founding fathers appreciated the advantages of competition for religious ideas and beliefs and added this amendment to safeguard against the kind of established church that dominated England at that time. Those beliefs that best satisfied the spiritual needs of the people would thrive in an open competitive environment where there is no state religion.

This "free-market" view of the First Amendment implies that public funds could be spent on the secular activities of parochial schools if they have to compete against public or other private schools. It also helps explain an inconsistency: Many programs do allow public funds to go to secular activities of religious groups. For example, patients can use medicaid and medicare benefits at church-sponsored as well as other private hospitals. And any religion that meets very minimal criteria can qualify for nonprofit status and gain exemption from local property and other taxes and regulations.

There are also precedents for including religious-sponsored schools in an education voucher system where taxpayers pay the tuition at schools chosen by students. The post-World War II G. I. bill covers the tuition of veterans at parochial colleges and universities. College students who receive Pell grants, federally backed loans, and other public support can use them to attend religious-sponsored colleges.

Some U.S. Supreme Court decisions indicate that the judiciary will allow public funds to be spent on parochial schools. For example, in *Mueller vs. Allen* in 1983, the court supported the constitutionality of a Minnesota law allowing parents to deduct their children's parochial-school tuition from their state income tax—clearly an indirect subsidy. Earlier decisions allowed public funds to subsidize the transportation of students to parochial schools and to pay for their secular textbooks.

Despite these decisions, there is still strong opposition to including parochial schools in an educational voucher program at the elementary and high school level. Some fear that students who attend parochial schools will be subjected to religious indoctrination. But a program could specify that no school would qualify for public funds if it required attendance at religious services or instruction in a particular religion. And public funds would be limited to secular subjects and philosophical aspects of religious studies.

Opponents of the inclusion of parochial schools also believe that it would increase the degree of segregation of students by race or creed. One important study, the book *High School Achievement* by James S. Coleman and his colleagues at the University of Chicago, finds that 90% of all students at Catholic high schools are from Catholic families. But they also show that these high schools are less segregated by race and income than are public high schools. Of course, parochial and other private schools that participate in a voucher or other school-choice program would not be allowed to discriminate in the selection of students on the basis of race, religion, or family background. Their right to exclude troublesome students could also be curtailed.

HIGH ACHIEVERS. If religious-sponsored schools were inferior, the educational advantages of including them in a school-choice program would be dubious. But the study by Coleman and his colleagues concludes that Catholic schools on average provide better education than public schools. Students from all races and family backgrounds score much higher on achievement tests than do comparable students from public schools, even though average spending per student by Catholic schools is a great deal lower. The advantage is especially large among students from less educated and poorer backgrounds. Catholic schools do better partly because they involve parents and the community more closely in school activities.

Sooner or later, the need to upgrade the quality of education available to the poor and middle classes seems sure to force many communities in the U.S. to include private schools in a choice program. It would be a shame to exclude religious-sponsored schools, which offer a superior education.

What Our Schools Need
Is a Healthy Dose of Competition

Disastrous results are often necessary before powerful special interests lose their political influence. The abysmal education received by many students in the U.S. has fostered a remarkable growth during the past few years of state and local systems that force public schools to compete for students.

Minnesota is phasing in a program that allows pupils to attend any public school in the state willing to accept them, as long as desegregation guidelines aren't violated. Other programs are in place in East Harlem, Massachusetts, Milwaukee, and Seattle. Some 20 state legislatures are considering plans that allow greater school choice.

The inner-city poor are the main beneficiaries of greater choice. If middle- and upper-income families don't like the public schools in their area, they already have many options. Many can send their children to private schools or move to communities with better schools. Poor families can't afford private schools or the move to expensive neighborhoods with good public schools.

LOSING CONTROL.   The opposition to school choice comes mainly from teachers' unions, school superintendents, school boards, and neighborhoods that fear an influx of undesirable students. All of these groups are worried about losing control, and the teachers and school officials are also disturbed by the prospect of competition. The recent report by the Labor Dept.'s Commission on Work Force Quality, of which I was a member, is silent on the issue of competition among schools because several commissioners were strongly opposed.

Greater choice among public schools is a major step in the right direction, but disadvantaged students should also be allowed to opt for private schools. On the whole, private schools do a better job of educating their pupils, as my colleague at the University of Chicago, Professor James Coleman, has shown in a massive study of public and private high-school education in the U.S. Catholic schools spend much less than big-city public high schools, yet they are more successful— because they're less subject to the political interference that limits disciplinary procedures, and they manage to get parents and the community closely involved.

Although teachers, school administrators, and many other groups have been adamantly opposed to including private schools in a choice program, a few states have been pioneers in this direction. The Post-Secondary Option Program in Minnesota pays the tuition and other fees of students who elect to receive all or part of their last two years of high-school education at private or public colleges and vocational schools. Last spring, Wisconsin Governor Tommy G. Thompson proposed to pay the tuition at any participating private school for as many as 1,000 low-income elementary school pupils in Milwaukee County.

The Milwaukee plan has the right orientation: It pays only for the private schooling of children from poor families. Means tests determine which families can qualify for various health and housing programs and should determine which pupils will get vouchers to attend private schools. Poorer families are most in need of the additional options that private schools provide.

SECONDARY ISSUE.   Even though opponents of school choice recognize that private schools would have to obey civil-rights laws to qualify for public funds, they still claim that such a system would add to the racial, religious, and social segregation of students. But how can a program that pays only for the private-school education of disadvantaged students raise, rather than lower, school segregation? Surely some private schools with mostly richer white students would agree to be in the program and accept more minority students if the government pays their tuition.

In any event, a school system should strive to provide quality education for all students, regardless of race, income, or other factors. If school choice improves the education obtained by disadvantaged groups, as apparently it has in East

Harlem and elsewhere, shouldn't the racial-ethnic-income composition of schools be a secondary consideration? Some excellent schools have only black and other minority students. Students in East Harlem can attend any public elementary or middle school in the district. The program has raised the ranking of its students from the lowest to about the middle level among the community districts in New York City.

I don't expect miraculous results from competition among schools. It is well documented that unstable family life and parental indifference greatly reduce the effectiveness even of the best schools. But Professor Coleman's study shows that Catholic schools succeed in raising the performance and cutting the dropout rates of disadvantaged pupils.

Competition among both public and private schools would help make good schools the norm rather than the exception. Parents would take their children out of weak schools and enroll them in strong ones. It could do more to improve the elementary and high-school education of disadvantaged students than all the proposals put forward by numerous commissions and academic panels.

GIVE ALL PARENTS A SAY
IN CHOOSING SCHOOLS

Under medicare, medicaid, and other federal and state health programs, total government expenditures to help cover the hospital bills of poor and elderly persons exceed $80 billion. Such payments are made directly to thousands of hospitals, about two-thirds of which are profit and nonprofit private institutions. The poor and elderly receive what amount to vouchers that they can use to pay for services at public or private hospitals.

Recently, Education Secretary William J. Bennett proposed a similar but more limited method of financing remedial education. Parents of students requiring such instruction would be given vouchers worth $600 a year that could be used at private as well as public schools. His proposal is a small step in the right 9orecent years amounting to more than $3,000 a year per public-school student—with vouchers for similar amounts that could be redeemed at private or public schools. Parents who wanted more expensive education could supplement vouchers with their own money.

At present, middle-class and wealthy families exercise considerable control over the schooling of their children. When these parents are dissatisfied with public schools, they have the means to enroll their children in private schools. Or they can move to communities with public schools more to their liking. Indeed, suburban communities compete for residents partly through the quality of their public schools.

COMPETING FOR STUDENTS.   Disadvantaged families cannot afford private-school tuition and can seldom move to communities with better public schools. Usually they must accept whatever public schools are available, no matter how bad. A voucher system would give these families some of the schooling alternatives now open only to middle-class and rich families. Minority families seem to realize this. In a 1985 Gallup poll, 59% of nonwhites, compared with 43% of whites, favored vouchers for education.

A comprehensive voucher system would require public schools to compete for students and to cover their costs with tuition revenue. Public schools could compete effectively only if they suppressed violence, instilled discipline, involved parents, offered a challenging curriculum, and controlled costs. If a public school could not attract sufficient students with tuition that covered costs, it would have to close or be sold to a private owner. Subjecting public schools to increased competition would especially benefit inner-city families who now must deal with monopoly providers of public education.

Through a voucher system, then, the government could help inner-city and other poor families pay for schooling without subsidizing public over private schools. True, a traditional argument for public schools is that only they are open to all races, religions, and incomes. But the fraction of children in public schools from poor black, Hispanic, and other families is larger than in private schools mainly because their parents cannot afford private schools. A voucher system would increase greatly the number of minority and lower-income families who choose private schools.

LESS SEGREGATED.   Moreover, geographic segregation of families by race, income, and other characteristics contributes to segregation within public schools. Professor James S. Coleman and his associates at the University of Chicago show in their book, *High School Achievement,* that students are less segregated by race and income—though more segregated by religion—in private high schools than in public high schools.

This study also indicates that children from poorer families do much better in private than in public high schools even after taking into account the tendency of more ambitious poorer families to choose private schools. Indeed, children from poor families appear to gain more from attending private schools instead of public schools than do children from rich families.

Some people worry that a voucher system would encourage frivolous classroom instruction. Yet in a study of a public and a private high school—both elite institutions—Professor Philip W. Jackson of the University of Chicago found that the private school had a more structured program of courses. Most poor families, given a chance to obtain good schooling for their children, will use vouchers wisely. To discourage an excessive number of frivolous courses, more state and local governments could follow the trend toward requiring students in all schools to pass minimum proficiency tests in basic subjects.

Some 30 years ago, Milton Friedman proposed a voucher system for schooling. Many critics considered his proposal wild and impractical, even while such a system was being implemented for hospital care and while British Columbia in Canada was beginning to use education vouchers. Education vouchers now seem rather tame compared with privatization of the postal system, prisons, public housing, and federal land (BW—Feb. 24). A voucher system for education is an idea whose time has finally come.

PART 5

Families

Since the family is the foundation of all civil society, the enormous changes in the stability and composition of families in recent decades has naturally been of great concern. Birth rates in richer countries have plummeted, the number of unmarried women with children, many on welfare, has grown rapidly, divorce rates have sky-rocketed, the labor force participation of married women has expanded rapidly, and social security pensions have enabled older parents to live separately from their children.

We address some of these changes in this part. For example, we argue that the well-being of children should guide all efforts to reform the welfare system. But the present system encourages the breakup of families, thus depriving children of frequent contact with their fathers. It also gives a financial inducement to poor women to have more children, which reduces the time, and paradoxically also the money, that mothers spend on each child.

The best way to help the children on welfare is to limit how long a family can collect benefits. Prolonged exposure to welfare creates a welfare "mentality," so that children as well as their parents become habituated to depending on the government for support. We also propose to create incentives for welfare mothers to treat their children better by penalizing those mothers who do not take their children to school regularly, or for regular health checkups.

Our proposal to use the private sector to collect child care payments from recalcitrant fathers elicited many letters. Some were from divorced women who applauded the proposal, but most of the critical letters were from divorced men. These men objected to greater collection efforts because they claimed to have little access to their children, and that they had been unfairly treated in other ways too by courts and by their former wives.

We sympathized with many of these men, and yet it was clear that their anger and prolonged battles with ex-wives had weakened their concern for the welfare of their children. The purpose of our proposal was not to redress the balance between divorced parents, but to ensure that the children had more adequate financial support. Even loving parents too often allow battles with each other to adversely affect their children—getting into arrears on child support in order to punish ex-wives is an apt example of what some men do to vent their frustration and anger.

Old age support is typically financed by a pay-as-you-go (PAYG) system, where social security and perhaps other taxes collected from workers pay for the support of retired persons. But PAYG is in financial trouble in many countries because benefits have become too generous, and the number of workers per retired person is declining, due both to low birth rates and extensions in the life expectancy of retired persons.

We propose reforming this system in a radical way by following the pioneering example set by Chile over 15 years ago, and since copied by several other nations. Chile essentially replaced the traditional PAYG by a system where workers save for retirement in their own accounts managed by private investment companies which compete for retirement funds. The Chilean system was greeted with enthusiasm by their labor force and it is working very well. It has obtained much higher rates of return on pension contributions than PAYG does because contributions are invested in stocks and bonds in the private sector. Moreover, an individual account system is also much less adversely affected by low birth rates than is PAYG.

FAMILY BEHAVIOR

THE BEST REASON
TO GET PEOPLE OFF THE DOLE

Economic systems that rely on private behavior and competitive markets are more efficient than those with extensive government control. However, the effects of a free-market system on self-reliance, initiative, and other virtues may be of even greater importance in the long run.

That's why economists and many other defenders of a free-market system in the 19th century often emphasized the system's effect on values rather than on efficiency. Alexis de Tocqueville, after a long visit to the U.S., observed in his remarkable study *Democracy in America* that "the principle of self-interest...disciplines a number of persons in habits of regularity, temperance, moderation, foresight, self-command; and if it does not lead men straight to virtue by the will, it gradually draws them in that direction by their habits."

These insights on the relationship between self-reliance and good habits should help guide the reform of public programs that corrupt the values of their participants. The welfare system is a good example, because leaders of both political parties agree it is not working well and needs to be changed. Although many families on welfare get off the rolls within a year, about 40% continue to receive benefits for longer than two years, becoming more and more dependent on government support.

People generally become thriftier and more self-reliant and develop other good habits when they are forced to make decisions and provide for themselves. But they lose the habits necessary to function well on their own—habits as simple as getting to work on time—when the government continues to support them. The importance of habits is revealed by the difficulties older workers in the formerly communist nations have encountered in adjusting to the different behavior needed to function in a free-market system.

TOO MUCH TIME? Many families appear to recognize the harmful consequences of becoming part of the welfare system: Several studies show that one of every four families eligible for welfare doesn't participate in the system. I believe the recently passed House welfare bill should have more sharply limited the length of time families can collect benefits. The present bill allows a family to be on the rolls for up to five years. Fortunately, many states will use the block grants this bill provides to impose lower time limits.

President Clinton has threatened to veto the House bill because it will follow the example set by a few states of denying additional cash benefits to mothers already receiving welfare when they have children born out of wedlock. The President and other critics claim that such provisions punish children in poor and broken families for their parents' mistakes since the parents would not have enough resources without government assistance to provide adequately for their children.

CORRUPTION.   The effect of welfare reform on children should have the highest priority, but these critics fail to appreciate how the present system corrupts the values transmitted to children. Changing the system to increase the responsibility and initiative of poor parents will help their children—even if the parents receive much less financial support from the government. Children use their parents as role models and absorb their parents' values. The values acquired by children have a much larger effect on their employment, education, and other achievements as adults than the amount of money their parents have.

Although I have used welfare to illustrate the harmful effects of government programs on the values of participants, programs that do not cater to the poor often also sap the sense of responsibility and other good values of participants. Examples include affirmative-action initiatives that help individuals get ahead not through their own accomplishments but because they belong to favored groups, aid to small and large businesses that subsidizes their profits and insures them against losses, and regulations that protect companies against competition. Social Security is another example, because it encourages many families to count on the government to provide their retirement income rather than saving for their old age while they are working—hence discouraging private savings, some studies show.

Voter pressure is forcing state legislatures as well as Congress to require evidence that the benefits of government programs and regulations tend to exceed their costs. Those calculations must take into account their effects on initiative, responsibility, and other essential values of a good society.

UNLEASH THE BILL COLLECTORS
ON DEADBEAT DADS

More than one in five U.S. children live in poverty. This is mainly because of a spectacular growth in the number of families headed by unmarried mothers, compounded by low or nonexistent child-support payments by noncustodial fathers. Fortunately for the children, as well as the mothers, it is possible to greatly increase the number of fathers who meet their obligations.

It is far too easy for fathers to dump the financial as well as the emotional burdens of raising children on mothers. More men will hesitate to father children if they know they'll have a tougher time evading the duty to support them.

Children can benefit emotionally as well as materially when their fathers support them. And if more dads were forced to pay up, they might be more likely to spend time with their kids—since they would no longer be avoiding detection.

A 1993 Urban Institute study estimates that incomes of many one-parent families would rise above the poverty level if all child-support obligations were met. But the American Fathers Coalition—a group of child-support payers—claims the delinquency figures are inflated by mothers' failure to report the payments they receive. This coalition also believes fathers sometimes fall into arrears because child-support awards are excessive.

This group makes some valid points, but it is still important to improve compliance with child-support obligations. Congress passed legislation in 1984 and 1988 requiring states to make stronger collection efforts, with the Federal government footing most of the bill. It is now easier to garnish wages, even when fathers have moved to other states, and to jail those who refuse to pay. Computer systems allow states to keep better track of where fathers live and how much they owe.

PATERNITY WARDS. As part of his welfare-reform package, President Clinton recently proposed stiffening these laws by establishing national clearinghouses to track interstate cases, by denying occupational permits and driver's licenses to fathers who don't pay up (some states already have such rules), and by requiring hospitals to establish and record who the father is for every baby born.

Although federal laws and state efforts have increased the numbers of fathers who pay up, statistics compiled by the Health & Human Services Dept.'s Office of Child Support Enforcement show that state agencies are collecting money in less than 19% of their child-support cases. Many fathers continue to successfully avoid detection by state governments—in some cases by fleeing to another state.

One reason for the low figure is that state collection agencies concentrate on helping mothers on welfare, including efforts to establish the identity of the fathers. States emphasize welfare cases because public spending is reduced when families receive enough child support to go off welfare.

But many women not on welfare are also failing to get the support due them. Some women who were not being helped by state agencies have turned to private collectors to track down the fathers of their children. These collectors have often been quite successful: They may garnish the wages of fathers or get local authorities to jail deadbeats until they pay up.

BOUNTY HUNTERS?   Private collectors usually charge a small nonrefundable fee, but their main source of revenue is a contingency payment that usually ranges from one-quarter to one-third of what they collect. This may seem like a big cut, but these fractions are not out of line with fees charged by companies collecting other kinds of debt. Yet some children's advocacy groups oppose the involvement of for-profit collection companies, because they hate to see large sums being siphoned off that should be going to the children. But mothers usually turn to private companies only after they fail to get what is due them through ordinary channels. And after all, 67% of what is collected privately is a lot better than 100% of nothing.

Private collectors often succeed where state agencies fail, because government officials lack financial incentives to track down fathers who are in arrears. Therefore, state agencies should take a cue from what some mothers are doing: Hire private companies to locate and collect from recalcitrant fathers.

Private collectors hunting down deadbeat fathers for state governments may evoke the notorious bounty-hunter system of the Old West, but it would be an effective response to the failure of state agencies. Privatization of state collection efforts has precedents in other kinds of debt: States have hired private companies to collect unpaid traffic fines, for example.

Congress should adopt most of the President's recommendations to strengthen the government's hand in collecting child support. But the laws already on the books would be much more effective in reducing the number of children raised in poverty if state governments and more mothers hired private collectors to track down deadbeat fathers.

FINDING FAULT WITH NO-FAULT DIVORCE

Both President Bush and President-elect Clinton repeatedly mentioned family values during the campaign, but neither proposed reforms that would significantly strengthen family life. Overlooked in the headline-grabbing attention to Murphy Brown, gays, and the family-leave bill are the pernicious consequences of radical changes in divorce laws during the past 20 years.

In 1970, California became the first state to allow no-fault divorce. Since then, practically all states have adopted similar statutes. No-fault makes it possible to obtain a divorce without the consent of the spouse and without proving guilty behavior, such as adultery. California's approach was hailed by women's groups and others as a civilized step that would be a great boon to women trapped in bad marriages.

It hasn't worked out that way. Scholarly research does not blame the no-fault provision for the boom in divorces during the '70s and '80s—that would have happened anyway—but it does hold no-fault responsible for many of the problems of divorced persons, especially women with children.

MUTUAL CONSENT. Under current law, a married woman with young children cannot stop her husband from divorcing her, no matter how much hardship she and her children would suffer. Since child-support payments are often meager, she faces a bleak financial future where she must work long hours or go on welfare just to make ends meet. The plight of these divorced women and their children—who now constitute almost 20% of all households—is among the most serious family problems in Britain, Canada, the U.S., and many other countries.

It is neither desirable nor possible to turn the clock back to the '60s, when most states did not allow divorce without proof of adultery, desertion, or abuse. What can be done to improve the situation of these families? The no-fault experiment should be abandoned and replaced by laws that allow divorce only when both the husband and wife agree—what is called divorce by mutual consent.

This change would greatly improve the bargaining power of the many married persons, especially women, who are hurt by no-fault. Consider a husband who very much wants a divorce and cares little about the harmful effects on his wife and children. Under present divorce law, his wife can do little to stop him, but if her consent were needed, she would have leverage. She could refuse unless the husband agrees to liberal child-support payments, a generous division of their assets, and other conditions. She need not agree until he convinces her that he would actually carry out his promises regarding child support. And she does not have to let him have his way in the marriage under threats that he will divorce her.

Children of divorced parents, especially boys, often suffer emotionally because of limited contact with their fathers. There is no perfect solution for this problem, but under the reform I propose, a mother concerned about how a divorce would affect her children could withhold consent until her husband pledged in writing to see them frequently, possibly through joint custody.

FAILED EXPERIMENT. No-fault divorce laws discourage married women from leaving the work force for several years to care for their young children, because they realize that they will need good jobs if their husbands ditch them. Under mutual consent, women would be more able to stay home for a spell after having children, if they wanted to, because they would then have much less reason to fear being left in a financial bind.

Judges now have a large part in divorce proceedings, even though they may not have enough knowledge to fit custody and support provisions to individual circumstances. Mutual-consent laws would reduce their role in divorce procedures, for couples would be required to work out their own terms as part of the consent process. There is every reason to expect that privatizing divorce proceedings—taking the judiciary out of them—would make them work much better, just as privatizing other activities has brought improvement (Economic Viewpoint, BW—Aug. 17).

No divorce law can solve all the problems created by failed marriages. A bitter or spiteful spouse may refuse to consent to a divorce, no matter how generous the terms—even if the husband and wife live separately for many years. This difficulty can be partially overcome by allowing a person to seek binding private divorce arbitration if the spouse has not agreed to divorce terms after several years of separation.

Most of the main changes in family structure during the past half-century cannot be reversed, for they are the inevitable result of the growth of women's employment, the decline in birth rates, and other developments I analyzed in my book *A Treatise on the Family*. But the widespread adoption of no-fault divorce is an experiment that failed. If no-fault were replaced by laws that require mutual consent to divorce, high divorce rates would cause much less harm to young children and to the women and men who do not want their marriages to break up.

REVAMP WELFARE TO PUT CHILDREN FIRST

Although the federal welfare program is called Aid to Families with Dependent Children, it isn't structured to encourage welfare families to help their children. The system should be reformed with the focus placed where it belongs: on children rather than on parents.

Several provisions of the traditional welfare system are not simply neutral with respect to children: They're damaging. In one well-known example, which was in effect until recently, more than half the states denied benefit payments to mothers who lived with their husbands. The unintended consequence was to encourage couples to split up in order to qualify for benefits—despite growing evidence that young children, especially boys, are harmed when reared only by a mother. Fortunately, a reform in the Family Support Act of 1988 requires states to allow intact families to be eligible for support.

We need to recognize that poor families respond to appropriate incentives—something implicitly denied by the present system. To provide welfare recipients with proper incentives, families that look out for the children's interests should get additional payments. For example, benefits might be larger if the parents take children for regular health checkups, if the children have good school-attendance records, if parents participate in school programs, or even if children get good grades and perform well on achievement tests. On the other hand, benefits could be cut or eliminated altogether if parents take drugs or drop out of high school.

There is plenty of evidence that performance in school is greatly improved when students attend regularly, especially if parents take an interest in school activities. Successful private and public schools have demonstrated that parental involvement can significantly raise the achievements of children from even the poorest families.

OPTING OUT. Proposed changes in California, Connecticut, Wisconsin, and other states—generally those with the most liberal benefits—would penalize families who do not do right by their children. New Jersey has recently taken a different tack by passing a measure that denies greater benefits to women who have additional children while on welfare.

Until New Jersey acted, all state-welfare payments increased according to the number of dependent children, which provided a motive for welfare mothers to have more and more babies. The New Jersey measure removes that monetary incentive. Perhaps more important, it sends a message that women who aren't self-sufficient should not have children. Of course, some women may have several children before going on welfare or while temporarily off.

Some critics claim that the radical changes proposed in various states pander to middle-class prejudices against poor families and welfare. Such attitudes probably have helped these measures gain support. Yet many poor families apparently do not like the present system, either. A telling statistic is that almost 40% of families eligible for welfare opt not to participate. Some may not know they are eligible, of course, but information about welfare eligibility has been widely circulated. I believe the majority of nonparticipants conclude that on balance, they would be made worse off by signing up.

ENDLESS CYCLE. How can a family be hurt by receiving monthly checks from the government? Among the tangible drawbacks are provisions allowing families on welfare to work only part-time and reducing benefits for those with larger earnings. And working less now reduces the chances of becoming self-sufficient later on. That's because future earning power is greatly reduced when a person has been out of work for an extended period, or has worked only part-time or sporadically. One cannot acquire needed job skills, which are developed only by working for a prolonged period at a job or in an occupation. Economist Seth Sanders of Carnegie Mellon University has shown that this helps explain why families refuse to go on welfare, as well as why families on welfare for several years are unlikely to go off: They become less and less capable of supporting themselves.

Some eligible families do not apply for welfare because it erodes a family's values and self-respect. This may be partly because of the social stigma of being on welfare, but I believe it is mainly because some parents conclude correctly that welfare handouts badly affect their own and their children's motivation to help themselves. They decide that the harmful effects are too large a price to pay for welfare checks.

If this is true, then families who do join the welfare rolls tend to be the ones who are least concerned about their children and least willing to help themselves. They most need financial and other pressures—both carrot and stick—to induce them to take better care of their children.

The American people want to help needy children, but they are right in sensing that the present welfare system fails to do this. Reforming the system to concentrate on improving the skills and health of children would remove much of the hostility to welfare.

SURE, SPEND MORE ON CHILD CARE. BUT SPEND WISELY

Child care has become a hot political issue. Washington is involved—and should be. The public has a clear interest in the care of the nation's children—especially poor or neglected youngsters.

Unfortunately, some of the proposals would help parents at the expense of children, and some wouldn't help those who need help the most. The many proposals for improving child care include President Bush's tax credit for low-income families with young children, Representative Patricia Schroeder's (D-Colo.) mandatory job leaves for parents with newborn or ill children, part-time mommy tracks at companies, and subsidizing child care—especially for the children of working women.

There is good reason to be concerned about what has been happening to children in the U.S. during the past couple of decades. Scores on both the verbal and mathematics parts of the Scholastic Aptitude Tests declined sharply during the 1960s and 1970s, although they have increased a little during the 1980s. The suicide rate among teenagers and young adults soared during the 1960s and 1970s, while the rate for all adults remained stable.

The number of children growing up with a single parent has multiplied as the divorce rate rocketed, and now almost 20% of America's families are headed by working mothers, the majority with low incomes. The incidence of pregnant, unmarried high school students has jumped, drug use has infected every community, and the barrage of other disturbing statistics seems endless. The same trends, although less dramatic, are found in Britain, Sweden, and other Western European countries.

PRECIOUS LITTLE.   President Bush's tax credit would award poor families a tax refund of as much as $1,000 per child under age four, but this only helps the children to the degree that the parents spend part of that additional income on the children. However, the children will see precious little more from parents who care mainly about themselves. Unfortunately, because the President's proposal ensures child support to divorced mothers, it could also encourage some poor families to split up.

Moreover, what happened during the 1960s and 1970s shows that merely throwing more public money at the child-care problem is not enough. The situation deteriorated markedly during those decades despite a rapid growth in federal, state, and local spending on children. It seems clear that we need to spend more resources on child care. But in my opinion, any increased public spending on such programs must be targeted to specified purposes that are likely to improve skills, training, mental health, values, and other human capital. This is the best way to reduce the chances that spending is not diverted to benefit other groups.

Probably the best way to ensure the most bang for the public buck would be some sort of system of vouchers that could be redeemed by poor families for those activities that improve human capital. For example, medical care, counseling services, and Head Start programs for children are promising candidates for a voucher program.

If Bush's tax-credit scheme is flawed, so are the other proposals for child care: Most help middle-class and richer families as well as poor families, or help parents at the expense of children. For example, government subsidies to child-care facilities favor all families with working mothers, not just poor families. No doubt children in some families with working mothers would gain from such subsidies because they would be placed in better care facilities. Clearly, the program is of no help when mothers stay home, for whatever reason, thus remaining outside the child-care program.

ABSENT MOM. Subsidies for child care encourage more mothers to work. Sweden has adopted practically all of the programs currently being mentioned in the U.S., including mandatory paid leaves for parents with young children, subsidized child-care facilities, separate taxation of the earnings of husbands and wives, and encouragement of part-time work by mothers. Sweden's experience shows that these programs have a huge effect on the labor-force participation of married women: More than 80% of Swedish married women with young children work, compared with 60% of American women and less than 40% of West German women. Labor-force participation rates of women in Sweden and Germany diverged rapidly after Sweden introduced these programs and Germany failed to implement them.

But there is a real question whether encouraging mothers to work is good for the children. Many psychiatrists and other professionals in the field of child care argue that young children often need their mothers' care, and a fierce debate is raging on whether many are hurt by their mothers' absence.

Public initiatives are clearly needed to safeguard the nation's most valuable resource—its children. However, Congress and the President should make sure that any new legislation is really aimed at helping children, not simply improving

the lifestyle of middle-class working women and other groups with sizable political clout.

CUT THE DIVORCE RATE
WITH MARRIAGE CONTRACTS

During the past 20 years, one of the more striking changes in Western countries
is the growth in divorce. If the current propensity to divorce is maintained, for
example, 40% of all marriages formed in the U.S. since 1975 will break up. A
number of reasons explain this phenomenon. Many married women now work
outside the home and are more financially independent (BW—May 13). The
number of young children in the typical family declined greatly after the 1950s as
birth rates declined, again reducing pressure on women to remain married, and
extensions of the welfare system gave poor women the equivalent of alimony and
child support payments.

Meanwhile, divorce laws changed radically. In 1970, California passed the first
unilateral, or no-fault, divorce law, and practically all other states have now followed suit. These laws permit a husband or wife to obtain a divorce without the
consent of his or her spouse and without having to prove that the spouse is at
fault. One might think that the change to unilateral divorce would increase the
divorce rate. But several studies, including a comprehensive one by Professor
Elizabeth Peters of the University of Colorado, have shown that apparently it did
not. In my book, *A Treatise on the Family,* I show that unilateral divorce is unlikely
to effect divorce rates much when wives or husbands can offer their mates financial and other inducements to remain married.

The change to unilateral divorce, however, did adversely affect the economic
well-being of divorced women. The study by Professor Peters and other studies
show that alimony and child-support payments have been lower with unilateral
divorce than they were where mutual consent or the need to prove fault are
involved. Although many women's groups initially supported unilateral divorce,
they should not have been surprised at this development. Husbands seeking
divorce no longer have to offer substantial settlements in order to obtain their
partner's consent.

BINDING DOCUMENTS.   Couples are likely to agree on financial terms
prior to divorce when divorce requires mutual consent or fault. By contrast,
courts are now filled with couples who litigate financial settlements while in the
process of divorcing. The number of lawyers who specialize in divorce proceedings has expanded enormously during the past decade. Judges are increasingly
asked to decide whether a divorced wife who worked while her husband went to

medical or business school is entitled to a sizable share of future increases in his earnings, or whether a woman who lived with a rich man is entitled to much of his wealth after they separate.

The courtroom is not a good place to make judgments about the unique circumstances of each marriage or relationship. We should replace judicial determination with marriage contracts that specify, among other things, the financial and child custodial terms of a divorce. Marriage contracts would become far more common if we set aside the legal tradition that they are not enforceable. In most cases they should be considered binding legal documents in the same way as contracts between business partners are usually binding. Contracts between couples who live together without being married should also be binding. In her book *The Marriage Contract*, sociologist Lenore J. Weitzman discusses the advantages of a contract and what it should include.

BLINDED BY LOVE. One objection to marriage contracts is that couples about to marry are unlikely to think clearly about the financial terms of a later separation. But such couples could start with a very general contract that provides for writing in more specific terms at a later date. Still, I agree that love's blindness may sometimes lead to unfair contracts. But is it better to delay discussions of financial and other terms until a couple is on the verge of divorce and one or both partners are angry and resentful?

Some people object to marriage contracts because they may increase the likelihood of a breakup by requiring couples to consider explicitly the terms of a divorce agreement. But most of today's modern couples are well aware that divorce is possible. For example, several studies show that wives are more likely to remain in the labor force and to delay childbearing when there is a sizable chance that their marriage may break up. Contracts that increase the security of wives could even reduce the number of divorces by encouraging women who are not interested in pursuing a career to have children earlier and withdraw from the labor force longer while caring for young children.

"Married in haste, we may repent at leisure," is how the 17th century English playwright William Congreve summarized the wisdom of the ages. We can reduce the suffering that hasty marriages often inflict with contracts that treat marriage as a long-term private arrangement between consenting adults. Such contracts would take into account the unique circumstances of each marriage. They would indicate the obligations of both husbands and wives. They would function far better than judges to specify the financial and other terms of divorce.

THE ELDERLY

How to Secure Social Security's Future

Social Security systems in the U.S., Germany, and most other rich countries are in deep financial trouble—not necessarily this year or the next, but surely by early in the next century. One problem is a sharp decline in the number of workers, whose taxes support a growing number of retired persons. Another is politicians who have saddled these systems with expensive benefits unrelated to the accumulated compulsory savings of the recipients.

Both problems can be solved by returning to the original goal of Social Security: to provide retirees with benefits that depend on their contributions to a fund while they worked. This revolutionary idea, which first surfaced in Germany at the end of the 19th century, mandated savings by working people so that they would not become dependent on public support as a result of failing to save enough out of their earnings. If today's plans were based on actuarial principles, retirement income and Social Security taxes wouldn't be determined politically. They would be based on the total contributions, retirement age, and marital status of family members.

For example, a person who earned a 3% real rate of return on the savings of 10% of earnings over 40 years and who then retired at age 67 for 15 years would receive a pension equal to almost two-thirds of earnings. So a family that saved $3,000 a year from annual earnings of $30,000 for 40 years would get almost $20,000 a year in retirement income. With any children grown, they may be able to live as well or better than before retirement.

SMALL GAP. Still, even with mandatory contributions, some retired workers would not have a decent standard of living because they earned too little when they were younger, perhaps because of long stretches of unemployment or ill health. To bring them up to an agreed minimum standard, the state would have to supplement benefits out of its general tax revenues. But with an adequate level of required contributions, such supplementation would be necessary for only one in five U.S. families.

Since all developed countries rely on pay-as-you-go Social Security systems—

where contributions from current workers support the retired—there is considerable concern about low birth rates. That means fewer workers will be available in the future to pay benefits to growing numbers of retirees. But there is a system where birth rates matter much less. In this approach, known as the actuarial system, each family funds its own retirement benefits from accumulated savings out of its own earnings.

Although this approach greatly helps in insulating a Social Security system from politics, it is possible to go further in this direction by allowing private companies to compete for the privilege of managing individual Social Security accounts. There are precedents in many countries where private companies compete to manage company pension funds. I chose the Vanguard Group over alternatives to manage my university retirement fund because it offers a rich menu of good investment options and provides monthly information on their performance.

SAFETY FIRST. The worldwide movement toward privatizing many diverse government activities makes it unnecessary to dwell on the advantages of introducing the competitive efficiency of private companies into the Social Security system. Retirees can be protected from excessive risk on their investments by requiring private management funds to have sufficient capitalizations and limiting investments to particular categories of securities.

A privately managed, actuarially based old-age system may seem wholly impractical and out of touch with political reality. But this is precisely what Chile introduced 15 years ago after people there became fed up with the state Social Security system. Argentina is on the brink of following Chile's example.

Many private funds actively compete in Chile for the right to manage the savings that workers are required to put aside for their old age. These funds have earned rather good rates of return on investment, and commissions have steadily declined over time as a fraction of contributions. During a recent visit to Chile, I didn't meet anyone who wanted to return to the old system, which taxed over 25% of earnings yet provided insufficient and somewhat arbitrary retirement incomes.

Of course, older workers who have been contributing for many years to the traditional system would have to be integrated into the alternative I propose. Chile offered its workers the option of either remaining in a government system or transferring to the competitive one along with a government bond that was valued in proportion to their accumulated contributions. Chile's transition went smoothly, and practically all older workers opted out of the traditional system— voting with their feet against state management.

The original aim of Social Security—to compel families to save out of earnings to provide for their old age—should be combined with the modern movement toward privatization of state activities. This combination would provide an effective retirement system that would be insulated in large part from politics, low birth rates, and funding crises.

WHAT KEEPS OLDER WORKERS
OFF THE JOB ROLLS?

During the past couple of decades, the government and the courts have become major players in determining the employment and pay of America's older workers. Legislation is being phased in that takes away an employer's right to retire most employees, and federal and state courts are filled with cases brought by older workers who claim discrimination. I believe that discrimination is only a small part of the problem, however, and that government interference has kept many of the elderly off the job rolls.

Government regulations and transfer payments, not company policies, explain the sharp fall in labor-force participation rates of men aged 60 to 65—from about 80% in the 1960s to less than 55% now. The relaxation of eligibility requirements for both disability pay and Social Security induced many workers in this age group to take early retirement. Why keep working if you can get almost as much income by retiring and collecting checks from Uncle Sam?

Employers' retirement rules don't even explain the big drop during the past 50 years in labor-force participation by men 65 and older. Japanese men are much more likely to continue to work than their American counterparts—36% of Japanese men 65 or older work, compared with only 16% in the U.S. Yet larger Japanese companies typically force employees to retire by age 55 or 60, which is considerably younger than what has been the prevailing practice in America.

VALUED VETS. The difference is that Japanese workers can find jobs with good pay after forced retirement. Many more jobs would be available to retired American workers if Washington did not impose expensive medical and pension costs on companies that take on elderly workers.

The federal government is extensively involved in the labor market for older persons through civil rights and other antidiscrimination programs. Yet no evidence exists of widespread discrimination against these workers. The low earnings and high unemployment of minorities arouse a strong suspicion of discrimination, but this smoking gun is not present for the elderly. Some older people may not get hired because of their high cost or low productivity, but they are not losing out just because of age. Men aged 60 to 64 who work year-round earn almost as much as those 45 to 54, and they earn much more than men aged 24 to 44. Unemployment rates among men over age 55 who want to work are way below those of younger men. The plain fact is that older workers form an elite who are generally valued by employers for their experience, knowledge, reliability, and loyalty.

Of course, some older workers do suffer when their productivity slips, when they fail to get along with new bosses, or when the demand for their company's product falls. Although laid-off senior workers frequently are recalled to their old jobs, they often take big cuts when forced to find new jobs. However, a study by Professor William Carrington of Johns Hopkins University indicates that discrimination is not the main reason for the big drop in earnings among older workers when they change jobs. Rather, their experience and expertise is often not readily adapted to new employers and different work.

The difficulties created by legislative and executive interference in the market for elderly workers are magnified by the courts. Lacking clear-cut guidelines as to what constitutes discrimination, judges and juries must improvise. Unfortunately, they do not have the requisite understanding of how labor markets operate, nor is enough evidence usually available to determine whether workers bringing suits have been unfairly treated or earn less than their productivity warrants.

CHRONIC DISADVANTAGE. The impossible task imposed on courts is compounded by the many intangibles that determine the worth of employees, especially older ones in responsible positions. These are hard to articulate to judges and juries, especially when they are sympathetic to workers who lose long-held jobs or are asked to take big cuts in earnings. Even when in the right, a company cannot easily prove to a skeptical jury that an older worker's demotion came about because his productivity was no longer up to snuff or that an unemployed older man was not hired because he could not fit into a new organization or his skills were not appropriate to the different type of work.

Fearful of court outcomes, companies now often settle age-discrimination suits even when they have done nothing wrong. And they guard against such lawsuits from older employees by simply not hiring them—although this course of action opens them to suits from those who weren't hired. So, in the end, the very policies supposed to protect the rights of elderly workers sometimes end up hurting them.

Governments can best help elderly workers by allowing them to collect full Social Security benefits even if they are working and by eliminating legislation that distorts their opportunities. The labor market for older workers will function much better if pay and employment are left to private negotiations among workers, unions, and companies.

Social Security Should Benefit Only the Elderly Poor

Sooner or later budgetary deficits and tax burdens will force the U.S. and other countries to do what has been until now politically unthinkable—to replace Social Security systems in their present form with systems of benefits only for the needy elderly.

It makes little sense to give Social Security benefits to the many elderly households with sizable earnings and assets. The conflict between annuity and redistributive goals has made Social Security a bad annuity system as well as an inefficient way to help the elderly poor.

Some will object to excluding the better-off elderly from Social Security benefits because they are under the impression that Social Security is fundamentally an annuity system. Retired people supposedly get back with interest more or less what they contributed through Social Security taxes on their earnings when they worked. But this impression is dead wrong. The present system greatly redistributes benefits toward the married elderly who live in households that have not earned much and have worked in covered employment for the minimum number of years (now about 10).

In annuity systems, benefits increase about in proportion to the amount contributed, but Social Security benefits don't. For example, according to the 1988 schedule of benefits, workers who earn $45,000 a year—the highest level of taxable earnings—and retire when they reach age 65 get only double the primary benefits of workers who earn just $7,000 a year and retire at the same age. Yet Social Security taxes on the first group are over six times higher than the taxes on the second.

MARKETABLE ASSETS.   Many retired families are well-off financially— fewer than 15% are classified as poor. Since Social Security benefits in 1985 provided less than 40% of the incomes of the top 40% of elderly households, they would remain reasonably well-off and much above the poverty line if they had no Social Security income.

Medicare has enormously reduced the financial burden to the elderly of hospitalization and other medical expenses. And many older households have marketable assets that can be drawn on in an emergency. The ratio of assets to income is much higher for retired families than working families, and fewer than 15% of older households have low incomes and few assets. Although housing is their most valuable resource, many older people own stocks and other financial assets.

The budget deficit and the tax burden on workers would greatly ease, and poorer households could be treated better, if only poorer households alone were eligible for Social Security income. Although the exact definition of the "elderly poor" has to be worked out carefully, federal expenditures in 1988 would have been reduced by well over $90 billion if the top half of older households were not eligible for benefits. Future reductions would be greater still because benefits and the number of elderly families are growing.

MEANS TEST.   If Social Security were to go only to the elderly poor, Social Security taxes could be folded into the income tax system. When all pretense is dropped that Social Security is an annuity system, separate taxes to finance benefits make as little sense as separate taxes to finance the food stamp program.

Those who object to a means test for Social Security benefits must explain why the elderly poor should be treated differently from the other poor who have to pass such a test, especially now that the elderly have to qualify for supplementary income benefits. To be sure, some elderly families would try to pass the test by saving less than they would save were Social Security benefits available to all retired persons. But these responses can be kept within tolerable limits—for example, by replacing only part of the gap between a family's resources and the poverty line. And many older families would be too well-off to try to qualify for poverty benefits.

Of course, since people who will retire in the next couple of decades have been counting on Social Security benefits, the new system should be introduced gradually.

A transitional period might be hard to manage politically since young workers would be helping to pay for benefits that they themselves would not end up receiving.

However, young families would at least have time to adjust spending and savings to provide for retirement. They could get more involved in private pension and annuity plans and give smaller gifts and bequests to their children. Some might even have the audacity to expect old-age support from their own children.

Obviously, no proposal to eliminate Social Security income for many elderly people is politically feasible at present. Eventually, however, a way will have to be found to overcome political opposition and reorient the system to help only those older people who are in need.

WHAT REALLY HURTS THE JOB MARKET
FOR OLDER WORKERS

Government regulation of labor markets has been growing rapidly in the U.S. and Europe in recent years at the same time that air travel, banking, and other industries have been deregulated. Most important is the increasing regulation of the market for older workers. A 1978 amendment to the Age Discrimination in Employment Act, for example, with a few exceptions prohibits companies and other organizations in the U.S. from forcing employees to retire before age 70. A bill introduced recently in Congress would greatly limit the power of organizations to establish any retirement age.

One might easily gain the impression from such legislation that private employers are reluctant to retain elderly employees. But the historical evidence proves the contrary. About 60% of elderly men were privately employed in the U.S. at the beginning of this century. A similar percentage of men over 65 were employed in Britain at that time. The employment of elderly men declined gradually from the Civil War to the 1930s, probably because wealth increased. Elderly persons with greater financial means are more willing to retire when their health deteriorates and as their family responsibilities decrease.

The rate at which men over 65 participate in the labor market declined rapidly after 1930 and is now well under 20%. And the participation rate of men aged 55 through 64 dropped from 87% in 1960 to less than 70% now. While many younger women entered the labor force during this period, the legislation under discussion prevented the participation rate of older women from growing. The reason for these rapid changes is not any growing discrimination against the elderly in modern industrial economies; the culprit is public policies that discourage employment of the elderly.

GOING UNDERGROUND.   Many persons age 65 to 72 do not want to work because their Social Security payments are smaller when they also earn income. Legislation adopted in the early 1960s lowered the age of eligibility for Social Security payments for males from 65 to 62, which explains the plunge in employment at these ages. The rapid growth of private pension plans—stimulated partly by tax incentives to defer income—has also lowered the number of elderly persons in the labor force. However, the lower marginal tax rates and related changes in the new tax bill, by reducing the tax advantages of retiring, will raise the employment rate of older persons.

Social Security and private pension plans affect the supply side of the market for elderly people, and other legislation exists that affects the demand for such workers. One example is the recent law that requires companies to maintain the health insurance of former employees for up to 18 months. This measure raises the risk of employing older workers, because their employers become obligated after the workers leave for what may be heavy medical expenses. This makes organizations reluctant to hire older workers, especially if they cannot retire them before 70. Moreover, federal laws with regard to employee eligibility for a company's pension plan reduce the willingness of companies with defined benefit plans to hire workers who will retire relatively soon. These regulations have led some older workers to find work in the underground economy. As a result, official figures must overstate, possibly by a lot, the actual decline in the number of elderly who are working.

Many large companies prefer to have fixed rules governing retirement ages for executives and other employees. These rules surely hurt some elderly persons who continue to be productive, but they are not motivated by a desire to discriminate against productive older workers. Rather, these rules are a recognition both of the decline in the health and productivity of a significant fraction of elderly workers and of the inability of most large companies to pick and choose among their older workers in order to retain only the productive ones.

SPECIAL DEALS.   Profit-seeking companies have an interest in employing older workers whose productivity warrants their earnings. Large companies in Japan traditionally retire workers at 55, yet the labor force participation rate of people over 55 has been higher than in the U.S. because many workers let go by one company are hired by others.

Smaller companies usually have flexible retirement rules, since they can more easily separate employees who continue to be valuable from those who should be retired. For example, before it was forbidden by the 1978 amendment, most universities had a rule that professors retire at 65. Still, many productive professors who reached this age were kept on through special arrangements.

The distortions in the labor market for older workers will not be cured by further government regulation. Indeed, such regulations and other public programs are mainly the source of the disease that has infected this market. Instead of additional interference, financial penalties for older persons who continue to work should be reduced and the extra financial burdens now placed on companies that hire older workers should be lightened. In short, what is needed is not further regulation but deregulation of the market for older workers.

PART 6

Discrimination

This part mainly considers the economic progress of blacks and women in the United States and other countries where they have suffered extensive discrimination. Both groups have made significant economic advances in recent decades because they improved their education and on-the-job training, and the discrimination against them has decreased. Civil rights legislation contributed to the decline in discrimination, but we argue that quotas and other rigid affirmative action programs have done more harm than good.

There are considerable differences of opinion about how much discrimination remains in different sectors of the American economy. One of the essays in this part raises serious questions about the quality of the analysis in a widely publicized study by the Federal Reserve Bank of Boston that claimed to find sizable bank discrimination against black applicants for loans. If banks discriminated by only funding financially secure black applicants, the loans to blacks should have lower default rates and yield greater profits than the loans to comparable white applicants. But although the Boston Fed collected many statistics, it did not try to get information on either default rates or profitability. Since the Boston Fed lacked the most relevant statistics, and since subsequent articles pointed out other defects in their study, the reputation it acquired as proving pervasive bank discrimination is without foundation.

DISCRIMINATION AGAINST BLACKS

END AFFIRMATIVE ACTION AS WE KNOW IT

Affirmative action is a hot issue in the Presidential race. The major Republican candidates are all firmly opposed to it, while President Clinton recently came out with a stirring defense. But it may not be too late to head off a divisive contest — if both parties will support affirmative-action programs that enable people from all backgrounds to compete effectively for better-paying jobs.

Polls show that a clear majority of Americans, including many from minority groups, are opposed to policies that impose quotas and set-asides. Yet they remain committed to civil rights legislation that reduces discrimination against minorities in schooling, training, and employment.

Even effective antidiscrimination laws cannot do much to address the main cause of unequal opportunities among adults: differences in childhood experiences. Some children, many of them not from minority groups, grow up in unstable families and vicious neighborhoods and receive low-quality education and training. The right kind of affirmative-action programs would raise their human capital so that they could gain the skills needed to compete.

CRIME DOESN'T PAY. Many types of human-capital investments could help such children do well as adults. For example, kids from poor families should be given tuition vouchers that they can use to get a decent education rather than having to attend inadequate local public schools. The welfare system should be reformed in ways that keep poor families intact. The crackdown on crime should continue, since it will eventually convince children growing up in slum neighborhoods that crime really does not pay. Programs that provide good diets and medical care for disadvantaged children, which have large payoffs in the long run, should be strengthened rather than weakened.

To be effective, programs for the disadvantaged must begin when children are very young, since their handicaps worsen with age. Public retraining and other programs for unemployed adults often have little effect, because they cannot offset the cumulative impact of bad habits and inferior schooling. Even the best affirmative-action schemes do not bring unprepared minorities up to the level of the students and workers who gain their positions on merit alone.

Universities provide clear evidence of these effects. Data published in *The New York Times* on June 4 show that, on average, because of affirmative action, black and Hispanic students entering the University of California at Berkeley—the most prestigious part of the California system—had much lower high school grade-point averages and scores on the Scholastic Assessment Test than whites and Asians. Black and Hispanic students admitted through special set-asides do much worse, too. The data indicate that the six-year graduation rate is only 59% for blacks and 64% for Hispanics, compared with 84% for whites and 88% for Asians.

RESENTMENT. The below-average records of blacks and Hispanics at Berkeley and other top universities caused by special admission standards undermines their confidence. It helps to perpetuate the worst stereotypes about minorities and feeds the resentment felt by whites and Asians who were not admitted because of minority set-asides.

But the inadequate performance of minorities in affirmative-action programs has nothing to do with the so-called Bell Curve or any other explanation based on the inferior mental capacities of minorities. White males also perform below average when they are admitted to universities and jobs with qualifications below those of others.

When I was growing up in the 1930s and 1940s, black, female, Jewish, or other minority doctors, lawyers, and business executives were presumed to be better than average. Only the best candidates were accepted under the limited quotas available to them. Affirmative-action programs have reversed such judgments about qualifications. The average minority professional or businesswoman is often presumed to be of lower quality than the average white male in a comparable position. This attitude has caused considerable resentment among successful members of minority groups who have overcome obstacles to get where they are. Perhaps this is why a black businessman, Ward Connerly, proposed that California abolish affirmative-action programs for minority admissions at public universities.

It is surely time for quotas and set-asides to go. But Americans should support devoting even greater public effort to improving the opportunities of minority and other children who come from disadvantaged backgrounds.

The Evidence Against Banks
Doesn't Prove Bias

A recent Federal Reserve Bank of Boston study says that banks discriminate against black and Hispanic applicants for mortgages. Although this study stimulated the Comptroller of the Currency to announce plans to ferret out such discrimination against minorities, it is flawed and does not provide persuasive evidence of bias against blacks or other groups in the mortgage market.

Discrimination in the marketplace is a serious problem that hurts minorities, but the use of invalid methodology is no help in fighting it. In my book *The Economics of Discrimination*, I set out principles for determining whether there is actual discrimination against minorities in labor, housing, or consumer markets. In essence, discrimination in the marketplace consists of voluntarily relinquishing profits, wages, or income in order to cater to prejudice. An employer discriminates when he refuses to hire applicants from a group even though they would produce more profit than those who are hired. Employees discriminate if they refuse to work alongside members of a group even though they can earn more by doing that. The corollary here is that if a company chooses not to hire members of a group, its decision may not be discriminatory if hiring others who are cheaper or more productive results in more profits.

HARD TO MEASURE. The flaw in all studies of discrimination by banks in applications for mortgages is that they have not determined the profitability of loans to different groups. Instead, they examine whether rates of denial to minority applicants for mortgages exceed those to whites with similar incomes, credit histories, and various other characteristics. These studies generally conclude that there is discrimination against black and Hispanic applicants because they are more frequently denied mortgages. In the Boston study, for example, 17% of blacks were turned down, compared with only 11% of whites with similar characteristics. Yet some of the studies find that Asian Americans are less likely to be turned down than whites, which is difficult to reconcile with discrimination by banks against minorities.

The conflicting results for Asian Americans and other minorities are probably because of the methods used. Although such "comparability" studies can be useful in finding a smoking gun and may be necessary when nothing better is possible, they are never decisive. Many characteristics unaddressed in these studies— such as any record indicating chronic late payments—could explain the differences in lending rates between groups.

A valid study of discrimination in lending would calculate default rates, late payments, interest rates, and other determinants of the profitability of loans. If banks do discriminate against blacks and other groups, they would impose stricter standards on loans to them than to whites with truly comparable credit backgrounds. The banks would be willing to finance only the most profitable of African-American applications. Were that the case, the mortgage loans approved for minority applicants should be more profitable than loans to whites, not less profitable or even equally profitable.

PARADOXICAL.   The Boston Fed's is the best of the conventional studies of mortgage discrimination. But since it chose to consider only recent applications, it did not have much information on default rates and other determinants of profitability. Apparently, the study did examine average default rates in different census tracts in the Boston area. It reports that it did not find greater default rates in tracts with a larger percentage of blacks and Hispanics.

However, the theory of discrimination contains the paradox that the rate of default on loans approved for blacks and Hispanics by discriminatory banks should be lower, not higher, than those on mortgage loans to whites. The reason again is that such banks only accept the very best minority candidates. Therefore, rather than supporting the banks' conclusion, the census-tract default data actually raise serious doubts about whether banks in the Boston area have been discriminating.

I am not claiming this proves there is no discrimination in bank lending against blacks and Hispanics, and it is obvious that there are many examples of discrimination against these groups in the overall economy. But I do say that serious methodological flaws make them of dubious value in formulating social policy.

A SIMPLE APPROACH.   Moreover, as far as I know, minority-owned banks and other banks that specialize in making loans to blacks, Hispanics, and other minorities have not tended to be particularly profitable. If this conclusion is correct, it, too, raises doubts about whether there is widespread denial of profitable applications from minority groups, since the banks that specialize in lending to them should do very well.

Economics all too seldom provides straightforward guidelines for designing and analyzing statistical materials on subjects of great social importance. Since the economic theory of discrimination does provide a simple approach, it is too bad that studies of whether banks discriminate in mortgage lending have not utilized these insights.

Productivity Is the Best
Affirmative-Action Plan

The recent Supreme Court decision upholding the right of employers to promote women over better-qualified men is a telling indicator of the court's thinking about permissible employment practices. But women's groups and many others will be disappointed when they discover that the decision will not have much impact on the economic position of the vast majority of working women in the U.S. The reason? Changes in the earnings and occupations of women in this country are much more closely related to changes in their productivity than to government action.

The history of the past 30 years supports this claim. The growth in the number of working women in recent decades has been spectacular: They increased from about one-fourth of the labor force in 1950 to almost half at present. Yet until the late 1970s, women remained in what were traditionally classified as female occupations, such as clerical work and elementary-school teaching. Few advanced into management positions, engineering jobs, or other male preserves. Further, until the late 1970s, women's earnings were stable at about 60% of the earnings of men.

Married women have had much lower earnings and lower-level occupations than men mainly because until the late 1960s most of them stopped working soon after the birth of their first child and did not return to work. They did not seek training in schools or in jobs that prepared them for careers. By contrast, single women generally remained in the labor force and acquired work experience. They have earned 80% of the salaries earned by single men of the same age and with the same amount of schooling.

REDUCING INEQUITIES.   Of course, women's lower earnings are in part the result of discrimination. Title VII of the Civil Rights Act of 1964 outlawed sexual and racial bias in employment and earnings. Subsequent congressional, executive, and judicial actions also undertook to reduce inequities in the workplace.

Yet most studies have found that Title VII and other government actions had little effect on women's economic position. Such a finding is not surprising given that the earnings and occupations of women improved little in the decade subsequent to Title VII's passage. In light of this evidence, why should we expect the recent high court decision on affirmative action to raise greatly the position of working women?

According to studies by Professor Robert G. Gregory of Australian National University and others, active government policies to promote the advancement of women have been most successful in countries where the government has a large role in the determination of wages and employment. Women have advanced rapidly in Sweden, where over half of employed women work for the government, compared with less than 20% in the U.S. They also have done well in Australia, where the government sets wages for practically all occupations and industries. In America, competition among employers and employees usually determines wages. Affirmative action and other programs in the U.S. to promote the advancement of women are unlikely to have a large effect without much greater government involvement in labor markets.

EXPERIENCE EARNS.　　Developments in recent years reinforce this conclusion. The Reagan Administration is philosophically opposed to some civil rights legislation, and it has consistently fought affirmative-action plans. It even filed a friend-of-the-court brief to support the male plaintiff in the court case just decided. Yet the earnings and occupations of women improved more rapidly during the past seven years than during any previous period. This year, for the first time, the hourly earnings of women employed full-time will exceed 75% of the earnings of men working full-time of the same age and with the same amount of schooling. Women also are making rapid strides into high-level jobs formerly reserved for men. Over 15% of lawyers and doctors are women, compared with less than 3% in 1970.

I am not suggesting that the rapid progress of working women is a result of the Reagan Administration's "benign neglect." Rather, most women now plan on participating for many years in the labor force. They are preparing for careers outside the home and are accumulating valuable work experience. Instead of shunning business, women make up more than one-third of business-school students. Stemming in large part from greater work experience and more career-oriented schooling and other training, the higher productivity of employed women is mainly responsible for their progress in the past few years.

I expect to see the economic position of working women in the U.S. rise further during the next few years as their experience and training continue to improve. Affirmative-action decisions by the courts will help the advance of women working for governments and, perhaps, large publicity-conscious companies. But while Supreme Court decisions are dramatic, the progress of most women will continue to depend on the quieter forces that encourage women to remain in the labor force.

Pretoria's Part in the
Black Economic Struggle

The country's Founding Fathers were concerned about the possible harm a strong government might cause unpopular minorities. Partly to limit such potential damage, they designed a system of checks and balances among the legislative, executive, and judicial branches. The founders also believed that government policies were largely the outcome of an intense competition by special-interest groups contending for political power. As James Madison wrote in *The Federalist:* "[Various interests] grow up of necessity in civilized nations, and divide them into different classes. The regulation of these various and interfering interests...involves the spirit of party and faction in the necessary and ordinary operations of the government." The founders' wisdom has been confirmed countless times during the past 200 years.

Consider the economic experiences of American blacks since Emancipation. As the economy grew during most of the past century, the earnings and skills of blacks greatly improved. Although the economic position of blacks even advanced considerably relative to that of whites, studies by James Smith of Rand Corp. indicate that blacks would have advanced more rapidly had it not been for Jim Crow legislation in the South and other forms of state and local discrimination that slowed gains in their education and training.

TELLTALE RATIO. Scholars dispute whether the affirmative-action legislation that began in the 1960s has had a sizable effect on the economic situation of minorities. However, no one can doubt that the elimination of most government discrimination against blacks has had far more to do with their rapid progress in recent decades than has affirmative action. Especially important have been improvements in the quantity and quality of black schooling (BW—Apr. 21). This improvement gave blacks the skills to compete for jobs on more nearly equal terms with whites.

The economic plight of blacks in South Africa tells a similar but more dramatic story. Their earnings and skills grew rapidly along with those of whites as the South African economy boomed during this century. Indeed, South African blacks are among the richest blacks in Africa. That's evident from the large immigrations from other parts of the continent. But while earnings of blacks relative to whites advanced slowly, the ratio is still below 30%, compared with more than 70% in the U.S.

Many factors contribute to the relatively low earnings of blacks in South Africa, but blatant and widespread government discrimination is unquestionably important. Blacks have been denied good schooling. And the law reserves most skilled jobs for whites and limits the access of blacks to many cities and towns. Competition among white employers for cheaper workers would have raised the economic position of blacks considerably if government policies came close to treating blacks on an equal footing with whites.

GROWING MUSCLE. The political importance of special interests lies behind the discrimination against blacks in both the U.S. and South Africa. Discriminatory legislation in the U.S. appealed politically to poor whites who wanted to weaken the economic competition from blacks and to white taxpayers who benefited from reduced expenditures on education for blacks. The elimination of this legislation during the past 40 years owes much to the growing economic muscle of blacks. That muscle provided the means to organize successful boycotts, force legal challenges, and promote other favorable political changes.

The influence of special interests is even clearer in South Africa's legislative history. A series of acts that began early in the 20th century and expanded in recent decades reserved skilled jobs in the mines for whites, strengthened the power of white trade unions, and weakened black unions. Apartheid legislation, by restricting the number of blacks who can live in urban areas, lessened the possibility of substituting black labor for white labor.

Many countries are now trying to pressure South Africa into relaxing discrimination against blacks. Whether that pressure will succeed remains to be seen. A more promising force may be the greater economic power of South African blacks and the divided economic interests of whites. Blacks there now organize boycotts of white businesses, call strikes, and put other kinds of pressure, including terrorism, on the government to change its policies. Sometimes the interests of blacks coincide with those of white employers and highly skilled workers. Both white groups are hurt by apartheid and other restrictions on black workers because employers are forced to pay more for less skilled workers, some of whom are used together with highly skilled whites.

I expect the most flagrant government acts that retard the economic advance of blacks in South Africa to give way before long in the face of the combined opposition from blacks, a segment of the white population, and perhaps also world opinion. South African blacks do not need affirmative-action programs. Instead they need elimination of the vicious laws directed against them.

THE AMERICAN DREAM MAY BE
COMING CLOSER FOR BLACKS

For more than a century, wave after wave of poor immigrants to the U.S. achieved rapid economic success. Germans and Irish in the middle of the 19th century, Italians and Jews in the late 19th and early 20th centuries—all reached economic parity with other Americans in three generations or less. Even Chinese and Japanese immigrants managed to climb out of poverty, in spite of powerful public and private discrimination.

Blacks originally came to the U.S. not as immigrants but as slaves. In *An American Dilemma*, published in 1944, Swedish economist Gunnar Myrdal focused on this unique experience of blacks to explain why they were the major exception to the American dream of up-the-ladder success. True, the earnings of blacks rose greatly from 1880 to 1940 as the economy developed. But my book *The Economics of Discrimination*, published in 1957, shows that during that long period their earnings did not rise much relative to those of whites.

JIM CROW LAWS.   Prior to 1940, severe discrimination by state and local governments kept the level of education available to black children abysmally low. In the South, Jim Crow laws dating from the turn of the century repressed blacks in many other ways. Extensive government discrimination combined with widespread prejudice in the marketplace to retard the economic progress of blacks. Economists have been able to demonstrate that competition in product and labor markets raises the cost of discriminating against people for reasons of race, sex, religion, or other characteristics. However, the persistence of such discrimination against blacks shows that competition and free enterprise do not by themselves eliminate the effects of prejudice in the marketplace, especially when the prejudice is deep and widespread and when governmental and private discrimination are mutually reinforcing.

Yet the timing of Myrdal's study is noteworthy because the early 1940s turned out to be a watershed in the economic history of American blacks. In a recent Rand Corp. study, James P. Smith and Finis R. Welch documented that the earnings of black males increased from less than 45% of those of white males in 1940 to almost 60% in 1960 and to 70% in 1980. Other evidence shows that black women are now close to earnings parity with white women.

Smith and Welch attribute the rapid advance of black males after 1940 to several changes in their circumstances. Especially important was the sizable increase in both the number of years blacks were able to spend in school and the quality of education they received. In 1940 black males averaged only 4.7 years of schooling, compared with 8.4 years for white males. Today the difference in schooling for black and white males is less than 1.5 years. Moreover, general prosperity during most of these four decades induced large numbers of blacks to abandon Southern agriculture. At the same time, it promoted rapid economic progress of the South itself, particularly after 1970. In 1940 more than 70% of all blacks resided in the South, with about one-third working in Southern agriculture. Now almost all blacks live in cities or suburban communities, and more than half live outside the South.

Unfortunately, not all the news about blacks is good. Unemployment among black men has remained at about twice the rate for white men, and in 1985 the rate exceeded 40% for black men under the age of 20. At first, the incomes of black families rose rapidly, along with the incomes of black men and women. But after the mid-1960s, the growth in individual incomes diverged considerably from that of families. By 1984 unmarried women headed half of all black families with children, compared with less than 20% for white families. The sharp decline in the number of black families headed by married couples lowered the income received by the average black family, compared with that of the average white family.

PESSIMISTIC VIEW.   Clearly, these trends in unemployment and family income give a more pessimistic view of black progress than do trends in individual incomes. Still, blacks have made substantial economic gains over the past 40 years. Moreover, the rise in the number of broken black families during the past 20 years is not mainly the result of discrimination by whites.

There is no reason to doubt that blacks can continue to make economic progress. A voucher system of financing education (BW—Mar. 24) would increase the quality of schooling available to inner-city blacks and other minorities. The instability of black families is partly related to the system of welfare payments and to the high unemployment of young black men. The welfare system can be changed to eliminate the penalty now imposed on intact families. Demand for the services of black men and women will continue to grow, and black unemployment will fall if economic growth becomes as rapid as it was in the period after 1940.

If all goes well, the beginning of the next century could see the end of this American dilemma—and the full participation by blacks in the American dream.

WOMEN

HOUSEWORK: THE MISSING PIECE
OF THE ECONOMIC PIE

Household production is an important part of the output of all nations, yet housework is not recognized when measuring the goods and services that make up the gross domestic product. This undervalues the contributions of women, since they are responsible for most of household production.

Families and other households are in effect small factories that even in the most advanced nations produce many valuable services and goods. They rear children, prepare meals, and provide shelter. They take care of sick members, give nursing and other assistance to the elderly, and perform many other helpful tasks.

Women contribute about 70% of the total time spent at these activities—even in egalitarian nations such as Sweden. They do virtually all the housework in poorer nations such as India. Some feminists argue persuasively that including housework in the GDP would raise the "consciousness" of women, especially in the less-developed world where women are badly treated. This would help to improve their bargaining position in marriage, since many housewives would "earn" more than their husbands if a woman's household contribution had a monetary value. Yet other feminists do not want explicit calculations of production for housewives, because that would conflict with their agenda of getting women out of the household and into the labor force.

LONG HOURS. It is time to recognize housework as part of the goods and services in a nation's GDP. The long hours spent at housework suggest that production in the home is a sizable percentage of the total output of all nations. After all, when a family hires someone to care for the children, clean the house, and cook, that work is counted in the GDP figures. When a parent does it, it is not.

There are several ways to quantify and measure household production. Although GDP only includes the production of goods and services that are bought and sold, they do include a value for owner-occupied housing by using the cost of rental housing that has comparable space and amenities to owned housing. The value of housework can be measured by what it would cost to buy services in the marketplace (such as baby-sitting) to replace those provided by parents.

These methods are used by Robert Eisner of Northwestern University in his careful study *The Total Incomes System of Accounts*. Eisner finds that the imputed value of household production in the U.S. exceeded more than 20% of gross national product from the mid-1940s to the early 1980s—the last year of his estimates. Much cruder calculations by the U.N. in its latest Human Development Report indicate that household production is worth more than 40% of world output.

SWEDISH SUBSIDIES. Neglect of household production in calculating the GDP distorts measures of economic growth. The huge increase in labor-force participation of married women during the past several decades came mainly at the expense of a reduction in the time women spent at unpaid household production. The rapid increase in GDP during these decades neglects the sizable decline in time spent on housework.

The substitution of market production for household production is clearly the reason for the rapid expansion of the child-care industry since the late 1970s. Working women reduced the time they spent caring for their own children by hiring other women to do it for them. Women cared for one another's children.

My colleague at the University of Chicago, Sherwin Rosen, studied a situation in Sweden, where the child-care industry is unusually extensive, partly because it is subsidized by the government. He does not take a stand on whether children are harmed when their mothers work. However, he does show that these subsidies caused considerable inefficiencies by artificially inducing many women to enter the labor force. For example, subsidies lowered the price to women of child-care services below its true cost. I found his conclusions persuasive, but they have been highly controversial in Sweden because many groups there want to "nationalize" the family by making government responsible for child care. They want to encourage mothers to enter the labor force so that they must hire other women to care for their children.

Including housework in measures of GDP would raise the self-respect of women and men who stay at home to care for children and do other housework. It would also provide a more accurate picture of GDP and growth and might lead to a different interpretation of public policies that affect the allocation of time between household work and market work.

WORKING WOMEN'S STAUNCHEST ALLIES:
SUPPLY AND DEMAND

Working women have plenty of problems in the workplace, as we were reminded so dramatically during the Clarence Thomas hearings. Yet those problems stand in stark contrast to women's rapid progress in occupations and earnings compared with men's since the late 1970s. The U.S. is getting much closer to granting equal pay for equal work, regardless of gender or family situation.

The proportion of married women who work has increased continuously: Now, more than 60% of married women with young children hold jobs. Women in the 1970s and '80s entered many professions at a breathtaking pace. They make up some 40% of the students in schools of law, medicine, business, architecture, and journalism, and are a small but rapidly growing share of those majoring in engineering. The percentage of male college graduates going on to law school has actually fallen since 1970, while females in the legal profession have risen from a negligible share in the early '70s to almost 25% now.

Median earnings of women working full time were comparatively stable from 1960 to 1979, at about 59% of the earnings of men—which means a gender gap of about 41%. But then, as reported in the Census Bureau's *Money Income of Households, Families and Persons*, the gap began a steady fall, dropping below 30% in 1990. I expect it to continue to fall throughout this decade.

Even 30%, however, overstates the true gap, since female full-time workers put in about 10% fewer hours a week than male full-time workers, and they have less previous job experience. The gap between men and women working the same hours and with the same experience is well under 20%.

LAME EXCUSE.   The most important reason for women's progress is their increasing presence in the labor force, as the nature of the family has changed. Birth rates have dropped more than 35% since the late 1950s, freeing women from child-care duties. Rapid expansion in the number of jobs in the service sector has let women combine child care with part-time work and flexible schedules. The exploding number of divorces after the mid-1960s forced women with dependent children to earn a living and provided a warning to married women that they should be prepared to work in the event their marriages should break up. Young women who have entered professions and other skilled occupations during the 1970s and 1980s continue to advance into more responsible positions, even if a "glass ceiling" has kept most from getting to the very top.

Not long ago, some women lost their jobs when they married. Women employees were paid much less than men, sometimes because of outright discrimination rationalized by the lame excuse that they were not the main breadwinners. The atmosphere created by civil rights legislation and the women's movement help combat such policies. These were not, however, the main forces behind their progress, since the gender gap in earnings did not begin to decline until more than a decade and a half after passage of the far-reaching Civil Rights Act of 1964. Women advanced most rapidly during the Reagan and Bush Presidencies—surely no more active in civil rights enforcement than previous Administrations. Moreover, not all minority groups advanced during the 1980s: Black men fell a little further behind white men.

Women's substantial progress during the '80s helped muffle the call for more radical legislation to aid them. There is much less support now than a decade ago for the silly system of government wage-setting figured on the basis of "comparable worth," the inevitably arbitrary judgments of statisticians and bureaucrats about what the pay should be in different occupations. Rapid entry of women into prestigious occupations has also quieted the call for quotas. Even supporters concede quotas aren't really what they have in mind.

MOTHERS' HELPER.   Instead, the drive to aid women is concentrating on other kinds of intervention in labor markets. Current favorites are mandatory, unpaid leave for parents when children are born or get sick and mandatory child-care facilities at work. Bills in Congress would make child-care leave available to either parent, but the example of Sweden—which has a liberal leave system—suggests that almost all would be taken by women.

Forcing business to provide leave is both inefficient and unjust. It in effect discriminates against single persons and against married women and men with no children or with grown children. It's one thing to call for a gender-neutral productivity test for pay hikes and promotions, but another to make business give preference to persons with young children. And while the present proposals are mild, everyone knows they are only a first step toward the Swedish system of requiring full pay for employees on child-care leave.

The law of supply and demand, along with civil rights legislation, is steadily improving the economic position of U.S. women. Extensive intervention in labor markets to help them is unwarranted and will do more harm than good in implementing the principles of equal pay and equal employment opportunities for equal work.

How the Market Acted
Affirmatively for Women

Between 1979 and 1984, the earnings of women compared with those of men rose at probably the most rapid rate in our history. Yet during much of that period, the Reagan Administration staunchly opposed the Equal Rights Amendment, hiring quotas, comparable worth, and most affirmative-action programs. The fact that such opposition failed to impede the economic gains of women suggests that largely silent market forces, not the political activity that captures so much publicity, have mainly determined the economic position of women in our society. Some economic perspective will make clear what has been happening.

The most striking change in U.S. labor markets during this century is the large increase in working married women. At the beginning of the 1900s, a tiny fraction of married women were employed outside the home. This fraction grew steadily until the 1950s, when its growth began to accelerate. Today, more than half of all married women are working. Stated differently, women were about 15% of the labor force in 1890, a little more than 25% in 1950, over 40% in 1980, and will be almost 50% of the labor force by the end of the decade.

Women have not only worked less than men but have also earned less. In 1950 men's earnings per hour in the U.S. were about 50% higher than those of women. Women's earnings apparently rose relative to the earnings of men during the first few decades of this century but then hardly changed between 1930 and 1980.

PREJUDICE HURT. It's not difficult to understand why the earnings of women lagged behind those of men. Schoolgirls, not expecting to spend much time in the labor force, shunned science and other studies that raised earnings, and flocked instead to subjects like home economics, English, and foreign languages. Women typically worked only until married, and then withdrew to have children and become full-time homemakers. As a result, most women did not acquire the work experience necessary to achieve higher earnings. Working women with household responsibilities were unable to compete effectively for those higher-paying jobs that required travel, night work, or rigid and long hours. Of course, discrimination against working women and the attitude that women belong in the home also kept both their earnings and their participation in the labor force low.

Women moved from home to the workplace in this century primarily because of developments in the American economy. Indeed, women stepped up their participation in the labor force in all countries that experienced strong economic growth. One reason is that as these countries became richer, the income women could earn by working outside the home increased. Also, more clerical, teaching, health care, and other service positions became available—jobs that appealed to women with homemaking responsibilities because they are less physically strenuous and provide more flexible hours than factory work. The time spent on child care and housework declined also because families in societies with advanced technologies have fewer children, and they spend more time in school.

MARKET HELPED. Broadly speaking, the evidence in Western countries shows that the growing commitment of women to the labor force, especially during the last few decades, reduced the difference in earnings between men and women. For example, from 1960 to 1980, the earnings of women compared with men rose significantly in Sweden, Italy, Britain, and many other European countries. In the U.S. the earnings of women were restrained in the 1960s and 1970s partly by the large growth in the number of employed women who had little work experience. But research by Professor Victor Fuchs of Stanford University shows that it has been rising at a rapid pace during the 1980s. During the past decade far more women have entered medicine, law, accounting, and other well-paid and highly skilled occupations.

What do these facts say about women's economic progress? In part, that the growth in the employment and earnings of women over time is explained mostly by market forces rather than by civil rights legislation, affirmative-action programs, or the women's movement. Such programs can hardly explain the steady growth in the employment of women prior to 1950, or its accelerated growth during the 1950s and 1960s, since neither civil rights programs nor women's movements were yet widespread. Nor can equal-pay-for-equal-work legislation alone explain the narrowing in the earnings gap between men and women in the past 15 years. For one thing, this gap also narrowed in countries, such as Italy and Japan, that did not introduce such legislation.

Since growing numbers of women in the U.S. are deeply committed to careers outside the home, we can expect the gap in earnings between men and women to close even more, primarily because of the economic forces discussed above. Responding to them, women are already spending far more of their time working outside the home than they did 30 years ago, and it is this choice that has dramatically changed their role in modern economic life.

PART 7

Crime and Addictions

Crime has become one of the most worrisome problems of daily living in virtually all major cities of the world. The essays in this part maintain that the rapid growth in burglaries and other crimes during the past few decades is not an inevitable part of modern life, but can be combated by proper public policies. These include stiffer punishments to felons convicted of serious crimes, especially when they use guns, and increased resources devoted to raising the likelihood of apprehending and convicting criminals. Recent studies support our claim in this part that the much higher rate of imprisonment in the United States since the early 1980s is partly responsible for the sizable decline in crimes, especially property crimes, during the past decade and a half.

However, the economic approach to crime outlined in these essays is not only about law and order, for it implies that crime is also reduced by better job opportunities for unskilled individuals. They will be less attracted to crime if work in the legal economy pays better. Therefore, our discussion in Part 4 of ways to improve education and training is relevant to the fight against crime.

The essays dealing with legalizing drugs also have a bearing on crime. These essays support the legalization of much drug use, even though legalization is no panacea and brings its own problems. Since the periodic "wars" on drugs by a succession of Republican and Democratic presidents have failed badly, radical new initiatives are worth considering.

Legalizing drugs will reduce street prices by more than 90 percent, which will make it unnecessary for addicts to turn to crime to support an expensive habit. Moreover, the greatly reduced price will also largely eliminate the huge profits made by successful drug dealers. This will reduce greatly the allure that selling drugs now has to young ghetto residents since it would no longer either pay better or be more attractive than the unskilled jobs they can get.

CRIME

Stiffer Jail Terms Will Make Gunmen More Gun-Shy

Gun control is a highly divisive issue that pits citizens who believe that the right to own guns for legitimate purposes is constitutionally guaranteed against those who want to sharply reduce the number of guns in circulation. But it is both desirable and possible to cut down on the guns in the hands of thugs and criminals without curtailing the right to own guns for other purposes.

An effective gun-control policy must try to deter the use of guns to commit crimes and to intimidate at school and elsewhere. The best way to do this is for states to impose a stiffer punishment on miscreants who use guns for criminal ends. A jail sentence—or additional time—should be added to the usual punishment for a crime if guns are involved.

If the normal punishment for robbery is a year in jail, for example, this sentence might be doubled, to two years, when guns are involved. The punishment for using guns could depend on the severity of the crime, whether the gun was fired, and even on whether it was likely to be fired.

Many gun-control advocates shrink from reliance on imprisonment and other punishments for the use of guns to commit crimes because these seem too indirect and uncertain to be effective deterrents. But considerable evidence, summarized by James Q. Wilson and Richard J. Herrenstein in their *Crime and Human Nature*, indicates that greater certainty of apprehension and conviction is an effective deterrent to robbery and most other serious crimes. For this reason, I have advocated much greater spending on police and courts to increase apprehension of criminals and expedite their conviction (BW—Nov. 29).

CLEAR SIGNAL.   To increase the certainty of punishment for criminal use of guns, it may be desirable for states to mandate the extra jail sentences, so that little discretion is left to judges, juries, and prosecutors. A rapidly growing number of states require additional punishments when guns are involved. True, some federal judges have criticized the mandating of sentences for federal crimes such as drug sales or white-collar crime, but a state mandatory term sends a clear signal about the risk of using guns to perpetrate crimes.

Harsher punishment for those who use guns to commit crimes does not penalize ownership of guns by shopkeepers and others who are vulnerable to criminal attacks. In the confrontation between criminals and their prey, this approach to gun control deals potential targets a better hand.

A heavy tax on gun sales or on the purchase of ammunition—as proposed recently by Senator Daniel P. Moynihan (D-N.Y.)—does not punish the use of guns. It just raises the cost of acquiring and loading them. Such taxes would not only reduce the demand for guns by shopkeepers and others who buy them legally, but they make it that much cheaper to acquire them illegally. Although these taxes have no direct effect on criminals, who buy their weapons on the underground market, they do have bad indirect effects. Taxes make guns and ammunition more—not less—readily available to criminal elements because more guns and ammunition will be siphoned off into the underground economy by people seeking to evade the taxes on legal sales.

LESS RESISTANCE? Even if taxes didn't increase the number of guns in the hands of criminals, they tend to raise the incidence of crime. Overall, criminals will expect less armed resistance from shopkeepers and homeowners if taxes reduce purchases of guns by people who want to defend themselves.

Some states require that all weapons be registered, and Congress recently passed the Brady Bill, which mandates a week's delay before applications to buy guns can be approved. Officials can use the delay to check an applicant's background for criminal records and other problems. Such procedures are worthwhile because they may cut down on impulsive gun purchases that lead to violence.

But they do little to keep guns out of the hands of teenagers and criminals who obtain their weapons underground, where guns are sold to anyone who can pay for them. This is the route by which arsenals of weapons have found their way into inner cities and elsewhere in the U.S. Guns continue to be smuggled onto the illegal market from abroad, from military stock, and from crooked gun dealers.

In other words, the fatal difficulty in relying only on registration and approval is that there are two almost completely discrete markets for weapons. The legitimate market caters to people who want guns for hunting and for protection against holdups and burglaries. The gray market caters to criminals who want weapons to help them steal, intimidate, rape, participate in gang warfare, and sell drugs. Cooling-off periods and other controls on gun sales by legitimate dealers have little effect on an underground market that ignores them.

The right approach to gun control can get widespread agreement and would not be subject to the bitter controversies that plague other approaches to this issue. This one supports registration and cooling-off periods, but it relies mainly on punishing those who use guns for crime and intimidation.

How to Tackle Crime?
Take a Tough, Head-on Stance

Fear of crime in the streets, at home, or at school has an enormous impact on the everyday life of urban residents in the U.S., and increasingly on suburban residents as well. Yet politicians only recently have begun to place crime at the top of their agendas.

The anticrime bill now moving quickly through the U.S. Senate authorizes spending $22 billion, including $9 billion to help cities hire up to 100,000 additional police and $6 billion for federal high-security prisons and other correctional programs. Other provisions ban assault weapons, require mandatory life sentences for certain repeat offenders, and expand the death penalty to cover additional crimes.

The book *Crime and Human Nature* by James Wilson and Richard Herrenstein summarizes many studies showing that appropriate punishments—especially raising the certainty of punishment via more police, quicker trials, and higher conviction rates—are effective in reducing the number of criminals who rob, steal, or rape. Still, some observers question whether punishment has all that much effect on crime. These critics point to an apparent large increase in violent crime during the 1980s, a decade in which the number of people in state and federal prisons almost trebled.

According to data compiled by the FBI from police reports, crimes of violence and crimes against property grew at a rapid rate in the 1960s and 1970s as the certainty of punishment plunged, partly because of an expansion in the rights of those accused of crime. But in the 1980s, the Supreme Court toughened its stance on criminal rights, yet crime appeared to continue to increase.

IDEAL JURORS. But more accurate data than police reports exist to measure crime. The National Crime Surveys of the Census Bureau ask households whether they have been victims of crime. These data show much higher crime rates than the FBI statistics do, but they also show that per capita violent crimes declined by 10% since 1979, although they have grown a little during the past few years. Crimes against property fell by more than 25% after 1979. So the Supreme Court's retreat on criminal rights during the 1980s and the corresponding growth in the prison population may have reduced crime.

Many politicians in the U.S. have shrunk from calling for a tough approach on crime for fear of sounding racist, since African Americans and Hispanics commit a disproportionate share of felonies. But it is just these groups who suffer the most from crime, and polls consistently show that they want more police protection and tougher treatment of criminals. A federal prosecutor once told me that he prefers to have older, employed, urban blacks as jurors in criminal cases, because they are least likely to show leniency toward defendants after having experienced so much crime firsthand.

The attitudes revealed by these polls have been reflected in recent local and state elections, with candidates responding more aggressively to crime. Both blacks and whites running for mayor and for governor in Atlanta, Detroit, Los Angeles, New Jersey, Virginia, and elsewhere promised to add many more police to patrol streets. Voters in the state of Washington approved a proposal to make life sentences mandatory for criminals convicted a third time for a serious offense. It is not surprising that politicians are taking a tougher stance on crime. The puzzle is that it took them so long.

HOODLUM NETWORKS.   Police, courts, and prisons account for only 6% of state and local government expenditures and less than 1% of the federal budget. Special interests that demand agricultural supports, entitlements, and other programs dominate such a large share of government budgets that little is left over for such essential services as crime control, which affects everyone.

More police and greater punishment are sometimes considered to be ineffective because criminals are said to be unaware of their chances of being caught and punished. But this argument confuses what law-abiding citizens know about these matters with what hoodlums know. Information spreads rapidly in their network when there is a police crack-down. They know firsthand that young offenders are usually not punished except for serious crimes. And the grapevine tells them that Judge X is tough on crime, while Judge Z is not.

Some intellectuals and politicians continue to justify paying less attention to police and punishment because they believe the highest priority should go to rehabilitation of criminals and amelioration of the root causes of crime: racism, unemployment, unstable families, and poor schools. But the evidence is overwhelming that it is very hard to rehabilitate habitual criminals.

Although root causes are important, social policy can do little in the short run to reduce the number of broken families, racists, bad schools, or people with poor job skills. The case for more police and additional punishment rests on the immediate impacts these measures can achieve. They do not take a generation to become effective: They can reduce crime straightaway.

MAKE THE PUNISHMENT
FIT THE CORPORATE CRIME

What is the rational way of setting proper punishments for business crimes? The Drexel Burnham Lambert Inc. plea-bargaining agreement that is said to impose a fine of more than $600 million for alleged mail and security fraud is the most current dramatic example of the policy dilemma confronting those who determine punishments, particularly fines. Fines are attractive in these cases because they compensate for damage and punish perpetrators at the same time.

Punishments for corporate crimes—indeed for all crimes—should include fines determined by the harm done to individuals, other organizations, and society at large. The penalty should be a multiple of, rather than simply equal to, the harm caused. That is because many violators of the law go unpunished. If companies that are convicted pay only for the damages they cause, the deterrent effect of fines would be too weak, because companies that are not caught pay nothing.

CAUGHT IN THE ACT.   The deterrent effect strikes the right balance only if convicted corporations also pay for companies that are not caught. For example, if it is known that only a third of a particular kind of security fraud is punished, those companies convicted of this kind of fraud should pay three times the damage they cause.

It might seem unfair to make convicted companies pay for the crimes of others. But companies that are committing crimes clearly assume that the odds are they won't be caught. Therefore, companies fined according to this formula do not overpay: In the security fraud example, guilty companies have a one-third chance of being caught and paying three times the damage they cause, and a two-thirds chance of escaping punishment and paying nothing.

Obviously, it is hard to estimate damages for many company crimes and even harder to determine the probability of conviction. However, these difficulties are shared by any system that tries to make the punishment fit the crime. Over time, estimates of damages and the likelihood of conviction will improve as the courts and others gain experience in this approach.

It may seem strange that the recommended fines do not depend on the gain from crimes. This is no oversight. The goal is proper deterrence, not vengeance. The object is to eliminate crimes that impose bigger costs on everyone else than the gains to perpetrators. This aim is accomplished with fines that are based only on the harm caused others.

Consider a steel plant that pollutes the water and general environment in the surrounding neighborhood. If each ton of steel produced causes an illegal environmental damage worth $100 to the neighbors, and if the probability of conviction for this pollution is one out of four, the appropriate fine should be $400 per ton produced.

Anytime there is a fine, there is always a chance the profit may exceed the fine. But this is not necessarily bad. In this example, the plant would still net $100 per ton after paying the fine if it profited by $500 per ton from the steel production. However, this net profit comes from the steel that people want, not from the damage that has been made to the environment.

I proposed this approach in an article published more than 20 years ago. It was endorsed in a discussion draft on business crime prepared last July by some members of the U.S. Sentencing Commission. The U.S. Supreme Court recently upheld the legality of this commission, which was created in 1984 by Congress to promulgate sentencing guidelines for federal crimes.

The commission's discussion materials include preliminary estimates of the social harm of and appropriate fines for various crimes. Although these fines are many times those currently imposed by federal courts, the commission tries to avoid excessive punishment by suggesting an allowance for any fines paid in civil suits brought by victims. Even so, the commission may have overstated the harm caused by some perpetrators of business crimes, as a few critics have claimed.

NO JAIL TIME.   If there are appropriate fines, there is no reason to jail officials of corporations that commit security fraud, antitrust violations, tax evasions, and similar crimes. Directors of companies that pay large fines for crimes committed by their officials have an incentive to fire them or force them to clean up their act. Imprisonment is inferior to fines because prisons are costly to maintain. In effect, imprisonment punishes taxpayers as well as criminals. Of course, officials should be jailed when their companies engage in murder and other heinous crimes that cannot be compensated for with fines.

Many companies oppose a rational approach to the punishment for business crime out of fear that it will lead to severe penalties. Proper fines are harsh for business crimes that cause major harm, but they are mild for the many crimes that have small harmful effects on others. Executives—as well as the public— who take the long view should support the members of the Sentencing Commission who are trying to put punishment of company crimes on a sound footing.

TAILORING PUNISHMENT TO WHITE-COLLAR CRIME

Although corporate white-collar crime does not arouse the fear and alarm stirred by assaults and robberies, we should not encourage such crime by imposing inadequate punishment. I propose a system of fines that would repay society for the harm that corporate crime inflicts on it. In the case of white-collar crime, the best way to accomplish this—and punish criminal acts—is to imitate what is done in civil suits, that is, fine guilty companies amounts determined by the damages from their acts.

Executives contemplating whether to commit a crime take into consideration not only the punishment they face if caught but also their chances of being apprehended. This suggests that the proper fine should equal the value of the harm caused—including the costs of prosecution—divided by the probability that a guilty company will be punished. For example, if the act does $1 million worth of harm with a 50% chance of going unpunished, then the fine would be $2 million. Fines of this size would force companies to think longer and harder before committing white-collar crimes.

Generally, punishments do reflect the likelihood of not being caught. For example, triple damages in antitrust cases are an admission that most violators of antitrust laws go unpunished. Moreover, the 1984 federal statute on criminal procedures permits companies to be fined twice their pecuniary gain from criminal acts, also an admission that many violators escape detection.

BILLION-DOLLAR FINES. Proper fines should run into hundreds of millions, and even billions, of dollars. Fortunately, the courts and regulatory authorities have become willing to levy such big fines. During the past summer a federal appeals court upheld a fine on Exxon Corp. of more than $2 billion for violating oil-pricing rules from 1975 to 1981. A few years ago, Weyerhaeuser Corp. was held liable for more than $1 billion in a private antitrust suit. The case eventually was settled for more than $50 million.

The white-collar crimes that raise corporate income by less than the expected fines would not be profitable. It follows that top management would try to avoid these crimes, because a reduction in profits lowers their income and wealth (BW—July 8). Stockholders also can sue the management of guilty companies for dereliction of duty. These suits seek levies on the personal assets of executives and may force corporate leaders out of their jobs. Faced with the prospect of proper fines and stockholder suits, top management would be more likely to stay well-informed about decisions that could lead to white-collar crimes—and to implement procedures reducing their likelihood.

When appropriate fines would discourage most white-collar crime, they might not discourage crimes that raise the country's wealth—that is, raise corporate incomes by more than the harm inflicted on society. Certain violations of antipollution laws could be an example of this. But even in such cases, fines would force companies to take into account the value of damages inflicted on others. Moreover, convicted companies would still have to compensate society. If guilty companies pay for the harm to society, why should we want to discourage white-collar crime that raises a country's wealth?

PAYING THE DEBT. It might seem unfair to punish guilty companies with only fines instead of with imprisonment or probation of guilty employees. My recommendation in favor of fines is based on the assumption that the principal aim of a reasonable system of justice is to compensate innocent victims for the harm they suffer from the intentional acts of others. At one time many statutes unfairly did permit individuals and companies to get away with small fines as substitutes for long jail sentences. But fines that force guilty companies to compensate society fully are not unfair punishment.

Proper fines for some white-collar crimes would be very large and would have a severe impact on the wealth of even major companies. Some companies would be forced into bankruptcy. The courts should work with these companies to help them pay off their debt to society in the same way that courts arrange for bankrupt companies to pay off their creditors. However, guilty managers—and other guilty employees—of companies that cannot meet their debt should be punished in other ways as well, including probation, restrictions on the jobs they can hold in the future, and perhaps even prison terms for those guilty of serious offenses.

This is where punishment for corporate white-collar crimes would differ from punishment in civil suits. These additional punishments are necessary to force managers of companies that cannot pay large fines to consider more fully the harm inflicted on society from criminal acts.

When bankruptcy is not an issue, proper fines do two things: deter companies from crimes that do more harm to others than good to themselves and compensate society for the harm from the crime. This is why companies guilty of white-collar crime ought to be hit where it hurts—in their pocketbooks.

THE ECONOMIC APPROACH
TO FIGHTING CRIME

Many intellectuals have argued in recent decades that little could be done about crime without radical changes in social and economic organization. Crime is unresponsive to conviction and punishment since it allegedly results from alienation and inequities, including intolerable conditions in prisons. In his book *The Crime of Punishment*, psychiatrist Karl A. Menninger bluntly states: "I suspect that all the crimes committed by all the jailed criminals do not equal in total social damage that of the crimes committed against them."

These views fostered a feeling of impotence about stemming the increase in crime—a feeling that appears to have influenced public policy. Rights of the accused were greatly expanded, judges and juries became reluctant to punish even obviously guilty persons, and the police increasingly were considered oppressors instead of protectors.

Whatever the cause, the evidence is clear that crime grew rapidly during the last few decades, and punishment of criminals greatly declined. The number of crimes of violence per capita more than tripled in the U.S. from 1930 to 1980. Crimes against property increased almost as much. Trends in other felonies have been similar. Moreover, between 1950 and 1980, the probability of apprehending persons responsible for robberies or other crimes fell by about 50%. The probability of convicting those who were caught also dropped significantly.

ATTRACTIVE `OCCUPATION.'   An older view of criminal motivation dates back to Jeremy Bentham, the great English philosopher of the early 19th century. This approach was revised and expanded by myself and other economists in the 1960s and 1970s. According to the economic approach, criminals, like everyone else, respond to incentives. More students go into business or engineering when earnings and other advantages go up in these fields. Similarly, in recent decades more persons were induced to commit crimes, or commit additional crimes, because crime became a more attractive "occupation" when punishment became less certain and less severe.

Numerous statistical studies have probed the relationship in the U.S. and other countries between crime and punishment, unemployment, and other variables to determine whether or not criminals do respond to incentives. These studies find that crimes of passion as well as crimes against property are reduced by making punishment more certain and more severe. The implication is that much of the growth in crime since 1950 has been encouraged by the decline in punishment.

The proportion of the population aged 15 to 24 increased from the mid-1950s to 1980. This also contributed to the growth in crime, since young persons are more prone to break the law. Here, too, the effect of incentives is apparent. The young are less likely to be punished when they are apprehended. In effect, the courts give each teenager at least one "free" crime. In addition, unskilled youths often turn to crime when they cannot find honest employment or can find only low-paying jobs.

DETERRED.   But the situation appears to be taking a turn for the better. Frustration and fear produced by the growth in crime in the 1960s and 1970s, and the revival of the economic analysis of crime, may have succeeded in changing public policy during the last few years. The probabilities of apprehending criminals and punishing those convicted have both begun to climb. The number of state and federal prisoners has risen by a startling 40% since 1980.

Both violent crimes and crimes against property have also stopped rising and begun to fall. This is consistent with the view that criminals are deterred by punishment, although the proportion of the population under age 25 began to drop in recent years as well.

Crime can be discouraged further. Many changes would be effective, but all require willing judges and legislators as well as favorable public opinion. Here are a few suggestions for changing the incentives of criminals. Since 1960, the number of police officers has declined more than 50% relative to the number of crimes. The certainty of punishment could be raised through modest increases in state and local expenditures to expand police forces.

In addition, we could continue the recent trend toward heavier punishment for serious crimes and encourage the courts to modify further some undesirable changes in criminal procedures introduced during the 1960s and 1970s.

In a different vein, we could exempt young persons from the minimum wage laws. These laws price unskilled youths out of jobs and so raise their unemployment rates. In turn, this unemployment encourages youths to engage in crime, especially crimes against property.

The economic approach indicates that we need not accept passively the current level of crime. By alleviating public fear, the reduction in crime from implementing these proposals would be well worth their economic and social costs.

ADDICTIONS

Gambling's Advocates Are Right
—But for the Wrong Reasons

Many state and local governments face even greater fiscal pressure to raise taxes than Washington does. In the scramble for additional revenue, Mississippi and Indiana, along with Boston, Chicago, New Orleans, and the District of Columbia, among other localities, already allow or are seriously considering the enfranchisement of casino gambling and other gaming devices such as lotteries. I support this trend toward legalizing gambling, although my reasoning has little to do with revenues.

Mayors and governors drool in anticipation of what gambling taxes can do for their budgets. Nevada, for example, collects more than $200 million a year from its casinos, the state's largest employer, and New Jersey better than $314 million. Several Indian reservations—notably in Connecticut and South Dakota—have become rich from slot machines, poker and blackjack tables, and other gaming devices. The U.S. Supreme Court ruled in 1987 that reservations could operate gambling facilities comparable to any others permitted in their states.

As casinos spread across the country, however, the number of communities competing for the limited tax revenues from gambling will increase. They won't be able to duplicate the financial success of Nevada, Atlantic City, or the Indian reservations.

State and local governments must forget about gambling as a fail-safe jackpot. There is no way gambling is going to solve their fiscal crises. It would only add a modest amount of tax revenue. But there is this to be said for legalizing gambling: It would enable the many people who wish to place a bet to do so without patronizing illegal establishments and facilities controlled by criminals.

VENIAL SIN. For me, the issue comes down to this: The arguments against legalized gambling are specious, so why not allow it? The assertion by religious and civic groups that gambling is sinful and hence shouldn't be encouraged is of dubious validity. Gambling is surely less sinful than smoking and drinking, since smoking damages health, and drunkenness causes automobile and job accidents and domestic violence. And assuming so-called sin taxes should be proportionate to the degree of sin, the sin component of gaming taxes should be below the sin-tax rates on smoking and drinking. Federal and state governments together tax about 20% of cigarette and beer sales, while Nevada collects about 5% of net casino revenues in that state.

More than 30 states already encourage gambling by running enticing advertisements for state lotteries. The poor bet on these lotteries—as well as on illegal gaming such as numbers and card games. The rich can speculate as recklessly as they wish through buying and selling equities, options, real estate, and other highly risky assets. It is principally the middle classes that are affected by present restrictions on casinos and other forms of gambling. But few families in this group bet much of their income and assets in the attempt to hit it big.

Some opponents paint a picture of gambling addicts frittering away their life savings in pursuit of the big killing of their fantasies. Analysis of the betting patterns of lottery and casino patrons, however, shows that addictive gambling is not common—surely much less so than addiction to tobacco and alcohol. Few people buy so many lottery tickets that they jeopardize their funds for food and other necessities. Most casino visitors are middle-aged folks having a good time with friends. Why deny them the pleasures—thrills, even—they get from modest betting on lotteries and other gaming devices?

GONE LEGIT.   Many of those opposed to legalized gambling don't care a fig whether the patrons would commit a sin or risk addiction. Their concern is with organized crime, which did, after all, create Las Vegas. But that was long ago, and nowadays reputable companies such as Hilton, Hyatt, Bally's, and Grand Casinos control most of the gambling facilities and hotel rooms in Las Vegas and Atlantic City and run the newly legalized casinos along the Mississippi River.

Organized crime thrives on illegal activities such as drugs and betting on numbers. Criminals have an advantage over honest businesspeople in bribing law-enforcement officials—and in using force to collect their debts. The influence of criminals on gaming would be reduced, not raised, if companies were able to operate casinos and other facilities on riverboats or anyplace else that is zoned for gaming. Many legitimate companies are eager to enter this industry as soon as it becomes a legal activity.

The fear of organized crime has encouraged state and local governments to operate state lotteries, the Off-Track Betting shops in New York City, and other facilities. But governments have been no more successful at these activities than they are at providing other services: New York's OTB offices are among the few unprofitable gaming establishments in the world. State lotteries have been slow to innovate, and they rip off their mainly less-educated clientele by paying out only 50% of their revenue. By contrast, privately run casinos in Las Vegas and elsewhere are forced by competition to pay out about 95% of the amount wagered.

HIGHER "SIN" TAXES:
A LOW BLOW TO THE POOR

Prompted by the large federal budget deficit and the financial difficulties faced by state governments, some economists have called for greater taxation of "sin"—smoking, drinking, and gambling. But I believe that the taxes on lotteries and cigarettes are already excessive and that only the tax rate on beer is clearly too low.

Lotteries have replaced "numbers" as the favorite method of gambling among the poor. There are 33 states with lotteries, and many others are discussing whether to introduce them. But only about half the amount wagered on lottery tickets is returned as prizes. From 30% to 45% of the revenue from lotteries, depending on the state, is tax. The rest goes for administrative expenses and for the cost of collecting the tax revenue. Why should states tax so heavily the pleasures poor bettors get from dreaming of a better life with less drudgery?

It is impossible to justify on equity grounds the heavy taxation of lotteries. A study of lotteries by Professors Charles Clotfelter and Philip Cook for the National Bureau of Economic Research shows that the poor bet a much larger share of their incomes. Yet, the authors also show that the typical low-income bettor does not spend much. Not many poor whites bet more than $10 a week, although a much larger fraction of poor blacks do. People who bet modest sums hurt no one, and those who gamble a lot mainly harm themselves and their families.

SOCIAL PRICE?   Inhalation of cigarette smoke does not cause auto accidents, absenteeism from work, or much other behavior that imposes large costs on society, although a big debate is raging about the harmful effects of passive smoking. And the taxes that account for about 30% of cigarette prices are regressive, since less educated and poorer people smoke much more than others. Perhaps smoking by teenagers should be curtailed if they are not capable of foreseeing the harmful consequences on their own health of their behavior, but why tax so heavily adult smokers who mainly harm themselves?

Excessive drinking does cause a large fraction of road deaths and much job absenteeism. The recent disastrous Exxon Valdez oil spill was allegedly partly the result of drinking by the ship's captain. Excise taxes account for a sizable 45% of liquor prices but only about 10% of wine and beer prices. The tax on beer seems low, for this is the alcoholic beverage favored by the drunk young people who cause many auto deaths.

However, heavy taxes on alcohol disproportionately penalize light drinkers and people who confine their heavy drinking to situations where they are not a threat to others. For this reason, I believe severe punishments to drinkers who cause serious auto and other accidents, rather than very high taxes, should be used as the main deterrent to inappropriate drinking.

Even though the federal and many state governments are looking for additional revenue to cut their budget deficits, they have shied away from raising taxes on groups that offer strong political opposition. Companies often use their political clout to keep down the taxes on their products.

NO PRESSURE.   In light of the importance of clout, it is easy to see why lotteries are highly taxed. Private companies do not run lotteries, so no company has much reason to lobby against the large slice of lottery revenues taken by states. Bettors are not well organized and do not spend enough to take an interest in the politics of lottery taxes.

The middle classes and the rich don't usually gamble through lotteries, but through stocks, bonds, futures, options, and other financial instruments. The low tax rates on financial transactions result party from stock and bond markets' serving other purposes than the desire of the traders to gamble—raising capital, for instance. But surely a crucial reason is also that groups such as the New York Stock Exchange lobby hard to keep taxes down.

The tax rates on cigarettes, beer, and wine are lower than those on lotteries not because of lower public hostility to smoking and heavy drinking than to betting. Rather, there is well-organized opposition to smoking because of the enormous harm to smokers. And everyone knows drunks pose serious threats to the innocent.

These forces aligned against smoking and heavy drinking would have led to higher federal taxes to raise revenue and cut down these activities were it not for the political power of beer, wine, and liquor producers, cigarette companies, and tobacco growers. They advertise, turn voters out on key political issues, and their political action committees contribute heavily to campaigns at all levels. Tobacco growers are even able to get large subsidies while Congress debates higher taxes on cigarettes, and the federal tax on alcohol has hardly increased in 30 years despite the large rise in consumer prices.

Government budget deficits may well justify higher sales and excise taxes, but taxes on lotteries and smoking—expenditures favored by the poor—are too high compared with the taxes on other consumer activities.

MORE PEOPLE ARE SAYING "YES"
TO LEGALIZING DRUGS

Cocaine and other drugs remain popular despite prisons crowded with drug dealers and military attacks on foreign sources of supply. Neither the Reagan Administration's high-profile war against drugs, nor campaigns in schools and the media, nor street prices that are many times the cost of drug production have succeeded in breaking America's costly habit.

More and more people recognize that the war on drugs has failed, enough so that quite conventional people are starting to consider what was unthinkable only a short time ago—legalization. In the 10 months since I wrote in favor of such a radical change in policy (BW—Aug. 17), support has come from the mayors of several cities and from articles in *Foreign Policy*, *The Economist*, and the British medical journal *Lancet*. *The New York Times* displayed a story on the sudden interest in legalizing drugs on its front page.

PUNISHMENT AND CRIME.   One difficulty with the present antidrug approach is that each new step to widen the battle only worsens other problems. The police spend about one-quarter of their time tracking down drug sellers instead of combating robberies and other crimes against persons. Despite widespread concern about whether our armed forces can adequately defend U.S. strategic interests, Congress recently passed bills that would broaden the military's mission to include attacks on drug smugglers and foreign sources of supply.

Calls for harsh punishment for pushers are popular with politicians, who are increasingly pressuring state legislatures to take action. A bill pending in New York would make possession of even a small amount of crack subject to a stiff jail sentence. But severe penalties encourage dealers to step up violent attacks on drug agents or anyone else seen as a threat to their freedom. An old dictum of criminal justice states that criminals commit worse crimes when lesser crimes are punished severely.

Some people are opposed to legalization for adults because they fear that children will then have ready access to drugs. But the present system encourages dealers to use children to sell drugs because children are dealt with more leniently than adult dealers. If drugs could be sold to adults, it might be easier to reduce drug sales to children, since the police and courts could then concentrate on apprehending and punishing people who sell to children.

Politicians are so intent on showing their opposition to drugs that they are even reluctant to sponsor measures that would provide drug users with sterilized needles to help check the spread of AIDS, one of the most serious health problems in the world. More than a quarter of AIDS cases in the U.S.—and about half of all AIDS deaths in New York City—originate not from sexual activity but from contaminated needles used to inject heroin and other drugs. Addicts would have ready access to clean needles if drugs were legal and sold openly.

No doubt drug use would expand if drugs became legal and street prices dropped. Drinking increased greatly after Prohibition ended in 1933, mainly because liquor and other alcoholic beverages became much cheaper. However, today's high drug prices force many heavy users to finance their expensive habits by theft, robbery, or dealing in drugs themselves. The association between crime and drug use would become much weaker than it is now if drugs were legal and cheap.

The harmful effects of greater drug use are mitigated by the fact that most

drugs are much less addictive than is generally believed. For example, the
National Institute on Drug Abuse says 95% of the 30 million Americans who
have tried cocaine either stopped prior to becoming addicted or managed eventually to break their addiction. And legalization would not necessarily lead to more
addiction, which is often caused by peer pressure, unhappiness, and stress. Many
people suffering from those ills now simply resort to heavy drinking or other
destructive behavior.

SOCIAL TAXES.   In our society, we have a more serious problem that is handled in a much more open way. Alcohol abuse is far more socially destructive
than cocaine, marijuana, and heroin rolled together. Many more innocent people
suffer from drunk drivers and drunkenness on the job and in the home than from
people who drive or work while under the influence of drugs. But we try to
reduce the social harm from heavy drinking through high taxes on alcoholic beverages and by punishing drinkers who cause accidents and merchants who sell
liquor to minors.

I think similar policies should be followed with drugs. As with alcohol, taxes
on the legal purchase and sale of drugs would have some dampening effect on
drug sales without making addicts financially desperate. This would be a so-
called social tax, similar to the ones successfully used against smoking and drinking. People who cause serious accidents while driving or working under the
influence of drugs, or who sell drugs to children, should be punished harshly. A
policy of legalizing drugs would then be both sensible and humane—and would
drastically reduce the social cost of the drug problem.

Should Drug Use Be Legalized?

Along with many other countries, the U.S. prohibits the sale and consumption of
many drugs, including marijuana, cocaine, and heroin. Repeated "wars" on drug
pushers have failed to stop the illegal trade in such drugs. The problems arising
from the failure to halt drug traffic are big enough to warrant serious attention to
other options. In this spirit, I advocate the radical solution used during the
Depression to end the prohibition on alcoholic beverages: We should remove all
restrictions on the sale to adults of marijuana, cocaine, and other drugs where the
legal ban has created more problems than it solves. Drugs, of course, should not
be available to children.

The constitutional amendment to end Prohibition was a confession that the
U.S. experiment in banning drinking had failed dismally. It was not an expression of support for heavy drinking or alcoholism. Similarly, my proposal to legalize some drugs does not indicate that I approve of addiction and drug use.

Rather, it is a way to combat the many severe problems created by the ban on these drugs.

EASE THE PRESSURE. Criminals, including highly organized networks, dominate drug traffic, just as they controlled the production and distribution of beer and liquor during Prohibition. If legitimate companies are allowed to take control of production and distribution of drugs, violence in the drug industry would end, just as it did with alcoholic beverages. Competition among these companies would reduce the monopoly power that pushers now wield over many addicts who do not have alternative suppliers. Defective drugs that cause poisoning and overdoses would be much less common if companies selling legalized drugs feared expensive lawsuits and the loss of their reputations. The present secrecy surrounding the use of illegal drugs also helps spread the AIDS virus. Addicts contract this disease from contaminated needles and go on to infect others.

Drugs are expensive mainly because their prices include a sizable allowance for the risks of apprehension and punishment and for the cost of bribing enforcement officials. The large reduction in drug prices from legalizing drugs would greatly ease the financial pressure on addicts. They would not have to turn to prostitution, burglary, embezzlement, and other crimes to support a habit that consumes all their resources.

Under the present system, users of drugs may lose their jobs and have trouble finding other work even when they continue to perform satisfactorily. A dramatic example is the banning or temporary suspension of drug-using players from major league basketball, baseball, and football. For repeated offenses players are banned regardless of their performance. Banned players must bear the financial and other burdens of any continued drug use while suffering enormous drops in income. If drugs were legal, users would be fired from professional teams and other jobs only for the same reason as drinkers: They can no longer do the job.

It is widely but wrongly believed that addicts and other regular users of drugs do not respond to changes in price. Although direct evidence is fragmentary, what is known about other highly addictive substances clearly suggests that the demand for drugs expands when their prices fall. For example, the level of smoking and heavy drinking is sensitive to the cost of cigarettes and alcoholic beverages. A study by Professors Philip J. Cook and George Tauchen of Duke University shows that imposing even moderate excise taxes on liquor greatly reduces death rates from cirrhosis of the liver, a disease associated with heavy drinking.

This price sensitivity raises the main argument against legalizing drugs: that making them substantially cheaper would expand their use. This would add to the number of automobile accidents, crimes, and other harm to innocent people caused by those under the influence of drugs. But the very sensitivity to price that stimulates greater use also suggests a partial solution to such problems.

Putting moderate excise taxes on the legal sale of drugs could curtail the demand
for them to manageable levels—and without imposing the financial burden on
heavy users that currently leads to so much social disorder. Taxation would also
contribute needed federal and state revenue.

HARSH PUNISHMENT.   People arrested for driving under the influence of
drugs generally escape with minor punishment. Evidence from several countries
indicates that harsh punishments for drunk drivers greatly reduce drunk driving.
For this reason, I am confident that punishment, including imprisonment, could
discourage many people from heavy use of drugs before driving or engaging in
other potentially destructive behavior.

Legalizing drugs will not solve every problem. But it is the best feasible solution. Following the example set by the ending of Prohibition, we should legalize
marijuana, cocaine, and certain other drugs we have failed to control. Excise
taxes and punishments could hold drug use to tolerable levels and discourage
their use prior to engaging in activities that might harm others.

PART 8

Antitrust and Cartels

Antitrust laws in the United States are excessively concerned with business practices such as mergers and price discrimination between customers that are alleged either to promote monopoly or to reflect the presence of monopoly power. But neither judges nor legislators have enough information to determine whether various common business practices promote or discourage competition. A much more effective way to control monopoly power is by encouraging entry of competitors, including competition from imports.

The paradox of present antitrust laws is that many price conspiracies are exempt from antitrust prosecution, even though such conspiracies are the one reliable sign of monopolizing intent. For example, regulation of college sports by the national Collegiate Athletic Association is largely a conspiracy to lower the compensation received by college athletes, especially football and basketball players. The NCAA justifies its actions on the grounds of equity, but we show that it is a strange type of "equity" to reduce the compensation of athletes, who are commonly from poor backgrounds, when universities with successful teams benefit greatly from sports revenues and publicity.

BASEBALL: HOW TO LEVEL THE PLAYING FIELD

Since the start of the strike by Major League Baseball players and the premature death of the season, sports writers, TV analysts, and fans have been busy assigning blame and taking sides—without addressing the underlying economic issues and special problems of baseball and other team sports.

The stubbornness and solidarity of owners during the strike have been blamed on the special exemption from antitrust laws granted to Major League Baseball in 1922 by the U.S. Supreme Court. But baseball isn't alone in its immunity to antitrust litigation: The Clayton Antitrust Act of 1914 exempted all unions, including sports unions. And other sports, even those subject to antitrust litigation, have had similar conflicts: Witness the 1987 National Football League players' strike.

The most important distinguishing characteristic of the economics of baseball has nothing to do with antitrust: It is that baseball fans, like fans of other team sports, often care less about the absolute quality of performance by players and teams than about their records relative to the teams they compete against. This consideration differs from those involved in most other products and services. Will the team they root for win a lot of games, make the playoffs, and possibly even win the World Series? Will their favorite batter lead the league, or will a star pitcher win more than 20 games?

A TIGHT RACE. The sensitivity of revenues from attendance and television to relative performance implies that revenues are greater when games are close, races are tight, and perhaps also when the teams that win the World Series or championships in other sports tend to change from year to year. Owners oppose free agency and unfettered competition for rookies, arguing that races would not be close because teams in large markets or with deep pockets would buy up the best free agents and rookies. Yet studies find that the tightness of races and difference in won-lost records have not changed much since baseball went to free agency in 1976.

The importance of relative performance also means that spending by teams can degenerate into an "arms race." Each team alone has an incentive to do a bit more to get a competitive edge, but no team may get an edge on the competition if all spend more. Just as nations can increase their weapons without changing the balance of power, the ranking of teams in a sports race may be unchanged when they all spend more on players, farm teams, scouting, managers, and in other ways.

Owners and players need to find a set of rules that limits spending and encourages competition without tilting the labor-management balance too much to either side. Owners believe the solution is a cap on team salaries, but players correctly perceive that such caps are too rigid.

Strikes and lockouts might occur even with the best of intentions, as players and teams struggle over the division of sports revenues. Although the median salary of players is about $500,000, even well-paid employees may want to strike and use other tactics to earn more, especially when their careers last only a few years. And while owners are frequently successful businesspeople who get a thrill from involvement in sports, they still want to keep down costs and earn a reasonable return on their investments.

FOR RICH OR FOR WORSE. Instead of a salary cap, baseball should tax total spending by major league teams on players, player development, and anything else that may improve a team's record. For example, they might impose a 33% tax on all spending for those purposes by a team above $40 million, approximately the average amount spent by Major League Baseball teams in these ways. At the end of the negotiations between owners and players, the union sprang this kind of tax on the owners.

Such a tax would discourage excessive spending of the arms-race variety. In addition, since the tax revenue collected by the leagues would be distributed to all teams, it would help compensate owners in small markets for the greater resources of the New York Yankees, Los Angeles Dodgers, and other teams in large markets.

But a tax on spending is not enough, for it does not give badly run teams an added financial incentive to improve their records and make the races closer. This can be accomplished with a second tax on teams that perform below average.

The more games a team lost in the previous year or two, the larger would be the amount it would be obligated to pay into the league's treasury. Such a tax would encourage weak teams to try harder, whereas the rookie draft and certain other rules of Major League Baseball favor rather than punish teams that do badly. When weak teams are favored, they have less incentive to become more competitive through their own actions—such as improving the quality of their decisions and management.

The predictable result: close and efficient competition without a salary cap and without shifting the balance of power toward owners.

THE PROBLEM IS NOT WHAT CEOs GET
—IT'S GETTING THEM TO GO

The recession and President Bush's trip to Japan with a cohort of highly paid CEOs focused the attention of both sides of the Pacific on huge executive paychecks. Although some business leaders are surely overpaid, I believe pay is a red herring. The main problem with corporate leadership—and hence competitiveness—is the difficulty in getting rid of CEOs who run their businesses badly. The best way to do that would be to give them fixed-term contracts.

Chief executives who perform poorly are hard to replace because they usually have indefinite tenure, subject only to the board of directors or the grim reaper. But CEOs control most board appointments and thus are protected against removal. Management's slate is unopposed in more than 99% of elections to boards of directors, and even in the small remainder of cases, management prevails over the opposition 75% of the time. The upshot is that, barring a takeover by another company, top management seldom is fired, even when the company does badly.

Legislators, governors, college deans, coaches of college and professional sports teams, and others make do with term appointments. It might be a good idea for college professors, too. And it would be better to replace the tenure of chief executives by a fixed-term contract, perhaps three to five years, which could be renewed. Prior to renewal, the board would evaluate performance—preferably with the help of outside consultants—and report its conclusions and some of their analyses to the shareholders.

The short-term contract wouldn't be a sure-fire remedy for bad management, since the CEO would continue to exercise much control over the board. Still, it would involve a systematic, regular review of performance that would help expose evidence of incompetent management to stockholders and workers.

HEAL THYSELF. I am not advocating that fixed terms be imposed by the Securities & Exchange Commission or an act of Congress: There is already too much federal regulation of corporate governance. Rather, I would like to see corporate boards take the initiative in providing fixed terms for CEOs, possibly in response to stockholder and public pressure. The performance of these companies could then be studied to determine whether term appointments really are a good idea.

Critics complain that executive pay usually does not fall much when a company's profits and stock plummet. But even though a hefty pay cut for top executives of a loss-making company might make shareholders happy and might improve the morale of employees who suffer losses in pay and jobs, it would not have much direct effect on profits, since executive pay usually is a minute fraction of total costs. And tying compensation more closely to performance would not magically cause an executive to make better decisions. It is possible, however, that linking pay closer to performance would attract more entrepreneurial executives to corporations.

The proposal by Governor Bill Clinton of Arkansas and some members of Congress to penalize a company that pays top executives more than a specified multiple of the earnings of the average worker would be an unwarranted intervention into the market. The issue it turns on—the relationship between executive and average pay—strikes a populist note but isn't particularly important. The same is true of the recent recommendation by the SEC that companies allow stockholders to vote on executive compensation, though their votes would not be binding.

A study by economist Steven N. Kaplan of the University of Chicago of top executives in large Japanese and U.S. companies indicates that the heads of Japanese companies appear to earn much less, yet their compensation is no more sensitive to performance than is the pay of American leaders. But Japanese CEOs typically serve for only 6 years, compared with almost 10 for Americans. This is because Japanese executives are older when they reach the top, and they are more likely to be forced out by poor stock performance and low profits.

LEADEN PARACHUTES. It is far more common in the U.S. than elsewhere to replace top management through friendly or hostile takeovers. Obviously, takeover battles are an uneconomic way to replace bad management. A much-criticized but more economic method of dislodging a CEO is to convert an unfriendly takeover into a cheaper friendly one through golden parachutes: liberal severance pay for top executives who are forced out.

It may be unfair to reward a bad CEO with a multimillion-dollar payoff. Yet under present conditions, that's often the cheapest, quickest, and most effective way to get rid of him and replace deeply entrenched management without a bruising fight. Clearly, fixed-term appointments would make it easier to oust incompetent CEOs more rapidly without takeover battles and golden parachutes.

Only bad leaders fail to cut their own pay when workers and stockholders are asked to sacrifice. But the poor performance of a corporation has less to do with executive pay than with the old problem of how to make a change at the top when leaders do not perform well.

IF COLLEGES ARE FIXING PRICES, IT'S A JOB FOR ANTITRUST

The Justice Dept. recently asked about 20 elite private colleges and universities for information on their tuition and financial aid. Apparently, this is part of a broad investigation into possible collusion by the best schools to rig fees and scholarships. If the fewer than 50 schools that compete for the top students (including the University of Chicago where I teach) have succeeded in raising their tuition and in limiting scholarships, this would constitute an anticompetitive practice akin to price-fixing agreements by companies.

During the past decade, the courts have struck down various collusive arrangements among hospitals, doctors, and lawyers. The government is heading in the right direction, for there is no good reason why nonprofit organizations such as universities and hospitals, or professionals such as doctors and lawyers, should continue their traditional exemption from antitrust laws. These groups, as well as profit-making companies, are tempted to raise revenues and cut costs through agreements to limit competition.

Companies often allege that price fixing is necessary to prevent "ruinous" competition, without defining what that means or why it is bad. Nonprofit organizations and professional groups defend their actions with several variations on this theme. They claim they need to avoid bidding wars, that students and clients should choose on the basis of quality of service alone, and that limited scholarships for the best students and higher fees for wealthy clients help make funds available to the needy.

These defenses are as shallow and fallacious as those advanced by companies. A "bidding war" is just a euphemism for competition—for top students, patients, or car buyers. In particular, competitive bidding by schools helps ensure that students are not shortchanged and do not have to pay more for a college education than is warranted.

COMPARISON SHOPPING. Nor is there a good reason why students should choose schools on academic quality alone, without regard to scholarships and tuition. If Harvard University offers twice the education quality of another university but charges four times as much, a student may sensibly decide to attend the cheaper school. After all, many students wisely choose state universities over better private universities because subsidized state schools are much cheaper.

It is as prudent to take account of cost in choosing among colleges, hospitals, doctors, and lawyers as to consider wages in choosing a job or price in choosing a home. I never regretted my attention to finances as well as academic quality when many years ago I turned down a graduate fellowship from an elite school in the Northeast partly because the University of Chicago offered more money.

It doesn't seem fair to force students who are in greatest demand to bear the burden of financing the aid to other applicants. These funds should come from general tuition revenue contributed by all students, government loans and grants, and donations, not from a conspiracy to prevent competition for the ablest students.

Faculty and deans who defend the practice of limiting competition for students would complain loudly about an agreement among schools not to compete for their professional services so that they could choose where to work solely on the basis of academic quality. There would be no end to the meetings and petitions to protest against such "unfair" practices. Indeed, these protests may soon begin, for Justice apparently is also checking into whether the top schools collude to reduce competition for faculty.

HIGHFALUTIN NONSENSE. Any efforts by the prestigious colleges and universities to rig tuition, scholarships, and faculty salaries seem innocent compared with the National Collegiate Athletics Assn.'s blatant restrictions on aid to student athletes and the severe punishments meted out to offending schools. These are defended by the same kind of self-serving, highfalutin nonsense that supports efforts to limit competition for good students—athletes should consider their education without regard to the aid they get, a lot of money is bad for young people, and scholarships to football and basketball players must be kept down in order to subsidize low-revenue sports like lacrosse and track.

If the current investigation by Justice is an indication that the government has stopped exempting colleges from antitrust laws, how can it avoid prosecuting the NCAA for its systematic and successful efforts to reduce competition for student athletes by almost 800 member schools? A few years ago, the U.S. Supreme Court established a precedent by striking down the NCAA's regulation of televised college football and basketball games.

Antitrust policy has wisely shifted away from a concern with business size toward price-fixing and related conspiracies to reduce competition. No one has advanced persuasive reasons why anticompetitive practices by universities and other nonprofit organizations should be excluded, and there are good reasons why they should be subject to the antitrust laws.

It's Time to Scrap a Few Outmoded Labor Laws

The Clayton Act of 1914 exempted trade union wage negotiations from antitrust laws. A conspiracy by competing companies to obtain monopoly prices is a violation of the Sherman Antitrust Act. Why should the efforts of unions in different companies to raise wages above competitive levels be treated differently?

People working for large, impersonal corporations often prefer to bargain over wages and work rules through unions rather than individually. In particular, workers who have spent many years with the same company may find a union helpful in protecting against management, especially new management, that tries to take advantage of the difficulties senior workers face in finding comparable employment elsewhere.

However, these legitimate and important bargaining goals of workers are attainable through a union of workers in the same company. They do not require workers in different companies to act in unison. Japanese workers, for example, have greatly improved their wages and working conditions by bargaining through company unions.

DUBIOUS VALUE. To allay the fear that company unions will bow to management, Congress and state legislatures can strengthen the right to a union shop and other protections for company union members. For example, if company unions were made fully subject to antitrust laws, right-to-work laws would not be desirable, even though they are a useful barrier between the workers and the power of unions that organize whole industries and occupations.

It is difficult to discuss unions dispassionately because they receive more credit and at the same time more blame than they deserve. Some unions have been a bulwark to workers against oppressive management, but advances in productivity, not unions, are mainly responsible for the improvement in earnings and working conditions of the average worker. Unions were unimportant in the American economy prior to 1930. Yet average earnings greatly increased from 1870 to 1930 despite the huge immigration of unskilled workers, who were more likely to be exploited than were native-born workers.

Unions that raise wages of their members above competitive levels lower economic efficiency by reducing employment in the unionized sector. And the higher earnings of union members usually come at the expense of poorer nonunion workers. Earnings gains to large numbers of union workers cannot come mainly out of profits because corporate profits are less than 10% of national income. Still, despite these harmful effects, unions should not be blamed for inflation and sluggish economic growth. The 1950s and 1960s had little inflation and rapid economic growth, even though unions were at peak strength. Unions are not a major cause of the monetary expansion that produces rapid inflation nor of the slow advance in productivity that leads to sluggish growth.

LESS CLOUT. The decline of trade union power during the past 30 years is as remarkable as it was unexpected. In 1955 one of every three members of the U.S. labor force belonged to a union, compared with 17% in 1987. This halving of union membership is partly due to structural changes in the economy and greater international competition. The growth of the service sector and the declines of manufacturing and mining in this period reduced the percentage of membership because service workers have not been easy to unionize. International trade expanded greatly during the past 30 years: Imports into the U.S. increased from 5% of gross national product in 1955 to 12% in recent years. Steel, auto, and other manufacturing industries lost out to imports from Asia and elsewhere partly because strong unions greatly raised costs of production.

But the most significant causes of decline in union membership since 1955 are laws that protect workers against unfair dismissal and the growth of unemployment compensation, Social Security payments, medicare, and other government transfer payments. Workers no longer need to rely on unions for protection against job loss and the expenses of ill health and old age.

Unions remain more powerful in Canada and Western Europe than in the U.S., but union strength also has begun to ebb rapidly in some of these countries. For example, during the past eight years unionized workers in Britain declined from about 50% to less than 40% of the work force, and Margaret Thatcher decisively defeated a long strike by the militant coal miners' union.

Union leaders were once powerful political brokers courted by members of both parties, but now they have less clout when challenged by business and other groups. A decade ago the National Football League could not have continued with replacement players, while almost all the regular football players were on strike, without fear of picketing violence and sympathy strikes. It is a good time politically to push for legislation that protects society against anticompetitive union practices and also strengthens a worker's right to join a union. Such a redirection of labor laws would help both the average worker and society at large.

ANTITRUST'S ONLY PROPER QUARRY: COLLUSION

During the 1980s both government and private antitrust cases have declined dramatically, while malpractice, product liability, and other business litigation has boomed. Specialists in antitrust law have shifted to other business areas as the once-prosperous antitrust field has fallen on difficult times.

The immediate cause of the decline has been the growing influence of economic analysis of competition and business practices on the thinking of judges and government officials. That analysis shows that competition usually promotes efficiency and the well-being of consumers and that anticompetitive behavior arises mainly from unwise public policies and a natural tendency for rival producers to collude on prices and production.

Conspiracies in restraint of trade tend to break down eventually without an active antitrust policy. Companies that are part of a conspiracy cheat on their output quotas, and high prices attract new companies into their industry. The experience of OPEC illustrates the spontaneous breakdown of an open conspiracy outside antitrust laws. However, antitrust policy can certainly discourage business conspiracies by imposing large fines and other punishments.

PREDATORY PRICING.   Political pressures often divert antitrust enforcement toward condemning business practices that promote efficiency but hurt weak companies. The U.S. Supreme Court said in the famous Brown Shoe case, decided in 1962: "It is competition, not competitors, which the [Sherman Antitrust] Act protects. But we cannot fail to recognize Congress' desire to [protect]...viable, small, locally owned businesses. Congress appreciated that occasional higher costs and prices might result from the maintenance of fragmented industries and markets."

The perennial complaint about predatory pricing illustrates the confusion of competitive behavior with unfair practice. Predatory pricing occurs when strong companies first price below cost to drive out weak competitors and later raise prices toward monopoly levels to recoup earlier losses. I do not know of any documented predatory-pricing case, although the government's 1911 antitrust suit against Standard Oil Co. began the long history of complaints about it. Typically, instead of predatory behavior, what really happens is that efficient companies take business away from less efficient ones by offering better deals to customers. What makes predatory pricing rare is that the high prices that are supposed to make up for the losses from selling below cost attract new competitors, foreign as well as domestic, who force prices down to competitive levels.

Rivals may merge to reduce competition, especially if the law prevents them from conspiring. But usually a far more important inducement to merge lies in improvements in organizational efficiency because of a larger scale of production, a more complete product line, or less-tangible synergies. Therefore, economic analysis suggests that antitrust laws should be lenient toward mergers. The incentive to merge for anticompetitive reasons will be weak if antitrust laws effectively attack implicit and explicit conspiracies. A more flexible merger policy was introduced a few years ago by Professor William F. Baxter of Stanford University Law School, then Assistant Attorney General for antitrust. It eased the conditions under which companies in the same industry could merge without Justice Dept. objection.

STIFF CHALLENGE. Wise antitrust policy tolerates business practices such as exclusive franchises even when companies cannot demonstrate that their practices add to efficiency. Competition will weed out inefficient behavior without government intervention. Antitrust action should only challenge behavior that obviously encourages collusion, such as agreement among rival producers to divide a market into exclusive territories.

The stiffest challenge to a domestic conspiracy often comes from foreign producers. Competition in the U.S. market for cars and steel increased when Japanese and other foreign companies became important players. Since domestic producers try to use their political clout to reduce foreign competition through tariffs or import quotas, an open trade policy is as valuable as antitrust laws in the fight against collusion and anticompetitive behavior.

Unfortunately, some groups have enough political influence to gain special privileges for their collusive activities. Thus colleges are allowed to conspire through the NCAA to keep down the pay of student athletes (BW—Sept. 14).

Unions that raise wages of members above competitive levels are protected from prosecution by the Clayton Antitrust Act.

Judge Robert H. Bork helped develop the economic approach to antitrust policy, especially with his book *The Antitrust Paradox*. If his nomination to the Supreme Court receives congressional approval, as it should, he will bring an understanding of economic issues that surpasses the knowledge of any justice in recent decades.

A strong dose of economic analysis helped clarify the goals of antitrust policy. It can do the same for product liability and other business activities where litigation has exploded.

THE NCAA: A CARTEL
IN SHEEPSKIN CLOTHING

You don't have to be an economist to understand the behavior of cartels. A cartel increases the profits of its members by assigning quotas that reduce production and raise prices. Some cartels hide behind highfalutin language and expressions of good intentions. Rival producers claim to be cooperating only to prevent chaos or to protect the health and safety of consumers and workers. An example is the group of independent doctors and other medical professionals who recently joined together to fight the spread of health maintenance organizations. No doubt many health practitioners sincerely worry about the effect of HMOs on patient care, but when these professionals organized, surely they gave some thought to the stiff competition they are getting from HMOs.

Governments often fail to oppose cartels that involve educational and other non-profit entities because these institutions are especially good at clouding the issues with self-righteous rhetoric. An excellent illustration is the National Collegiate Athletic Assn., a group of almost 800 colleges and universities and more than 100 conferences and related bodies. Some college coaches, faculty, and administrators do worry about the effects of big-time athletic programs on academic quality and the education athletes receive. NCAA's regulations, though, by reducing competition for players, TV contracts, and tournaments, raise the profits that member schools realize—or cut the losses they suffer—from their athletic programs.

In 1984 the U.S. Supreme Court to some extent saw through the NCAA's claims of good intentions, declaring its restrictions on televised college football games an illegal conspiracy in violation of the Sherman Antitrust Act. The court said that "good motives alone will not validate an otherwise anticompetitive practice."

UNLAWFUL CONSPIRACY.   The effect the court's decision had on the market for televised games supports its conclusion about the monopoly power of the

NCAA. Since the decision, the number of college football games broadcast on the primary network and cable carriers has increased dramatically, while the average fee per game paid to schools declined sizably. Moreover, such popular schools as the University of Oklahoma and the University of Notre Dame have increased their share of televised games at the expense of less popular schools.

In a dissent to the majority opinion, Justice Byron R. White argued that the court's majority was inconsistent in ruling against the NCAA while permitting it to retain its power over compensation to student athletes. I agree that the majority opinion was inconsistent, but White should have called for abolishing restrictions on compensation, not maintaining the NCAA's power over TV broadcasts.

Regardless of good intentions, the NCAA's restraints on pay to athletes clearly reduce the competition for such people. There is little doubt that scholarships and other compensation would increase if the court were to decide that these restraints are also an unlawful conspiracy. The increase would be especially large for the top athletes, who generally come from poor families.

HARD TO BELIEVE.   As schools compete in a more open and honest fashion, under-the-table payments to athletes and other subterfuges devised to cheat on the NCAA would disappear. This could end the so-called scandals that plague the NCAA, such as the latest involving Auburn University.

Defenders of the present system claim that if colleges could compete freely for athletes, the athletes' education would suffer, they would be spoiled by large incomes, and the financial stability of many athletic programs would be jeopardized. It is hard to believe that even the strongest defenders of the NCAA take these objections seriously. Under the present system, many of the best athletes never graduate from college, while those who do often cheat to get through or are steered into programs with little educational value. A recent book by Lawrence Taylor, the great linebacker for the New York Giants, confesses his own cheating at the academically respected University of North Carolina. Big incomes do no more harm to student athletes than to young professional athletes or other young people. Would anyone advocate a cap on the earnings of young traders on Wall Street so that they don't get into trouble from having a lot of money? And why should the best athletes be forced to support athletic programs by accepting low pay—rather than alumni and students supporting them through contributions and higher ticket prices?

Economists disagree about many things, but they strongly agree that cartels raise prices, lower outputs, and are bad for society. The effect on prices and output of explicit cartels like OPEC are direct and obvious. The harmful effects of cartels that hide behind the smokescreen of good intentions are more difficult to detect, especially when nonprofit institutions are involved. The NCAA is a prime example of such a cartel. It is time that all the NCAA's restrictions on competition for athletes and sports revenues be declared an unlawful conspiracy in violation of the antitrust laws.

Low-Priced Oil Is Still a Good Deal

Just as nature abhors a vacuum, so do special interests and naysayers abhor good economic news. In many quarters of the Western world these days, doubt has replaced the initial joy that greeted the plunge in oil prices. Restating a few simple economic truths about the consequences of the recent change in world oil prices might help dissipate some confusion.

In 1985 the U.S. imported about 3 million bbl. of crude oil a day, plus 2 million bbl. of oil products. The decline of some $14 a bbl. in the world price of oil during the past few months will increase annual gross national product in the U.S. by $26 billion, provided that imports remain constant and the cost of oil products also declines by $14 a bbl. This $26 billion increase is less than 1% of GNP. By contrast, the OPEC-engineered hike in oil prices of $9 per bbl. in 1973 decreased GNP in the U.S. by some 2%, based on the 1973 level of oil imports and on a $9-a-bbl. increase in the cost of imported oil products.

The initial gain from lower oil prices is much smaller as a percent of U.S. income than was the 1973 loss because the explosion in oil prices from 1973 to 1981 reduced the relative importance of oil imports in the U.S. economy. It stimulated domestic oil production and discouraged oil consumption. In the same way, a lower world price will discourage production in the U.S. and encourage both households and companies to use oil more liberally. These responses in production and consumption will raise the demand for oil imports. This anticipated rise in oil imports reflects the gain the U.S. will derive from replacing higher-cost domestic oil with lower-cost imported oil and from substituting the cheaper foreign oil for gas, coal, and other resources.

INJURED GROUPS. The plunge in oil prices will obviously benefit most those countries that import all of their oil. Yet even in a country such as Japan, which is entirely dependent on imported oil, the decline of $14 a bbl. will increase its GNP by only about 2% at its current import levels of crude oil and oil products. It follows that while the lower oil price is important to oil-importing countries, including the poor ones, it will not decisively determine what either the inflation rate or real income will be in those countries.

Clearly, the drop in oil prices has also hurt some groups in the industrial countries. Yet even within the same industry the effects are mixed. U.S. domestic oil producers have been hurt badly, for example, but refiners benefit from the cheaper price of their major raw material. Banks with extensive loans to domestic producers or with loans to Mexico and other oil-producing countries will suffer, while banks with loans to heavy fuel-using sectors or to Brazil and other oil-importing countries will prosper. The real and lamentable difficulties experienced by some groups should not make us forget the overall benefit to industrial countries from lower energy prices. Moreover, domestic producers in this country profited greatly in the early 1970s when oil prices exploded, and the real price of oil is still higher than it was at the beginning of 1973.

RELAX AND ENJOY. For a time, OPEC was more successful than are most cartels. But even successful cartels break down eventually as members violate cartel agreements, production by outsiders grows, and higher prices reduce consumption. OPEC has finally succumbed to these forces. Cartels sometimes revive after they break down, but they seldom fully regain their economic power. For these reasons, I do not believe that the plunge in oil prices is mainly a short-term tactic by Saudi Arabia any more than the recent collapse of the tin cartel was a temporary expedient engineered by Malaysia and other major tin producers. Saudi Arabia possibly decided that it is better off with sales of, say, 4.5 million bbl. per day at $15 a bbl. than with 2 million bbl. or less at $28 a bbl.

The U.S. should be taking steps to maintain and even extend the gains it is deriving from low oil prices. It is true that raising dependence on foreign producers stirs legitimate concerns about national security. Yet the U.S. can deal with worries about our vulnerability to future embargoes, Middle East conflicts, and other threats by adding to the strategic petroleum reserve and perhaps also by encouraging continued exploration for domestic oil reserves. The so-called windfall profits tax on oil companies should be scrapped. Most important, we should abolish all the remaining, incredibly complex controls over the pricing and distribution of natural gas.

President Reagan is right to oppose a tariff on oil imports. A tariff is simply a fancy way to subsidize domestic oil producers, just as "stabilizing the world price" of oil is a euphemism for helping such producers by raising world prices. In the 1960s and 1970s, oil-import quotas, domestic price controls, rationing, and windfall taxes slowed and distorted the U.S. adjustment to high fuel prices and helped OPEC maintain its power over the oil market. Instead of repeating these mistakes and adding new ones, why don't we just relax and enjoy the benefits we are receiving from low oil prices?

COLLEGE ATHLETES SHOULD GET PAID WHAT THEY'RE WORTH

In the spring a young man's fancy may turn to love, but in the fall it almost surely turns to football. Inevitably, though, his daydreams of the spirited competition of the college football season are marred by public accusations that some schools have disobeyed the rules of the National Collegiate Athletic Assn. that govern payments made to athletes.

In 1984 the U.S. Supreme Court held that the NCAA violated antitrust laws with its restrictions on televising the football games of member institutions. Certainly, that was a monopoly, but at least college football faces a lot of competition for audiences—both on TV and in the stadium. The NCAA's real monopoly power is over its athletes.

This is why the association's rules on payments to college athletes are a more serious restraint of trade than were its restrictions on televising football games. The NCAA limits not only the number and size of athletic scholarships but also such matters as compensation to athletes for summer employment, when colleges can approach high school players, and when transfer students from other colleges are eligible to play. These rules are designed mainly to reduce the competition among colleges for players in football and basketball—the two top revenue-producing college sports.

An association of companies that limits payments to employees and punishes violators would usually be considered a labor-market cartel. Why should the restrictions on competition for athletes among the approximately 800 members of the NCAA be any different? And especially since these restrictions primarily affect the low-income athletes—most of whom are black or from other minorities—who dominate big-time college football and basketball.

LOWER SALARIES.   One answer is that some institutions would have to drop football and other sports if they were forced to pay market prices for athletes. Clearly, the same argument would justify lower salaries and increased teaching loads for professors to ensure the survival of many academic programs.

But programs should not be saved through artificially low wages to athletes, professors, or anybody else for that matter. Why should the viability of athletic programs depend on what amounts to subsidies from athletes rather than on such resources as larger gifts from alumni, higher tuition from students, bigger subsidies from taxpayers, or higher ticket prices for spectators?

A second argument used to defend the NCAA is that athletes should choose a college for its educational quality rather than for what it will pay them to play. Presumably scholarships awarded to students for academic achievement, as well as the salaries paid to faculty and even college presidents, should also be kept low and uniform so that these people choose colleges on the basis of academic quality rather than monetary rewards. It is presumptuous to argue that college athletes are less capable than other students to choose the particular mix of monetary compensation and educational quality that best suits their talents and interests. Nor should college athletes be held to a higher standard than are other members of academia.

BIG-TIME PROGRAMS.   Such an argument also suggests that a lot of effort is devoted to the education of athletes. Although some colleges do have excellent records in this area, many with big-time athletic programs do not seem concerned about the education their athletes receive. Indeed, less than one-third of the athletes in revenue-producing sports graduate from college, according to Richard E. Lapchick of Northeastern University's Center for the Study of Sport in Society.

In his dissent from the 1984 decision on the televising of college football, Justice Byron R. White—himself a former college athlete—claimed that competition for college athletes should be limited to preserve the amateur nature of college sports. But why should all college athletes be amateurs? Currently the Ivy League has tougher academic standards for athletes than most Division I schools—universities with big sports programs. The University of Chicago is a member of a conference that essentially prohibits athletic scholarships altogether. Open competition for college athletes would only slightly affect these schools and the many others that actually use amateur athletes.

Open competition would widen the range of college athletic programs and would permit schools to be honest when they use professional athletes—who may also be students. Many schools, in fact, already use professionals. They often violate either the letter or the intent of the NCAA rules through such practices as gifts to parents, providing athletes with well-paying jobs that require little work, and pressuring teachers to give athletes passing grades.

The NCAA's efforts to justify its restrictions on competition for athletes should be viewed with suspicion because they increase the financial benefits colleges receive from football, basketball, and other sports. I would have expected greater hostility from Congress and the courts to a policy that lowers the earnings of young black and other athletes with limited opportunities.

WHY MANAGERS HAVE
THE SHAREHOLDER AT HEART

The current takeover wave is causing increased attention to whether top executives of large corporations promote their own interests or those of the stockholders. In the 1932 study *The Modern Corporation & Private Property*, Adolf A. Berle Jr. and Gardiner C. Means argued that widely dispersed stock ownership gives top management considerable leeway to pursue aims that are contrary to stockholders' interests.

The Berle-Means thesis was supported by early empirical studies that found only a weak relationship between corporate profits and the income and wealth of top executives. But recent theoretical and empirical evidence makes a strong case that Berle and Means greatly exaggerated the conflict of interest between management and shareholders and that contemporary writers continue to exaggerate it.

A good introduction to this new research is provided by the April, 1985, issue of the *Journal of Accounting and Economics*. The studies discussed in this issue are on firmer ground than the earlier ones because they take into account important theoretical developments in the pricing of corporate shares, and also contracts that reduce conflicts between executives and stockholders.

An effective way to align executives' incentives closely with stockholder interests is to link management bonuses and other compensation to company performance, as measured by the market value of a company's shares, and to encourage top executives to invest heavily in those shares. The studies show that much of top executives' total compensation does come from bonuses linked to performance and from investments in their company's stock. In effect, management and stockholder interests are aligned by the very stock market that, according to Berle and Means, makes management more independent.

STRONG IMPACT.   A study by Professor Kevin J. Murphy of the University of Rochester examines the evidence on the relationship between executive compensation and company performance. It looks at the total compensation received by more than 400 executives in more than 70 large manufacturing companies from 1964 to 1981. He finds that superior company performance has a strong impact on bonuses. A 10% increase in the rate of return on the company's stock raised bonuses awarded to top executives by 12%, while a 10% increase in sales raised them by almost 10%. The size of bonuses is even related to rates of return on the company's stock relative to those of other companies in the same industry. Moreover, other studies find that the departure of top executives prior to age 65 is hastened by poor performance of the company's stock.

If top executives are using compensation methods that benefit themselves at the stockholders' expense, the market value of the company's stock should fall when new methods are introduced. The studies in the *Journal of Accounting,* however, show the opposite, that the market value of shares generally rises when new methods of compensation are made public.

Mergers, takeovers, and proxy fights also help discipline entrenched managers who fail to satisfy stockholders. Various studies in recent years have shown that when companies are about to be acquired, their shares typically appreciate substantially prior to the acquisition. Indeed, the shares of an acquired company rise so much that it is likely that expensive takeover contests are used only when companies have been performing much below their potential.

GOLDEN PARACHUTES.   It is true that management sometimes resists mergers and takeovers that appear to be in the interests of stockholders. In most cases, however, management has an incentive to agree to those deals that would raise the value of their company's stock, since they usually have invested heavily in that stock. Golden parachutes further discourage opposition to mergers and takeovers, and they also compensate departing management for long service that will be less valuable at other companies. Though golden parachutes have been criticized, a study in the *Journal of Accounting* shows that when a company announces a golden parachute contract with its top executives, the price of its stock typically goes up.

An obvious way to evaluate the Berle-Means argument about how broad stock ownership increases management independence is to see if top management is better compensated in companies with more dispersed stock ownership. The few available studies on this topic, including one by Professor George J. Stigler of the University of Chicago on compensation during the 1930s, suggest that this is not the case. Moreover, it is reasonable to suppose that the independence of management from stockholders should have declined over the past 20 years because the growth of pension funds and other institutions that control large blocks of shares has increased the concentration of stock ownership.

In short, while the case that the interests of management and stockholder are closely linked is not yet proved, the growing evidence is convincing that they are less in conflict than many students of the corporation have assumed.

PART 9

Special Interests and Politics

This part discusses various special-interest groups that promote laws and regulations that benefit their members. For example, the elderly in most developed countries receive generous government medical and pension subsidies because they exercise considerable political clout. Similarly, various industries have supported an "industrial policy" because it would help reduce competition from imports and often leads to additional government subsidies. Still another example are the advocates for the homeless in the United States who for a while gained public attention and political support by grossly exaggerating the number and plight of the homeless.

These and other examples show how naive are the economic theorists who believe that politicians and bureaucrats are mainly interested in discovering how to promote efficiency and social welfare. Yet objective analysis of the effects of public programs and regulations can have a large influence in the long run, even though its influence on policies is usually minuscule in the short run.

Gary's work on the military draft many years ago shows the relevance of the distinction between short- and long-run influence. During the summer of 1957 he wrote a paper for Rand Corporation called "The Case Against Conscription" that came out strongly for a voluntary armed forces. The Air Force was then the main financial supporter of Rand, and they did not allow Rand to publish this study because they believed the draft helped the Air Force recruit highly qualified "volunteers." Gary became convinced by this experience that a voluntary army was not politically feasible, and he simply put the manuscript in his files.

But political views on how to recruit for the military changed radically after the Vietnam War began because many young men violently opposed being drafted. Their opposition forced President Nixon to convene a commission which recommended that the United States convert to having a fully voluntary armed forces. In 1979 the draft was abolished and replaced by an all-volunteer armed forces, a change that was politically inconceivable in the 1950s. The voluntary army has worked so well that many other nations followed the United States's lead and also abolished conscription.

SPECIAL INTERESTS

How the Homeless "Crisis" Was Hyped

In 1982, Mary Ellen Hombs and Mitch Snyder, advocates for the homeless, estimated in their book *Homelessness in America: A Forced March to Nowhere* that between 2 million and 3 million people in the U.S. were then without a home. The magnitude of that figure helped create a perception that the number of homeless people was one of the major failures of U.S. social programs.

On the face of it, such an assertion—implying that more than 1 out of every 100 Americans in the 1980s had no place to live—simply wasn't credible. Indeed, a few years after publishing the estimate, Snyder conceded that it had no basis in fact. He admitted that he had simply pulled the number out of a hat to satisfy people pressing him for specificity.

Still, his fabricated estimate was accepted by many. Residents of large cities were receptive in the early 1980s to exaggeration about the number of homeless because their own anecdotal evidence was that a lot more people were sleeping on sidewalks and in public buildings and pushing their belongings around in supermarket carts during the day. But most Americans don't live in big cities, and homeless persons are much less common in the small cities and towns scattered throughout the U.S.

The implausibility of the Hombs and Snyder guesstimate did, however, stimulate efforts to obtain more precise numbers. One of the first, by Peter H. Rossi, then at the National Opinion Research Center in Chicago, counted the number of homeless in Chicago in the mid-1980s by sending interviewers out in the middle of the night. They found about 3,000 persons, less than one-eighth the number claimed by some local homeless advocacy groups. These groups in turn attacked Rossi for being uncaring and for slanting his estimates toward the low side. But his methods were much more scientific than those used by his critics.

URBAN PERCEPTION.   Rossi's estimates and those of others are carefully reviewed in an excellent recent book, *The Homeless*, by the sociologist Christopher Jencks. He shows how difficult it is to define, let alone estimate, the number of people without homes. But he concludes that during any week in March, 1990—

the date of the latest estimates—about 300,000 Americans were homeless in the sense that they slept either in free shelters or in public places not intended for habitation, such as bus stations, sidewalks, or abandoned buildings.

Jencks's review does indicate that homelessness greatly increased over time, which surely contributed to the perception among denizens of New York, Chicago, and other large cities that it is so common. The number of people without a home seems to have more than doubled from the late 1970s to the mid-1980s, and probably increased in the 1960s and 1970s as well, but it does not seem to have grown much during the latter half of the 1980s.

Contrary to another myth propagated by television and homeless advocates, families with children make up less than one-fifth of the homeless population—the rest are mainly single males—and virtually all families stay overnight in shelters. Even people who sleep on the streets or in public places generally can go to shelters—unpleasant as they may be—if they choose.

Jencks provides a good analysis of why homelessness increased over time and makes sensible suggestions for reducing its incidence and increasing the fraction who sleep in shelters. However, I am not concerned here with the causes and cures of homelessness but with advocacy groups' ability to convince a gullible public and media that homelessness had become a huge problem in America.

COMMON SENSE. In fact, the rather small size of the homeless population in reliable estimates indicates that, although the growth in homelessness is disturbing, it has been a much less serious social trend than several others that received little attention until the past few years. Those include the rapid escalation in the '60s and '70s, especially in cities, of robbery and other crimes against persons, the sharp fall during the past two decades in the earnings of high school dropouts, and the collapse in the quality of inner-city schooling.

The public is constantly bombarded with exaggerated claims not only about the number of homeless but about many other subjects, such as the number of people who will get AIDS, the financial savings from radical changes in the health-care delivery system, the damage to health from various ingredients added to foods, and the size of the world population in the year 2050. It isn't easy to assess the validity of confident assertions on complicated issues, but two common-sense checks often help in gaining perspective. An obvious one is to assess whether persons making the claim gain any advantage from exaggeration. A second, more difficult one is to look at the basis for the claims, since even a little digging often reveals the shallowness of their foundations.

If early assertions about the incidence of homelessness had been examined in this way, Snyder and others could not have so badly misled the American public.

CUT THE GRAYBEARDS
A SMALLER SLICE OF THE PIE

Getting old is better than the alternative, the adage has it. But while growing old still has plenty of disadvantages, its attendant burdens have been lessened over the past several decades through technological advances in medical care, age-discrimination legislation, and increased Social Security, disability, and medical payments. Obviously, society should assist the old who need help, but the U.S. and other rich nations have gone too far in catering to elders who are reasonably well off. This is imposing a heavy burden on young people that before long could lead to open warfare between the generations.

Social Security benefits and government spending on the health of the elderly total 7% of gross national product and 30% of federal spending in the U.S., up from only 20% of federal spending in 1970. Similar percentages are found in Germany, Sweden, and other rich countries. Spending growth on these entitlements is an important cause of the budget crises in the U.S. and many European countries.

Spending on the care of older persons also is partly responsible for the rapid rise in medical expenditures during the past decade. Coming health-care reform may or may not lessen this impact. Even though persons over age 60 constitute only about 12% of the U.S. population, they absorb some 40% of spending on medical care. Since older persons are more susceptible to life-threatening illnesses, it's in the nature of things that they will claim a big chunk of medical spending even in an ideal health-care system. But some health experts argue that too little is spent on preventive care and too much on helping the elderly cling to life a little longer.

LARGER SHARE. It's easier for a country to be generous to its senior citizens when they are a small fraction of the population, but that is not the case in industrialized countries, where a declining birth rate has combined with increasing life expectancy to raise the proportion of the population that is over 60. In the U.S., this proportion was under 10% in 1960; it is projected to rise to 20% by 2020. In Japan, it is expected to reach almost 30% by 2020, while in Germany, the elderly may exceed a third of the population by 2030.

This trend implies that a growing tax burden to pay for benefits to the elderly will fall on a smaller fraction of the population. According to estimates in the recently released U.S. federal budget, those born in 1920 paid less than 30% of their lifetime income in taxes, after netting out Social Security and other payments from the federal government, while today's teenagers will pay almost 37%. These demographic trends are surely going to continue, so according to the same estimates, people in their prime 20 years from now may pay over 66%. Other estimates show that before long, Social Security taxes in Germany will have to rise to 30% of wages just to keep pensions at promised levels.

Transfers of wealth from the young to the old won't be the only source of friction between the generations. The Age Discrimination Act of 1967 in the U.S.
unleashed a stream of litigation by older workers charging unfair employment
discharge and discrimination in pay and promotions. Suits by older employees
have become one of the fastest-growing and most successful forms of litigation in
the federal courts. Juries have considerable sympathy toward older workers,
even though as a group they have the lowest unemployment rates, are the best
paid, and have the most sought-after jobs.

LOBBYING CLOUT. In 1986, Congress passed an amendment to the Age
Discrimination Act that eliminated forced retirement, though various exceptions
were granted for occupations and industries that require physical strength and
other characteristics of youth. The stated purpose of the amendment is to enable
the economy to continue to benefit from the skills of older workers and to reduce
the drain on the Social Security system by keeping more older persons in the
labor force. But the irony is that other legislation, notably generous Social
Security and disability programs, caused the sharp decline in labor-force participation by persons over 60, despite overall improvement in their health.

Senior-citizen lobbies wield such political clout in most countries that despite
growing complaints from taxpayers, governments have shrunk from reducing
benefits to the elderly—though Britain recently eliminated a few perquisites, and
Germany is hoping to reduce slightly its generous system of transfers. The
Clinton Administration seems to have shied away from proposing even modest
reductions in Social Security benefits despite the fact that it is desperately seeking ways to finance welfare reform and expanded job-training programs.

I believe that the young eventually will rebel against tax and other burdens.
They will demand restraints on transfers to the elderly and, possibly, even major
modifications in age-discrimination and retirement legislation. To avoid an ugly
clash between the generations, politicians should begin to reduce these entitlements and other privileges to older persons now.

CHANGE AT THE WHITE HOUSE?
PLUS CA CHANGE...

Will Bill Clinton's victory over George Bush make a difference in what the federal government does? Not much, suggests evidence from the past.

In democracies, when power shifts between political parties, there is scarcely a
ripple in public policy. The actions of Harold Macmillan, Edward Heath, and
most other Tory leaders after World War II are difficult to distinguish from those
of Clement Attlee, Harold Wilson, and other British Labor leaders. The lone—

admittedly huge — exception, Margaret Thatcher, had to stage a coup within her own party.

The same could be said of Democratic and Republican Administrations in the U.S. during the past 50 years. Richard Nixon professed to support free markets, but he was the first President to impose wage-and-price controls during peacetime, and he presided over one of the most rapid expansions of business regulation by the federal government. Ronald Reagan is rightly credited with encouraging deregulation and the buildup of the military, but both movements began under Jimmy Carter.

There is no more apt illustration of this thesis than the Bush Presidency. During his term, labor, market, and environmental regulation expanded remarkably rapidly, as did federal spending. I doubt if these trends would have been much different had Michael Dukakis won in '88. While Bush vetoed 33 bills passed by Congress, the Democrats, who controlled Congress, counted on many of his vetoes to bail them out of grandstanding tactics.

CENTRIST PULL. This Tweedledum-and-Tweedledee stability of policies should not be lamented, however, because the political system would be chaotic if government spending and taxing radically changed every time a new group took over, and the consequences for economic and social decision-making would be catastrophic. Companies would be unable to plan their investment and employment decisions if tariffs, pollution-control requirements, and other regulations were drastically altered with each new Administration.

A stable political system, with its slow shifts in voting patterns, is the direct result of stability in the distribution of power among many competing special-interest groups. Pressures on Bush to maintain generous Social Security and medicare expenditures, continue welfare and food-stamp programs, support agricultural prices, and cut competition from Japanese cars have been every bit as strong as they would have been under a Democrat.

UNEXCEPTIONAL. Clinton wisely recognized that American voters did not want the sizable expansion of the federal government advocated by the interventionist wing of the Democratic Party. His economic appointments so far are moderates, with the glaring exception of the new head of the Council of Economic Advisers. Although big spenders have been chosen to head the agencies in charge of transfer payments and social services, I suspect the liberal wing of his party will be unhappy with much of what Clinton does. Similarly, Bush appreciated that there was no groundswell of support for the large rollback of programs advocated by free-market Republicans.

Both planted their feet firmly in the political middle, differing mainly in details. So it would be surprising if the election's outcome makes a big difference, especially in the domestic programs that dominated the campaign.

Historians discuss these issues on a grander scale when considering the role of great individuals. Of course, exceptional figures—such as Franklin Roosevelt, Reagan, Thatcher, and Mikhail Gorbachev—matter a great deal. They capture and promote major shifts in popular opinion and the configuration of political forces, though in part, they simply speed up changes that are inevitable. However, most of the time, it is not the individuals in office who determine what happens but the underlying economic and social forces—the political "fundamentals," as stock market jargon has it. With the greatest of respect for their considerable talents, neither George Bush nor Bill Clinton is in the truly exceptional class.

This doesn't mean that people who identify with particular political parties are misguided. The party in power does make some difference. Clinton will be more disposed than Bush has been to federal spending on roads and other infrastructure, to environmental claims about the greenhouse effect, to subsidizing industrial product development, to protectionist trade restrictions, to easier access to abortion, and to judges who are less enamored of free markets. But the differences won't be easily detected from statistical trends in federal policies.

Such skepticism about the impact of a Bush, Clinton, or Perot won't sit well with those who devoted time, effort, and emotion to their favorite candidate. But the stability of Western democracies is far preferable to a system in which the enthusiasms of campaign workers and contributors radically alters public policy.

NAFTA: The Pollution Issue Is Just a Smokescreen

Opponents of the North American Free Trade Agreement (NAFTA) in the U.S. claim that weaker environmental and labor-market regulations in Mexico give an unfair advantage to producers there. Although calls for a level playing field between developed and developing nations are politically seductive, weaker regulations in the latter do not justify trade restrictions.

Consumers in all countries gain from free trade. Those in developing economies benefit when they get easier access to the high-quality goods that rich countries produce. As long as the goods are safe, consumers in developed nations generally don't care if goods imported from poorer countries are cheaper because they have fewer labor-market and environmental regulations.

Some people argue that free trade produces an "artificial" division of labor among countries because it encourages exports based on weaker environmental and other regulations. But it is as natural for poorer nations to spend less than richer ones on clean air, minimum-wage laws, and other regulations as it is for them to spend less on education and training. No one complains, though, that world specialization is greatly influenced by differences in investments in human capital.

GREEN INK.   Studies have shown a strong positive relation between a country's per capita income and its spending on preserving the environment. Such expenditures have already grown sharply in Mexico under the government of President Carlos Salinas de Gortari to more than 1% of its gross national product. Since NAFTA will benefit Mexico, it will increase that country's efforts to protect the environment.

The U.S. has a legitimate concern about Mexican pollution that spills over the border. This is one reason why NAFTA contains so many environmental provisions that it may be the greenest treaty ever negotiated. A glaring example of transnational effects is the extensive pollution from the *maquiladora* program established in the 1980s that permits factories on the Mexican side of the border to export freely to the U.S. One advantage of NAFTA is that it will lessen border pollution because some *maquiladora* plants will move to the interior, since they will no longer have to be along the border to get access to the U.S. market.

The White House and many members of Congress want to have a NAFTA commission that will investigate whether certain imports from Mexico result from weaker environmental and labor regulations there. But the political process cannot determine objectively which goods have succeeded in penetrating into a market because environmental and other regulations are less extensive in exporting nations. The investigations into dumping of goods by foreign producers in the U.S. and Europe is not reassuring, for these have been dominated by political considerations, not by careful analysis of the evidence.

In considering NAFTA and other trade agreements, it is important to recognize that labor-market, and even some environmental, regulations have become excessive in most developed countries. Free trade curtails some of the excesses because developed countries then have to compete harder against imports from developing nations. Unions and several powerful lobbying groups in the U.S. oppose NAFTA partly because it will cut back their influence over policy.

Regulations desired by most citizens do not get enacted in developing nations controlled by dictators or cliques. It may be sound policy to curtail trade with these countries, just as many nations refused to trade with apartheid South Africa. But political democracy prevails now in Mexico, Chile, Argentina, much of eastern Europe, and many other parts of the developing world looking for access to better markets, so popularly demanded regulations will tend to get enacted there.

Workers and consumers in democratic nations should be free to make their own judgments about the quantity and kinds of regulations that are required without undue pressure from economically powerful nations. This is an especially sensitive issue in negotiations between the U.S. and Latin American countries because in the past the U.S. has sometimes dictated their domestic policies.

MUCH ADO.   Undoubtedly, NAFTA will harm certain sectors of the U.S. economy, for some plants will be moved south after Mexico receives greater access to the U.S. market. The perennial complaint of business and unions about unfair competition is politically more potent when imports come from economies with less onerous regulations.

However, the Office of the U.S. Trade Representative found only 11 U.S. industries out of more than 400 examined that would be vulnerable under NAFTA to differences in environmental rules, lower tariffs, and other regulations. Although one can quarrel a bit with their conclusions, it is clear from this and other studies that the treaty will have a small although overall positive impact on the U.S. economy. NAFTA will help the U.S. and will not encourage unfair competition from Mexico. The U.S. should sign the treaty quickly and without further modification.

HOW IS AFFIRMATIVE ACTION
LIKE CROP SUBSIDIES?

Many conservative intellectuals are passionately opposed to quotas and other parts of affirmative-action programs, while liberals just as fervently advocate them. Yet the depth of emotion on this issue seems misplaced when affirmative action is recognized for what it is: a federal regulation that probably causes less harm than many other programs but does hurt some individuals, as it caters to minorities with political clout.

I don't like group quotas and other aspects of affirmative-action programs, but I am puzzled by the handwringing and anger of those who are opposed, especially some intellectuals. Although no one has even rough estimates of the social costs and benefits of these programs, I strongly suspect that certain other subsidies and regulations do more damage. Examples include tax and other breaks to the housing industry, the declines in labor-force participation of elderly persons induced by the tax on Social Security benefits, and higher consumer prices due to quotas on imported cars, textiles, computer chips, and, until recently, steel.

Opposition to affirmative-action programs may be strong because their effects can be so visible: for example, when such programs are used to admit students with weak records to law schools, medical schools, and premier universities or to help promote minority members into high-level jobs, while people who are more qualified are passed over. The harm from most other programs is indirect or hidden from view.

ETHICAL APPEALS.   Some opponents argue that affirmative-action regulations are worse than other government programs because the criteria are inborn characteristics: race, gender, national origin, and the like. But other programs that have nothing to do with inherited characteristics often in reality help only a small group. For example, hardly anyone not brought up on a farm ever becomes a commercial farmer. Thus, subsidies to agriculture are in a sense unavailable to people who grow up in cities.

Supporters of affirmative action deny that it is the result simply of political power. They argue that justice demands compensation for the horrors of past discrimination. Opponents argue just as strongly that quotas violate our culture's principle of equal treatment for equal skills, and they reject the notion that the present generation can be held responsible for discrimination in the past.

Both sides in this debate make valid points, but arguments about benefits are usually couched in terms of moral and ethical justifications, partly to gain the support of other voters. When was the last time you heard anyone defend a government program simply on the grounds that the person wanted to have the benefits? Although Republican opposition to quotas has helped the party make political inroads at the national level among white male blue-collar workers who traditionally voted for Democrats, clearly affirmative-action programs would not be politically viable if they had the support only of those blacks, women, and others who benefit.

SHADOW OF DOUBT. Most other government programs could not have been implemented without support from persons not much affected by them one way or the other. Surely, management and employees at Chrysler Corp. did not have enough clout by themselves to get the large federal bailout a decade ago. Alone, the small number of sugar growers in the U.S. would not have had much chance of getting the restrictive quotas on sugar imports that have been in effect for the past 70 years. This need to inflate self-interest into a broader moral and ethical point is why no business executive pleads for government subsidies by explaining that otherwise he might lose his job or have to take a big cut in pay. Instead, he complains about unfair competition from abroad or frightens voters with tales of defense vulnerabilities or the loss of jobs and stockholder equity if help is not forthcoming.

Opponents make much of how affirmative action detracts from the achievements of the most qualified members of minority groups. These able people suffer psychologically from skepticism about whether they deserve their success. Stephen L. Carter, a black professor at Yale Law School, in his book *Reflections of an Affirmative Action Baby*, poignantly describes his experiences with this attitude.

Of course, the doubt cast on the qualifications of successful minority members is unfortunate. But every government program hurts someone—often even some members of the groups that benefit. Studies have documented, for example, that programs involving acreage restrictions on agricultural crops benefit rich farmers sometimes at the expense of poor farmers who do not get their fair share of the allotments.

Recognizing that affirmative-action programs are government regulations with a complicated incidence of costs and benefits does not resolve the dispute over whether or not they are desirable. But it may help focus the debate on the real question: Do they cause as much harm or do as much good as other government programs that generate very little debate?

WHY POTHOLES AND POLICE
GET SUCH SHORT SHRIFT

Even ardent conservatives agree that government spending on infrastructure is critical to a healthy and growing economy. Our governments protect us from external enemies, combat crime, ensure the safety of people and property, and provide roads, bridges, sewers, and schools.

Until 50 years ago, more than half the spending at all government levels in the U.S. went to schools, roads, sanitation, police, fire fighting, and the military. But despite defense expenditures swollen by the cold war, the percentage of the federal budget spent on infrastructure has fallen sharply since World War II and now accounts for only about 30% of public spending. The rest goes to pay for Social Security, medical care, welfare, subsidies to agriculture and housing, and thousands of other special-interest and social programs.

Of course, a rich and fair society should have social programs. But can anyone doubt that the U.S. provides inadequate protection against crime, that public schools hardly educate many young people, and that roads and bridges in major cities and on many interstate highways are maintained badly?

OBSTACLE COURSE.   I began to reflect on these issues recently after my wife and I drove from Chicago to a summer home on Cape Cod. We installed a car alarm partly because we know that a loaded car, parked outside restaurants and motels, is an inviting target for thieves. I had checked to make sure that we had sufficient automobile insurance, keeping in mind it takes several years to litigate an accident case through the crowded court system. Potholes and bumpy roads made the short trip out of Chicago a challenging adventure. The Indiana Turnpike was in good shape, but Interstate 80 in Pennsylvania was, as usual, a hopeless obstacle course, and much of the Connecticut Turnpike was only moderately better.

Bluntly put, many of our vital government functions are badly neglected. In addition to unsatisfactory roads, court delays are so pervasive that private arbitration is spreading to circumvent the court system. The use of guards, alarms, and other protection devices has grown rapidly to offset a weakened police and correctional system. The fact that many ordinary citizens are not sure they can rely on police protection against robberies and assaults is one of the few persuasive arguments against strict gun control laws.

Military spending in the U.S. has only partly recovered from its reduced level during the 1970s. The experts disagree about whether the military is capable of meeting a surprise nuclear attack or of fighting an extended conventional war. For what it's worth, this amateur's instincts side with the pessimists.

People choose to live in suburbs and small towns for many reasons, but the high crime rates and appalling public schools in major U.S. cities surely are important factors. Residence in New York City would be far more attractive to families with school-age children were crime as infrequent, public schools as good, and streets and sidewalks as maintained as they were during the 1940s.

NEGATIVE EFFECT.   Federal, state, and local governments in the U.S. spend about one of every three dollars of national income. Inadequate infrastructure in the midst of such abundant government spending might seem paradoxical but nevertheless is easy to explain. Infrastructure suffers precisely because those governments are doing so many other things, distracting attention from the performance of the government officials who manage the infrastructure. At the same time, the rapid increase in social and special-interest programs has stimulated strong movements to reform taxes and reduce marginal tax rates. The large budget deficits of recent years have further increased pressure to cut spending where it has been politically feasible.

Unfortunately, budget deficits and opposition to high taxes not only prompted cutbacks on many peripheral government programs but also on spending for roads, schools, judges, police, and the military. Those parts of the infrastructure that are not supported by pressure groups will suffer more from the cutbacks in spending.

Since the private sector can manage schools, hospitals, arbitration, prisons, roads, and many other types of infrastructure better than the public sector, the privatization movement has been a useful byproduct of the pressure on government spending. But public treasuries still provide most of the financing. States support the growing number of privately run prisons and patients receive medicare and medicaid for their stays in private hospitals. The quality of privately run infrastructure also suffers when public financing is inadequate.

It is not realistic to expect much weakening in the political power of the special-interest groups that fight for agricultural price supports, Social Security, and most other large public programs. For this reason, the prospects are dim for dramatic improvements in roads, protection against crime, and other vital government functions. But until other government programs are scaled back more, the infrastructure will continue to be neglected.

INDUSTRIAL POLICY

MEMO TO CLINTON:
JAPAN INC. DIDN'T MAKE JAPAN STRONG

During the 1980s, many books and articles in the West sang the praises of Japan Inc., lauding what they believed to be a new form of capitalism wherein government and companies join to produce a powerful economic machine. The Japanese began to believe their press clippings and became convinced that in a short time they would overtake the U.S. as the most powerful economy in the world.

Industrial-policy boosters gave much credit to the guidance that the Ministry of International Trade & Industry (MITI) and the Finance Ministry provided for industrial and financial development. MITI supposedly picked out promising technologies and promoted them to the private sector. Yet it was never clear how Japanese bureaucrats managed to be so much more successful than their Western counterparts in technological breakthroughs.

The Western experience shows that government officials who spend taxpayers' money tend to make worse investments than private investors who spend both their own money and funds raised from banks and stockholders. For example, the governments of both Britain and France wasted a lot of money trying to develop a commercially profitable supersonic airplane. And the U.S. government has had to shut down Synthetic Fuels Corp., the company it created to develop substitute fuels for oil and coal.

LOST HORIZONS. The Japanese are apparently no longer convinced that their bureaucrats, however well-trained and professional, are successfully guiding the economy. The program MITI began in the mid-1970s to create startups, is conceded to be a failure. It is also recognized that the same ministry probably slowed Japanese adaptation to the telecommunications and biotech revolutions. Even the head of MITI recently said that the state must abandon its attempts to plan the economy.

Thanks to evidence of widespread corruption and the most serious recession in a long time, Japanese voters recently kicked out of office the political party that held power for 30 years. A major goal of the new government is to deregulate retailing and several other sectors where it believes government intervention has worsened performance.

Unfortunately, the Clinton Administration believes that industrial policy in the form of promotion of new technologies by the federal government is a promising way to improve the growth rate of the U.S. economy. A joint effort with the auto industry to develop cars that get more than 80 miles per gallon of gasoline was recently announced with much fanfare. In light of the extensive history of U.S. failure at industrial policy, I don't see how the U.S. can expect to succeed where Europe and even Japan have failed.

The Japan Inc. model also includes control of financial markets by the Finance Ministry. But Tokyo concluded in the latter part of the 1980s that many regulations were hindering rather than helping Japanese financial intermediaries compete against New York and London. The government then deregulated and opened these markets to foreign banks and investment houses.

BURST BUBBLE. Still, the control over financial markets exercised by the Finance Ministry has been greatly exaggerated. U.S. money managers who lost a bundle by being short during the extraordinary rise of stock prices on the Tokyo exchange in the 1980s were convinced that the government—especially the Finance Ministry—rigged this market, as well as the market for land. But it defies common sense to think that such decentralized markets could be rigged by the Japanese or any other government. I expressed that skepticism in these pages in May, 1990. The collapse of land and stock values and the failure of several government efforts to revive them have poured cold water on the claims of rigging. Stock and land prices had been bid up in a kind of South Sea bubble beyond any reasonable estimates of their worth. The present recession began after the bubble burst a few years ago.

On a recent visit to Tokyo, I was struck by how sharply the mood has veered from optimism to pessimism and concern, with calls for political and economic reform. Japan does need to deregulate several markets and make other changes, but carefully. After all, despite a slowdown in its growth rate in recent years, Japan's economy has been a stellar performer for several decades. The current recession has been made especially painful for Japan's export sector by a sharp rise in the value of the yen relative to other currencies, but that disparity may not last.

The recent pessimism is excessive, because Japan Inc. was always far more myth than reality. Japan earned its economic success the old-fashioned way, by combining a skilled, hard-working labor force with innovative companies that compete in a predominantly private-enterprise system—not by pioneering a new type of capitalism. That formula will again propel Japan forward in the future.

Although Japan was never as strong economically and politically as some experts would have us believe, it does not need radical surgery to remain one of the economic powerhouses.

IF IT AIN'T BROKE, BILL, DON'T FIX IT

Some observers believe U.S. companies are hopelessly ineffective when competing internationally, especially against Germany and Japan. This belief is even fallaciously extended to include the woes of IBM and Sears, Roebuck & Co. — companies that dominated their markets not too long ago.

The truth is IBM and Sears lost ground not to foreign companies but to major domestic competitors such as Apple, Microsoft, L. L. Bean, and Spiegel. They declined because they were slow to recognize major trends in their markets. Sears became a giant by pioneering catalog sales to rural families, and it never adjusted well to the upscale demands of more affluent urban households. In the '60s and '70s, IBM controlled the world market for large computers, but did not foresee the growing significance of PCs and workstations.

In any country, successful companies tend eventually to lose their creative energies. In much the same way that the old saw has it about families — "From shirtsleeves to shirtsleeves in three generations" — sooner or later, companies begin to decline. The fate of the Great Atlantic & Pacific Tea Co. is particularly instructive. A&P was such a dominant force in the grocery business in the '20s and '30s that an ill-advised and costly antitrust lawsuit was brought against it by the Justice Dept. However, A&P is today a minor player in its industry because it failed to adapt quickly or successfully to the growing penetration of its market by stores springing up in shopping centers.

CATCHING UP.   Listening to the critics, one might think that German and Japanese companies are way ahead. And it's certainly true that many companies in Germany and Japan are very well run — otherwise they would not have been so successful. The Japanese have been superior to other countries in producing automobiles, consumer electronics, and certain other goods, whereas the Germans are whizzes at high-quality products, especially machinery.

Yet the German economy has grown more slowly than that of the U.S. since the late '70s, while the gap between the rates of growth in manufacturing productivity in the U.S. and Japan has been sharply reduced in recent years. Service industries are much more productive in the U.S. than elsewhere, and this sector now accounts for more than half of all jobs in advanced countries.

Indeed, it could be tempting to misread the temporary difficulties of the German and Japanese economies as portents that their companies can no longer compete effectively for world markets. But it isn't necessary to deprecate the prospects of companies elsewhere to recognize that U.S. business is not losing its edge. American companies remain world leaders in many products and services, including aerospace, chemicals, software, telecommunications, pharmaceuticals, and securities markets. In the international division of labor, each industrialized nation tends to specialize in those goods and services in which its companies are the most efficient. Although no country can dominate all manufactured goods and services any longer, the decline of U.S. business has been grossly exaggerated.

A decade ago, the Midwest was written off as an important manufacturing center. But the region recovered and has led the boom in U.S. manufacturing exports during the past decade. And while the U.S. allegedly has lost its leadership in high tech to Japan, the trade surplus in what the Commerce Dept. calls "leading-edge products" more than doubled, from $16 billion in 1986 to $36 billion in 1991.

MR. FIXIT?   Other indictments of U.S. business include the charge that executive suites pay too much attention to short-term profits and not enough to long-term planning, that they pay top executives too much, that they fail to involve lower-level employees sufficiently in decision-making, and that they have started to neglect investment in research and development. But despite these assertions, U.S. companies must be doing something right because they are performing well enough in the competition for foreign markets.

As I see it, neither international competition nor bad management poses the biggest danger to U.S. companies. The overall record of U.S. business speaks for itself. Obviously, some U.S. companies have been badly run and need restructuring. Yet many are holding their own against the best from elsewhere, even though competition for world markets has intensified during the past couple of decades.

The real threat is from an entirely different direction. It is often argued that U.S. companies don't receive enough support from the federal government. But surely we do not need more misguided government efforts to regulate and assist business. Unfortunately, some members of the new Clinton Administration believe that the government can help U.S. business compete better in international markets by subsidizing promising technological developments, mandating greater on-the-job training of workers, imposing stricter environmental controls, and in other ways. On the contrary, I believe U.S. companies will continue to do just fine in world markets as long as they do not get too much interference from government.

The Myth of Industrial Policy

A bandwagon is getting rolling in the U.S. for a new type of industrial policy that involves government subsidies for early development of technologies that can help America compete in the global marketplace. But I doubt whether the public sector will do a good job of directing applied research toward projects with commercial value. Entrepreneurs and investors should risk their own money, not taxpayers', in the competition to work up profitable technologies.

The fascination with technology policy has gained support from a recent report, *The Government Role in Civilian Technology.* In it, a panel created by the prestigious National Academy of Sciences recommends, among other things, that the federal government establish a "civilian technology corporation" to support applied projects at an early stage. I am a member of the academy but disagree with the recommendation, although the panel's discussion is more judicious than most treatments of this subject.

I believe that state sponsorship of technologies is doomed to fail, because it encourages companies and industries that have new projects to compete in the political arena for taxpayers' assistance. Politicians will become advocates of pet projects, and bureaucrats will shy away from other ventures that have long lead times.

ASIAN MODELS.   The Western world's experience with state efforts to promote novel technologies offers little support for such an industrial policy. In 1980, several years after the oil-price shock, the U.S. set up the Synfuels Corp. to develop synthetic fuels to replace oil and other fossil fuels. But Congress had not anticipated the sharp fall in oil prices and the politics involved in supporting alternative fuels. The corporation quietly went out of business in 1986.

Britain, France, and Germany, together poured billions into Airbus Industrie to help raise their technological base for the production of advanced aircraft. After years of turning in losses, Airbus is finally managing to sell a reasonable number of planes, but it is doubtful whether this has done much for the technological base of these countries. This joint venture came after the ill-conceived Concorde supersonic project sponsored by the French and British.

We are told by advocates of the new industrial policy to disregard these and other failures and to look instead to Asian countries for models. Singapore is singled out for praise for the central direction of its economy toward state-of-the-art technology. No one can doubt that its performance since the late 1950s has been remarkable in many ways, with annual growth in per capita income that averaged more than 6%.

Singapore started building a manufacturing base in the late 1950s with simple textiles but then rapidly upgraded—first to elementary electronics, including radio and TV production, then to advanced electronics involving computer chips.

In recent years, Singapore has gained a major world position in international financial markets and is now targeting the biotech industry.

SWEET TALK. This rapid change in product mix was orchestrated by an explicit government policy of promoting advanced technologies through liberal subsidies to foreign companies in targeted industries. The government gave long tax holidays and low tax rates, controlled the unions and industrial disputes, and provided many other inducements.

Yet behind Singapore's glittering numbers and fancy industries is a bottom line that is not so impressive: In a recent study, economist Alwyn Young of Massachusetts Institute of Technology shows that Singapore has had almost no productivity gains in overall output of manufactured goods since 1960. The rapid growth of per capita income came almost entirely from an expansion of its capital stock, resulting from the generous subsidies to foreign corporations that invested there. These companies did very well but left little imprint on the economy's productivity.

Hong Kong, Asia's other trading entrepôt, had no industrial policy but experienced equally rapid growth in per capita income. Young shows that even without such a policy, Hong Kong had spectacular expansion in productivity and in domestic manufacturing companies.

No one advocates the new industrial policy without citing Japan. But private industry in Japan supplies more than 70% of the funds spent on research and development, which exceeds the private sector's share in Britain, France, or the U.S. I believe that the role of the Ministry of International Trade & Industry and other government bodies in directing and advancing technological developments in Japan has been enormously exaggerated. The Japanese government has no more orchestrated the productivity advance there than it has rigged prices on the Tokyo Stock Exchange.

The new industrial policy is the latest fad in the many proposals to give governments a bigger role in promoting economic development. We shouldn't be taken in by the sweet talk: Public support of R&D should concentrate on basic research without commercial value, while the private sector should finance and develop profitable technologies.

THE BEST INDUSTRIAL POLICY
IS NONE AT ALL

Depressed economic conditions in much of the world since 1973 make it possible to observe the ways in which special-interest groups use political clout to obtain subsidies, favorable regulations, and other government help that enable them to resist making adjustments to adverse economic conditions. Such groups—farmers, industrialists, managers, and workers—are able to influence government action in their own behalf in capitalist, socialist, and communist systems, but they are most successful in countries which exercise extensive public control over economic activity.

These conclusions cast serious doubts on the wisdom of pervasive government involvement in economic decisions, particularly government planning through an explicit industrial policy. Many people have proposed that the U.S. and other capitalist countries adopt such a policy. The Reagan Administration has little use for it, but if the U.S. economy slips into a serious recession with a weakened manufacturing sector, industrial policy advocates will be heard from again. Yet experience in the U.S. and other countries suggests that workers, management, and other interest groups will manipulate any industrial policy to promote their own interests rather than those of the whole country.

SLOW DEATH.   The U.S. steel industry provides a good example of how special interests in a mainly private-enterprise system influence government behavior. Most integrated steel mills in this country are no longer able to compete against steel from abroad. During the 1970s these mills contracted, but less rapidly than they should have, as management united with well-paid workers to lobby for a sequence of federal programs—notably, quotas and tariffs on imported steel, loan guarantees to steel companies, and government-directed programs to reinvest profits. These programs had the effect of raising domestic steel prices and slowing the contraction in employment and output.

The state-owned coal industry in Britain is a striking example of inefficiencies that can arise when government is directly involved in management of an industry. Pressure from miners has forced the government to keep many inefficient pits open through such policies as restrictions on coal imports and massive subsidies, including preferential use of British coal by the state-owned electric power industry. In the early 1970s striking workers helped bring down a Conservative government, and a recent strike dragged on for more than a year before the union acquiesced in closing the most grossly inefficient pits.

The situation in Israel illustrates how government responds to interest-group pressure under democratic socialism. Israel's economy grew rapidly from its founding in 1949 until the early 1970s. Then growth slowed to a crawl while inflation soared to one of the highest levels in the world. It is obvious that the government should cut sharply various subsidies, regulations, transfer payments, and perhaps even military expenditures. So far, however, the political clout of groups benefiting from such programs has prevented Israel's two major political parties from taking these necessary steps.

Interest groups also influence communist economies. The Soviet economy expanded rapidly during the 1950s and 1960s, but faltered badly during the subsequent two decades. Collective farming has been unable to meet the domestic demand for food, and industrial goods have been shoddy. All Soviet leaders after Stalin have recognized that farmers, workers, and managers lack adequate incentives, but none of them has been able to do much to improve the situation. Although little is known about the internal politics of communist countries, entrenched bureaucrats, party members, and military leaders apparently have successfully resisted reform.

These examples clearly bring out that state-owned industries and private industries able to rely on government assistance often perform well during good times but adjust more slowly to adverse conditions than do private industries not helped by the state.

RADICAL SURGERY. Consider the case of the video game industry, which virtually collapsed in the early 1980s when personal computers emerged as a superior substitute. Presumably, the industry could not marshal enough political support to make it unnecessary to adjust to competition. Manufacturers of the games either went out of business or shifted into related products. For example, one small company, General Computer Co., dropped games and began producing disk drives for computers.

Since the evidence shows that industries that rely heavily on the state adapt slowly to bad times, the expansion of federal involvement in the U.S. economy over the past 50 years inevitably has reduced the economy's flexibility. Planning future development of the economy by means of an industrial policy would further reduce the economy's ability to cope. An industrial policy would become a servant of special interests rather than a guardian of the general interest and would delay rather than hasten the economy's appropriate adjustments to changing conditions.

MILITARY

LEAVE THE DRAFT WHERE IT BELONGS: ON HISTORY'S JUNK HEAP

The resounding success of the U.S. military during the gulf conflict should silence for a while the many voices that called for reinstatement of the draft after the U.S. responded to Iraq's aggression.

The gulf conflict was dominated by highly sophisticated weapons with advanced computers and guidance systems. To use these weapons successfully, men and women in almost all military occupations, including the infantry, must be well-trained and experienced.

New recruits cannot operate complicated and expensive weapons with only a few months of training. This is why during even the height of the draft, highly skilled tasks were performed mostly by volunteers who made a longer commitment to military service. And occupations requiring lengthy training have proliferated as reliance on sophisticated weaponry has increased.

SUPERB MORALE. In the early 1980s, Congress voted a large pay increase for enlisted personnel as part of the Reagan-initiated military buildup. By paying better and offering attractive working conditions, the military managed during the ensuing decade to recruit remarkably well-qualified men and women with superb morale. Almost all are high school graduates, compared with less than 80% of civilian workers, and the military chooses graduates with better scores on aptitude tests. During the draft era, the military was forced to take many high school dropouts, since most college graduates and many high school graduates were able to avoid the draft. Drug use is much lower in the military than in the civilian sector, in sharp contrast with the Vietnam period.

The military has been criticized for relying too heavily on minorities and for not distributing the task of defending the country fairly among social classes and racial groups. It is true that blacks constitute over 20% of the armed forces compared with only 12% of the civilian work force. But the Army is not staffed mainly by the lower classes, as demonstrated by the preponderance of high school graduates and by the fact that almost half of all recruits come from families with above-average incomes.

I believe the military deserves praise rather than criticism for offering black men and women better work opportunities than they can find in the private sector. About a third of noncommissioned Army officers are blacks, as is the chairman of the Joint Chiefs of Staff. In contrast, the number of blacks who head top corporations can be counted on the fingers of one hand.

Some critics of present recruitment policy want to use military service to help overcome illiteracy, to instill patriotism, and to guide confused young people toward finding themselves. Military service is ill-suited to accomplish these laudable goals.

They are inconsistent with the main purpose of a military force—to resist aggression successfully with a minimal loss of lives and material. There is much evidence in all wars that disgruntled and low-quality recruits, let alone illiterates, do not perform very well.

SOCIAL PROBLEMS.   The education system, like the military, has come under pressure to help solve intractable social problems. Once again, praiseworthy aims, such as achieving racial and social balance or serving as substitute parents, have little to do with the goals of education: teaching students to read, write, and analyze. Luckily, military leaders were more successful during the past decade in fending off well-meaning but diversionary pressures.

Critics of voluntary military service, such as former Navy Secretary James H. Webb Jr., see a populist advantage to the draft: It makes it harder to wage unpopular wars that would be resisted by potential draftees and their families. The Vietnam experience offers some support to that view. But the other side of the argument is that in pursuit of a popular cause, the draft may encourage war and even reckless sacrifice of life with its provision of cheap and ready manpower. Put crassly, this argument holds that commanders of volunteers will show greater concern for the lives of their troops, if only because volunteers are highly trained and were recruited with attractive pay and working conditions. For whatever reason, the top brass seemed more intent on minimizing coalition casualties in Desert Storm than it had been in Vietnam, where most troops were draftees, though sensitivity to criticism at home was also a factor.

The skills of a voluntary force are most needed in the early stages of *blitzkrieg* warfare, when the first few days—even hours—may be crucial. On the other hand, during a fully mobilized and protracted war such as World War II, millions of soldiers are needed. The high pay required to attract so many recruits voluntarily would sharply raise taxes and impose a serious strain on the budget. During that kind of mobilization, a draft eases the pressure on the budget and taxes by shifting much of the cost to young people.

The gulf war apparently has convinced some military reformers in the Soviet Union that a voluntary army may have higher morale and fight more efficiently than a conscripted one. It would be a paradox if that lesson was better learned by the Russians than by Americans eager to bring back the draft.

Defense Spending Isn't Stunting the U.S. Economy

Does the U.S. role as world policeman weaken its capacity to compete on the economic front? The paltry and grudging contributions being made to defray the costs of the war against Iraq by Germany and Japan, America's main economic competitors, raise precisely the question that was forcefully addressed in a best-seller of several years ago, Paul Kennedy's *The Rise and Fall of the Great Powers.*

I do not know whether the U.S. has been spending an appropriate amount on defense, including development of new weapons. And perhaps more responsibility for defending against aggression should be shifted to rich countries such as Germany and Japan. But the numbers do not support the claim that America's economic growth has been seriously stunted by its spending on defense.

Many commentators, including Robert B. Reich of Harvard University, place a great deal of emphasis on the negative effect on the private sector of the extensive federal support of research on new weapons. Until the mid-1970s, America spent a larger fraction of its gross national product on research and development than did either Germany or Japan, but these two countries have increased their research spending during the past 15 years. And about one-third of the U.S. R&D effort was devoted to military research, whereas our competitors spent little on the military.

GUNS VS. BUTTER?   The significant resources devoted to developing new weapons by the U.S. may appear to be a big drag on efforts to improve civilian productivity. Yet surely only a small part of any reduction in military research spending would have been allocated to support advances in the private sector. Since such spending takes a small share of income, government spending for research on new weapons is about 4% of the federal budget and less than 1% of GNP. Military spending is hardly big enough to deter greater public efforts to promote private productivity.

The U.S. spends about 6% of its GNP for defense, compared with 1% by Japan. If the U.S. were to cut back its military spending to that level, it is folly to assume—as many do—that all the savings would go into investment. Instead, we need to start with the more reasonable assumption that such a defense dividend would be allocated between consumption and investment in roughly the same 4-to-1 ratio as GNP. Thus, if U.S. defense spending were reduced to the Japanese level, only 20¢ of every dollar cut from the military would go into investment.

Even after that additional capital spending, Japan would still be investing a much larger portion of its GNP than would the U.S.

Although the usual practice is to compare R&D spending as a fraction of a country's GNP, the actual amounts spent may be more relevant. Spending on R&D in the U.S. almost equals the combined spending of Germany and Japan, with France and Britain thrown in for good measure. American industries are typically larger—the U.S. economy is about four times Germany's and twice Japan's. And big economies do not have to spend much more on research than smaller economies to generate equal advances in productivity. An innovation can cut costs by 10% whether an industry is big or small.

SPIN-OFFS. Progress in military technology sometimes spills over into the private sector. Computers, jet engines, radar, and sequential analysis in statistics are just a few of the major advances that arose from military-sponsored research, and numerous products, such as Velcro and Teflon, were developed for the military. There is no doubt that many U.S. businesses got a strong head start in international competition because of products developed out of government-funded research for the military.

It is true that America's role as world policeman places extra burdens on its industry, including restrictions on exports to hostile countries, exposure to terrorism, and the loss of markets. On the other hand, such a role helps in negotiating favorable treatment of U.S. goods and citizens by other countries and in making the U.S. a haven in times of world stress, which increases the foreign demand for dollars, U.S. real estate, and stocks and bonds of American companies.

Research by Harvard's Robert J. Barro, who compares per-capita-income growth among more than 60 countries since 1960, supports the conclusion that military spending does not explain why some countries grow more slowly than others. He finds that countries that spend a large portion of income on the military grow about as quickly as others, even when comparing those at the same stage of development and with similar levels of schooling.

There are other reasons why Germany and Japan have grown faster. Japan has been especially successful at adapting ideas and processes developed elsewhere, often in the U.S. Both countries have top-notch educational systems, provide extensive apprenticeship and on-the-job training, and have a strong work ethic. Both are sticklers for high-quality merchandise and services. Germany and Japan have done well, but not because they spend little on defense.

WHY A DRAFT WOULD
ONLY DAMAGE THE ARMY

The improved prospects of a nuclear arms agreement with the Soviet Union increases the importance of the U.S. Army and other conventional forces. The all-volunteer system is working extremely well, but calls for a return to the draft abolished at the end of the Vietnam War are being fueled by budgetary pressures to reduce government spending and by a belief that the Army and Navy are having difficulty obtaining quality recruits.

Pressures to balance the federal budget encourage hidden taxes and congressional mandating of expenditures by the private sector. Future military pay is likely to lag behind civilian pay as Congress continues to strive to reduce the deficit. The resulting decline in volunteers would then lead to more calls for reinstating the draft. Some politicians already support its reinstatement.

Unfortunately, like other hidden taxes, the draft does not reduce the true cost of obtaining recruits. It only shifts the cost to the draftees. For example, if the military pays just $4,000 a year to a draftee who could earn $10,000 annually on the outside, the draftee must forgo $6,000 of income. In effect, this draftee is paying a hidden tax of $6,000 for each year of service. Young people are hardly in a financial position to afford such steep taxes. To make matt.ers worse, the taxes paid by draftees often greatly exceed the explicit taxes with a voluntary force because a voluntary system attracts the recruits who are most willing to serve. Draftees, on the other hand, are reluctant to give up excellent civilian opportunities.

MEETING GOALS.   A fully voluntary army is not desirable during a big and protracted war. The high tax rates needed to finance a large voluntary army during such a war would greatly discourage long hours of work and high savings. It is thus desirable in a major war to use the draft and impose more of the burden on young people. But a moderate-sized armed force prepared for limited conflict is better manned with volunteers than with draftees.

Poor education of recruits, rampant drug use, and low morale did plague the voluntary system during its first half-dozen years. But the increase in pay, training, and education benefits during the Reagan Administration radically changed the picture. Recruitment goals are now easily met by the Army and Navy as well as by the more glamorous Air Force and Marines.

Enlistment normally declines when the economy is strong, yet recruitment goals were met even in the past few years when the economy boomed and unemployment among the young fell sharply. The beneficial effects of the rise in pay and other benefits on the number and quality of volunteers confirms the evidence anmmvailable from various studies: The supply of volunteers is quite sensitive to compensation and working conditions.

COMPLEX WEAPONS. More than 90% of the young men and women enlisting during the past few years graduated from high school. This exceeds the percentage among young civilians, it is much higher than the percentage among enlistees prior to the increase in pay and other military compensation, and it is also higher than the percentage among draftees in the early 1970s. Although weapons have become extremely — perhaps excessively — complex, young recruits now seem to handle them surprisingly well.

Intangible measures of quality are also upbeat. Drug use by recruits has declined greatly during the past several years and may now be below the use by young civilians. Absences without leave and desertion rates are the lowest in many years, which reflect the enormous improvement in the morale of recruits. There is also no reason to believe that the patriotism of volunteers is less than the patriotism of draftees.

Blacks enlist and reenlist more readily than whites because military pay is relatively good and opportunities for blacks to advance appear to be as good as or better than in civilian jobs. Yet fewer than 20% of new recruits are black, compared with 15% among all young persons. About 6% of officers are black. Racial strife among recruits has moderated and may well be less than elsewhere in America where blacks and whites work together.

I don't understand why many people interpret the higher enlistment and reenlistment rates among blacks as evidence against the voluntary system. If opportunities for blacks are better in the military, shouldn't the concern be directed toward their civilian opportunities rather than toward their enlistment rates under the voluntary system?

I wrote a report entitled *The Case Against the Draft* when I was a consultant to Rand Corp. 30 years ago. The Air Force sponsored my research, but it favored the draft and refused to issue the report under its auspices. The subsequent experience with both drafted and voluntary forces has greatly changed military thinking. The services now all recognize that decent pay and working conditions will attract high-quality volunteers who are superior in many ways to draftees. Such a report written now might have the enthusiastic backing of the Air Force as well as of the Army, Navy, and Marines.

PART 10

Government and Taxes

Governments should have the major responsibility for basic aspects of modern living: protecting citizens against crime and foreign aggression, and helping families who do badly through no fault of their own. Unfortunately, governments nowadays are not discharging these responsibilities very well because the scope of government activities has grown enormously to include areas such as supporting farm prices, subsidizing consumption in old age, and regulating labor markets. These additional responsibilities leave governments with little money and time to adequately perform their main responsibilities.

The expansion of government power undermines political credibility by tempting politicians and bureaucrats to abuse their power. The political corruption scandals that have erupted in so many countries illustrates this process. Government officials are sometimes offered generous bribes and other financial inducements because their decisions have such a large impact on the fortunes of companies and individuals. Since most officials are not saints, some of them succumb to these offers and in effect sell political favors.

Term limits have been supported as a way to cut corruption and also to bring political representatives closer to the needs of ordinary citizens. We believe, however, that term limits are likely to have the opposite effect because politicians in office for a limited time may be even more tempted to sell out to special interests. Moreover, representatives serving for a short time lack the incentive to invest in the knowledge necessary for informed decisions on national defense, taxation, environmental protection, and other complicated government issues.

The growth of government increased greatly the power of judges because they must interpret a vast amount of vague legislation. An independent judiciary through indefinite terms for judges was a good idea when the Supreme Court and other federal courts dealt mainly with fundamental constitutional issues. It is less attractive now when judges effectively legislate through their own interpretations of statues. This is why we advocate fixed but relatively long and renewable terms for federal judges that would make them more responsive to voters and legislators without making them subservient.

GOVERNMENT

IF YOU WANT TO CUT CORRUPTION, CUT GOVERNMENT

New evidence of corruption by leading politicians and businesses is surfacing in virtually every corner of the globe. The list of kickback, payoff, and bribery scandals seems endless: Korea, Japan, Mexico, and Nigeria are in the news now, but few countries have escaped unscathed. There is no magic bullet to cure this disease. Nevertheless, much smaller, democratic, and businesslike governments would help a lot.

People like to think the bribery in their country is unique—that their politicians, bureaucrats, and businesspeople are especially venal. But the source of official corruption is the same everywhere: large governments with the power to dispense many goodies to different groups.

Every regulation, law, and public program, whether it's a government contract or an export subsidy, can be manipulated to favor particular interests. Companies try to influence these decisions through legitimate lobbying and by arguing their case for government help. But some are also tempted by the huge sums involved to bribe and use other unlawful means to influence the outcomes.

The process of competing for government favors is called "rent-seeking" in the literature on political economy. It has a long history and is inevitable whenever governments affect the destinies of companies. But rent-seeking has grown dramatically because public spending and regulations are now so extensive. Politicians and bureaucrats may be no more mercenary than other groups, but they face unusually strong temptations to sell their power for money and other gains. Some businesses are willing to provide these temptations, perhaps justifying their behavior with the excuse that others are also doing it.

FIERCE WATCHDOGS. Corruption distorts the functioning of an economy because it leads government officials to take actions that are not in the general interest. Corruption can even choke off economic development by discouraging honest entrepreneurs and by sharply and arbitrarily raising the cost of doing business.

Dictatorial regimes often appear to have little corruption, but that is an illusion caused by suppression of dissent and the press. It is no accident that evidence of extensive bribery surfaced in Argentina, Brazil, Korea, and Mexico only after effective opposition parties and free presses developed. Democracies generally have much less corruption than closed systems: Opposition parties have the incentive and ability to expose the misbehavior of the ruling party.

Yet the huge gains from rent-seeking guarantee that democracies also have disturbing levels of corrupt behavior. Some democratic countries, including Japan and Italy, have seen widespread cases of public officials accepting money in exchange for favors to business friends. Although instituting large cuts in the scope of government is the only surefire way to reduce corruption, that is seldom mentioned by the Republican leaders in the U.S. who advocate much smaller government. Highlighting the effects of corruption may boost support for government retrenchment—even among those who would favor a large public sector in a more perfect world. Corruption scandals in Japan, for example, helped increase pressure for deregulation.

AUCTION BLOCK.   Still, some reforms are possible even without huge reductions in government. Subsidized lending to large or small businesses is not necessary under a competitive banking system, and these subsidies are an open invitation to official corruption. Apparently, the supply of cheap loans from a government-controlled banking system was a major source of the scandals in Korea.

Open bidding should be required whenever valuable assets are transferred from the public to the private sector. In particular, rights to broadcast over radio and television spectrums and to use public lands for oil exploration or timber production should go to the highest bidders, subject only to environmental and other safeguards. Production quotas, whether they refer to fishing (BW— Sept. 18), pollution, imports, or crops, should also be sold in open markets, not given to groups with political clout.

Unfortunately, all countries continue to give away rather than sell valuable public properties. I believe the reason is that politicians and bureaucrats are well aware that this raises their power over business, and voters have not been demanding that business be forced to bid for quotas and other privileges.

The worldwide trend toward democratic governments is helping to expose political corruption more quickly. But it will remain disturbingly high as long as governments continue to have so much power over the fortunes of business.

BEDTIME FOR BIG GOVERNMENT

After the overwhelming Republican victory last November, the pundits said that not much was going to be accomplished, that politicians' talk was a lot cheaper than actions, and that it would be, more or less, politics as usual. But the hard-headed experts were wrong.

The House and Senate have agreed on a plan to cut taxes over the next several years and propose to sharply limit spending on medicare, medicaid, welfare, and many other programs. A surprising number of senators and representatives are advocating either a much flatter income tax or, more radical still, the complete replacement of the income tax by a consumption tax. Congress is calling for systematic evaluation of the costs of major federal regulations and apparently will succeed in deregulating the telecommunication and banking industries, and in placing caps on punitive damages in civil cases.

Although the Republicans are taking the lead, many Democrats also sense that voters demand change. Some Democrats in Congress are supporting the Republican initiatives, and President Clinton's proposals to cut federal spending and taxes during the next 10 years are similar to what Congress is doing.

I have been skeptical that even the powerful voter mandate for change could overcome the dedicated opposition of groups with a vested interest in the status quo. After all, the convoluted tax code with its numerous loopholes and government programs that subsidize thousands of interest groups, from the elderly to the merchant marine, resulted from rough infighting during the past several decades. How could an election reverse what had evolved over time out of a complicated political process?

EASY VICTORIES. Some have attributed what is happening in the U.S. to the growing power of the religious right, with its conservative social and economic agenda. Others say Americans gave up on politicians and the big government they created because of repeated scandals. Still others claim the middle class and white males are finally rebelling against the social experimentation that began with Franklin D. Roosevelt's New Deal and culminated in Lyndon B. Johnson's Great Society.

However, explanations based on the religious right and other uniquely American developments cannot explain the successful attacks on big government in many other nations. The Progressive Conservative Party just won a resounding victory in the Canadian province of Ontario, a traditional hotbed of liberal thinking, even though the party was ridiculed by the ruling liberal New Democratic Party as Republican wannabes. The French conservative Jacques R. Chirac easily won the contest for President, a post the Socialists held for 14 years. A former socialist, Fernando Henrique Cardoso, used a largely market-oriented platform to gain a big victory in a contest against a leftist opponent for the Brazilian presidency, while the Peronist Carlos Saul Menem easily was reelected President of Argentina after six years of freeing the economy and maintaining strict control over inflation and the printing of money.

COSTLY LESSON.   The most impressive evidence of the reaction against big government may be the sensible policies followed by Nelson R. Mandela in South Africa. Despite being imprisoned for 27 years by an Afrikaner government that discriminated outrageously against blacks, Mandela's program so far is surprisingly pro-business. He apparently appreciates that the discrimination there was not due to capitalism but to government laws designed to protect white workers against competition from South African blacks.

Voters all over the world may have learned through 50 years of social and economic engineering, highlighted by the total collapse of central planning and communism, that extensive government spending and regulation heavily damage the economy and undermine values and morale. It may seem a bit surprising that it took half a century to learn this costly lesson. But the harm from big government only slowly became apparent to the general public partly because voters had to see through a smokescreen of rhetoric by intellectuals, politicians, and the media that ridiculed opponents of big government as either lacking in compassion or as tools of business interests.

I am not yet ready to concede fully that we skeptics were wrong about the likelihood of major reductions in the role of government in modern economies. But the trend of the past half-century toward relying on big government to solve economic and social problems could be ending not only in the U.S. but in many other nations as well. If this reversal continues, I would be delighted to digest an abundant portion of crow.

HOW BAD STUDIES GET TURNED
INTO BAD POLICIES

Economists cannot design research projects that decisively answer important policy questions. They have to rely on the limited knowledge that can be extracted from the effects of government policies and other events. Yet politicians are all too quick to grasp preliminary results of these studies as justification for regulations and other interventions that sometimes do damage to the economy.

A good example is a 1992 Federal Reserve Bank of Boston analysis of discrimination against applicants for mortgage loans. The senior author was Alicia Munnell, a respected economist who was then in charge of research at the Boston Fed and recently was nominated by President Clinton to fill a vacancy on the Fed's board. After reviewing what happened to some 4,500 loan applications in 1990 by banks in the Boston area, the authors claimed to have found evidence of extensive discrimination against black and Hispanic applicants.

The publicity that this study attracted led the Comptroller of the Currency to closely monitor banks for evidence of discrimination in their lending practices and to investigations of banks by the Justice Dept. and the Massachusetts Attorney General. Such scrutiny and political pressure resulted in legal actions against a few banks. One involved a consent decree last August with a Maryland bank for supposedly "shunning" loans in urban areas. Another involved settlement of a case against Chicago-based Northern Trust Corp., which alleged the bank gave greater assistance to white applicants who were attempting to qualify for mortgage loans.

Such political reactions would be justified if the Boston Fed found convincing evidence of bank discrimination. But the study—despite being lauded as conclusive—contains many omissions and data errors. An economist at the Federal Deposit Insurance Corp. took a close look at a sample of the actual lending records used by the Fed and concluded that the data are so inaccurate (owing, in part, to errors in copying), that it is impossible to determine whether or not banks had discriminated against blacks and Hispanics. Another analysis found that the Boston Fed's results are dominated by two banks that had relatively high rejection rates of minorities only because they specialized in soliciting loans from marginally qualified minority applicants.

Some of the evidence found by the Boston Fed contradicts their claim of discrimination against minorities. For example, average default rates found in this study were about the same on loans in census tracts with a large percentage of blacks and Hispanics as in predominately white tracts. Yet if the banks had been discriminating against minority applicants, default rates on loans to minorities should have been lower than on loans to whites, since banks discriminate in part by accepting minority applicants only with exceptionally good credit histories and employment records. They would reject marginally qualified minority applicants while accepting marginal white applicants. The implications of the theory of discrimination for default rates and other behavior are spelled out in my Nobel prize acceptance lecture entitled "The Economic Way of Looking at Behavior," published in 1993.

WAGES OF ERROR.   I am not claiming that all the additional studies of bank lending practices concluded that banks do not discriminate, nor am I suggesting these studies "prove" banks generally do not discriminate. But the additional analyses do show the difficulties in reaching recommendations on controversial policy questions by generalizing from highly imperfect evidence.

These difficulties are further illustrated through recent discussions of the employment effects of minimum wages. The most basic law in economics states that a rise in the cost of labor, capital, or other inputs lowers demand for that input, a law that has been verified by the experience of thousands of companies

all over the world. Yet Labor Secretary Robert B. Reich cites controversial studies that claim to find rises in minimum wages have sometimes not reduced, and
may even have increased, employment of low-skilled workers. My discussion of
some problems with these claims appeared in *Business Week* of Mar. 6, 1995.

The effective responses to the allegations that banks discriminate and that
higher minimum wages do not reduce employment should be a lesson to economists not to advocate major policy initiatives on the basis of very limited and
imperfect evidence. Politicians are only too eager to promote results based on the
flimsiest of evidence to attract support for policies that help voters and interest
groups they favor.

Never Mind Congress—
The Real Reform Action Is in the States

Overshadowed by the House Republicans' efforts to implement the Contract
With America are revolutionary proposals by states and cities that may have a
greater impact than what ultimately happens in Congress.

Some 30 states are planning to reduce taxes, while New Jersey, Michigan, and
a few others have already begun the process. California, New York, and
Massachusetts were leaders during the past 30 years in expanding state spending
and regulations. But all now have Republican governors—Pete Wilson in
California, George W. Pataki in New York, and William F. Weld in
Massachusetts—who are strong advocates of cutting taxes and red tape.

I was a member of the Governor's Task Force on California Tax Reform &
Reduction appointed by Wilson in 1994. We suggested, and he endorsed, a 15%
across-the-board cut to be phased in over a three-year period in state personal
income and bank and corporation tax rates. In New York, after years of growth
in taxes, Pataki was recently elected on a platform that pledged to cut state
income taxes by 25% during the first four years of his term. Weld has renewed
proposals for tax cuts that are expected to be approved in some form by the state
legislature. Democratic governors have also heard the voters' message, and some
are advocating tax and spending cuts.

FORCED TO WORK. Total state and city government tax revenues are
almost as large as the federal government's and have risen at about the same rate
since the 1970s. However, part of the growth in state spending has been mandated by federal programs such as medicaid. This is why governors from both political parties are urging Congress not to impose additional mandates on them.

Local governments are not limiting their reforms to taxes. Massachusetts,
Virginia, California, Wisconsin, New Jersey, and other states are seeking radical

alterations in the welfare system. The Virginia legislature recently passed a law modeled after one enacted in Massachusetts that forces recipients to work, eliminates benefits to parents who have been on the welfare rolls for two years, and denies aid to children born to mothers already collecting relief.

Some states are also ahead of Congress in cutting regulations and making drastic changes in the tort system. Governor Wilson wants to cap punitive damages in tort suits at three times the direct losses to plaintiffs and encourage litigants to use private arbitration instead of the courts. He also hopes to discourage frivolous suits against defendants who have deep pockets and who might settle rather than go through costly litigation.

California is planning to reduce its onerous regulatory burdens intended to protect the environment. It will propose a constitutional amendment to require a two-thirds vote by the legislature to approve all laws imposing new compliance costs. The state also will require an economic analysis of the benefits and costs of all suggested state environmental regulations.

LIGHTING A FIRE. The Republican mayor of New York, Rudolph W. Giuliani, facing an enormous budget gap, is slashing city spending. Giuliani wants to privatize several city-owned hospitals and cut medicaid spending and other social services.

These state and city tax and spending cuts are partly responses to the same voter discontent with politicians and government that is lighting a fire under Congress. But local governments are also motivated by a consideration unique to them: growing regional competition to attract business and skilled workers. Computer, electronics, biotechnology, insurance, engineering, scientific research, and other manufacturing and service industries are footloose and don't need to locate near raw materials, ports, or other transportation facilities. They choose where to locate partly on the basis of the tax and regulatory climate.

The California Task Force's proposals for tax reduction were partly motivated by competition from Utah, Oregon, and other Western states with better business climates. Business migration to these states is expected to accelerate if California does not lower its taxation of individuals and businesses and reduce regulatory burdens. Other states are also reexamining how their taxes and regulations measure up relative to neighboring and more distant states competing for the same business.

Competition for people and business in the decentralized spending of a federal system of government helps force local programs to be more responsive than national programs to the wishes and needs of citizens.

To Root out Corruption,
Boot out Big Government

In several countries I visited in the past year, major scandals centered on corruption charges against prominent politicians and businessmen. Everywhere, I was told that their business leaders were uniquely venal and their political system especially vulnerable to corruption. But corruption is common whenever big government infiltrates all facets of economic life, never mind the political and business systems.

In modern economies, profits often are determined more by government subsidies, taxes, and regulations than by traditional management or entrepreneurial skills. Huge profits ride on whether companies win government contracts, get higher tariffs and quotas, receive subsidies, have competition suppressed, or manage to have costly regulations eased.

Companies respond to the importance of government's role by striving to influence political decisions. It often is effective just to lobby politicians, and human nature guarantees that sometimes businesses bribe officials and politicians in return for government favors and profits.

"Rent-seeking" is the way economists describe all efforts by special interests to benefit by influencing political decisions. The expression applies to any group that depends on government handouts and other favors. Paradoxically, rent-seeking can serve a social purpose. It may prevent policies that would cause considerable social harm or promote policies that make an economy more efficient. For example, if all the detailed regulations regarding construction in the statutes and codes of most U.S. municipalities were followed to the letter, construction would virtually cease because of the costs of compliance. And communist economies would have performed much worse than they did—and their record was bad enough—had bribes not greased the wheels and overcome the most outrageous government controls over the economy.

BUMPY ROAD.   But bribery and other illegal rent-seeking usually do considerable damage. They always divert the time and resources used by high-powered lobbyists and fixers away from the production of useful goods and services. They also often promote policies that distort the operation of an economy.

Organized criminals extract monopoly prices for the goods and services they control through bribes and intimidation. Roads are badly built or diverted to less useful routes in order to reward builders and landowners who influence officials making the decisions. Loans from government banks and agencies go to companies with political clout rather than where they can be invested most profitably. Evidence of these and many other acts of political corruption have been highlighted by the scandals in Brazil, Italy, Japan, South Korea, and other countries.

In several countries, politicians and parties caught with their fingers in the till were ousted this past year. The reaction has been so strong in Italy that the largest party of the political center, the Christian Democrats, may be permanently damaged. Recent elections in Rome and other Italian cities have been dominated by ex-Communists and fascists, a pathetic choice between two political extremes.

The party that ruled Japan continuously since the 1950s has splintered into several competing groups. The Brazilian Congress impeached the nation's first democratically elected president in 30 years, Fernando Collor de Mello, because of revulsion at the widespread corruption in his government.

SEVER THE LINK. Voting out crooked politicians and punishing people in business who illegally influence policies discourages corruption. Reform movements that come to power often make good for a while on their promises to clean up the process and eliminate corruption. During such crackdowns, businesses and other rent-seekers must rely on campaign contributions and other legal ways to influence outcomes.

But corruption always reemerges wherever governments have a major impact on economic conditions. The momentum behind reform movements peters out as politicians, officials, and companies become tempted once again to risk exposure and disgrace by giving and receiving bribes and engaging in other corrupt acts.

There is only one permanent way to reduce undesirable business influence over the political process: Weaken the link between business and politics. It is essential to simplify, to standardize, and especially to eliminate many of the regulations affecting economic activity. Surely this explains why new governments recently elected in Japan and Korea have pledged to deregulate, and why a new Italian political center is forming around demands for privatization and increased competition.

Evidence of widespread corruption can be a blessing in disguise if it is the catalyst for reducing government control over large segments of the economy. But if all it does is to help elect politicians who promise to be more honest and diligent than their predecessors, experience shows that before long, political and business corruption will rear its ugly head again.

THE SPENDING MONSTER STILL HAS
TOO LONG A LEASH

Despite misgivings about higher taxes, Americans generally support President Clinton's proposals for tax increases because he has convinced them that they will significantly reduce the budget deficit. But if the past 12 years are any guide, federal spending is likely to expand as tax revenues grow.

Federal expenditures at the end of Jimmy Carter's Presidency in 1980 were $591 billion, and taxes brought in $517 billion, so the deficit was $74 billion. By the end of Ronald Reagan's second term in 1988, tax revenues had risen to $909 billion despite—or because of—the Tax Reform Act of 1986. That would have created a large budget surplus if federal spending hadn't risen even more, increasing the gap to more than $150 billion.

The trend during the past four years is even more revealing, since the defense buildup—started under Carter and accelerated by Reagan—tapered off. But notwithstanding the 1990 budget accord between Congress and President Bush in which he was persuaded to break his vow not to raise taxes, the deficit grew sharply, to $300 billion, because spending grew faster than taxes did.

And it did so despite the fact that the government shunted large expenditures onto the business sector. It mandated business outlays for environmental cleanup, aid to handicapped employees, old-age support, health care, and other programs.

HEAVY PRESSURE.   President Clinton says he will both raise taxes and reduce spending, but his proposals put much more emphasis on tax increases than on spending cuts. But the net reduction in expenditures amounts only to a little over $100 billion, even after including the $55 billion in spending cuts Clinton says he will accept if Congress agrees to higher spending on jobs, roads, and other "investments." According to the Administration's estimates, the proposed hike in energy and income taxes will bring in about $250 billion of additional revenue during the next five years. And during the next two years, the Administration is not even asking for any reduction because the President wants an additional $30 billion to be spent on stimulating the economy—despite the strong 4.8% growth in gross domestic product during the last quarter of 1992 and 2%-plus growth during the whole of last year.

The heavy weighting of the President's proposals toward higher taxes and the deficits experienced during the past dozen years are not accidents, nor do they only reflect partisan conflicts. There are enormous pressures on Congress and Clinton to spend on thousands of programs favored by groups with political clout. In addition to the two biggest components, health and retirement benefits, the full list would take up many *Business Week* pages: It would include education and training programs to help children; a delicatessen of pork, featuring roads, public-transportation systems, and airports; the environment; assistance to the handicapped, minorities, and the poor; improving life in the cities; fighting drugs and crime; supporting Big Science and university research; and helping industry develop commercially viable technologies.

LONG ODDS.   The President sought to weaken the opposition to new taxes and to make the proposed tax increases more popular by concentrating the hike in income-tax rates on the so-called rich, saying they do not bear their fair share of the tax burden. However, the White House greatly overstates the effect of these rate increases on government revenue because it neglects the adjustments to a steep rise in the tax rate from 31% to an effective tax rate of well over 40% when one includes the higher tax for medicare and the limits on itemized deductions. High-income families will convert more of their income into tax shelters, and some workers who have spouses with high incomes will drop out of the labor force.

Whatever additional revenue is actually produced by the income- and energy-tax increases will set off a battle in Congress and among the President's advisers over the wish to cater to the many powerful interests clamoring for greater government benefits, vs. the political advantages of lowering the deficit. Over the past dozen years, this battle has consistently been won by the advocates of more spending.

I do not claim that there is an iron law of democratic politics whereby expenditures always expand by more than added revenues. I say that powerful forces clearly push in this direction. It is stark testimony to the strength of this spending impetus that the Clinton team's search for programs that don't work or are no longer needed found only 11 in a budget of almost $1.5 trillion. Along the way, the plan exaggerates the feasible reduction in defense spending, disguises some tax increases as spending cuts, and attempts to shift the onus of cutbacks onto the opposition by challenging the Republicans to suggest programs to be slashed.

It appears that Congress has received the message sent by the public in the last election and is now determined to reduce spending by much more than President Clinton has proposed. I certainly hope so. But I wouldn't make book on it, taking into account the incredible appetite for government spending in the U.S. and all other democratic countries.

REFORMING CONGRESS: WHY LIMITING TERMS WON'T WORK

Critics on both the right and left agree that Congress is not working properly. The hostility is evident in the hackles raised by the relatively modest $12 million pay raise members voted themselves last year and in the sharp decline in voting in congressional contests during non-Presidential election years.

Some of the blame is often placed on the advantages incumbents have over challengers. According to opinion polls, most Americans favor a constitutional amendment to limit congressional service to a few terms—one or two for senators and three to six for representatives. Although I agree that Congress should be reformed (BW—Apr. 16), surely limiting members' terms is not the way to do it—and could even be counterproductive.

During the past 50 years, the probability that an incumbent will win reelection has risen dramatically—to over 90% for representatives and more than 70% for senators. These numbers overstate the true advantage, since incumbents who expect to lose tend not to run. In 1986, six senators out of the 33 with terms ending and more than 50 representatives did not seek office again.

LEARNING THE ROPES.   Even so, incumbents clearly have enormous advantages over challengers. They have name recognition, opportunities to go on television and radio, ranking privileges, power to do favors for constituents and other interest groups, and much easier access to campaign funds than challengers do.

But longer congressional service is also part of a general trend in the U.S. and other modern economies for workers to remain at the same jobs. Skilled workers with more than a few years' experience seldom change jobs. They need so much training and knowledge to perform well that frequent job changes would greatly reduce their productivity.

Members of Congress, too, need many years to learn the ropes. For example, mastering the intricacies of military affairs to weigh the seemingly plausible arguments of brass hats who have spent their adult lives in uniform takes a long time. Members need the background to see through self-serving pleas, whether from environmental activists or chemical industry spokesmen. These are reasons voters would be likely to return incumbents to office even if they did not have other advantages over challengers.

Critics concede that increased skill often comes with congressional seniority. They contend that these real advantages of incumbency are outweighed by the pernicious influence of political action committees and other special-interest groups that help finance campaigns. But limiting congressional terms might increase rather than reduce the political power of such interest groups because candidates unable to rely on the various advantages of incumbency might become yet more dependent on promising favors in exchange for votes and campaign contributions.

In addition, those in Congress who are unable to hope for lengthy careers will be tempted to favor groups that can provide employment or consulting fees when their careers on Capitol Hill are over. Lawyers and other officials who leave government agencies often become employed by groups they had dealt with, and a similar pattern is probable for senators and representatives forced to retire after short stints.

POLITICAL FAVORS.   Supporters of limited terms sometimes claim that members who did not have to worry about reelection would become more dedicated proponents of the social interest, instead of advocates of partisan positions. But isn't it much more likely that members who cannot look forward to a long tenure will take less interest in their work and spend their time arranging future careers? Only an unrealistic view of human nature and how people respond to incentives could presume that taking away the right to continue at a job will improve performance.

Congress has serious problems not because incumbents have immense advantage, but mainly because thousands of groups look to the federal government for political favors. Legislatures in other democracies also succumb to the political pressures of various special interests, although candidates elsewhere usually are much more subject to party discipline and do not have to rely so heavily on raising campaign contributions from interest groups.

The posturing and silly behavior in Congress may vastly exceed those of representatives in other countries, but the bottom line is whether tariffs and import quotas, agriculture policies, and other legislation are worse in the U.S. I don't think so: At least the U.S. has avoided high marginal income-tax rates, extensive nationalization programs, and many other examples of bad legislation found in European democracies.

Effective reform must reduce the political power of voting blocs and special interests so that Congress can concentrate on issues that cannot be handled adequately by states or the private sector. I do not know of any easy way to accomplish this. However, it seems clear that reducing incumbents' advantages will not significantly improve how Congress works, and it could well make matters worse.

FEDERAL PAY: ONLY TOP-TO-BOTTOM REFORM WILL DO

We need a full reform of the federal pay structure. Federal pay should be determined by what it takes to attract qualified personnel, not by the size of the budget deficit. But even though the Quadrennial Commission's recommendations to raise the pay of top government officials should generally be accepted, bringing the federal pay structure in line with private compensation would reduce expenditures over the longer term.

The reason is that most federal employees earn more, not less, than they could get in the private sector. Federal employees tend to make 5% to 10% more than workers in the private sector who have the same amounts of education and other measurable human capital, as shown in recent work by Professor Alan Krueger of Princeton University and others. The low quit rates and long queues for federal jobs also suggest that federal workers earn a premium. Yet this premium is hardly a stimulus to greater effort since federal workers are almost never fired or demoted.

I believe most federal workers get a pay premium because they're an effective special-interest group. It isn't surprising that they would have political clout, considering their control over the enforcement of legislation and Presidential directives.

Nevertheless, top executives in the federal government do much worse than private executives with apparently comparable responsibilities. No federal executive earns more than $100,000, while the average CEO in *Business Week's* annual pay scoreboard (BW—May 2) earns $965,617 in salary and bonus. Even executives in the nonprofit private sector make a lot more than government workers in comparable positions.

TEMPTATION. Recruitment for many top government jobs is difficult, and turnover rates are increasing. The Justice Dept. can't hold on to ambitious and experienced lawyers who earn less than newly graduated associates in many law firms. Even the most dedicated government executive must be tempted by the much-better financial opportunities in the private sector.

Some conservatives, wary of the considerable powers of ambitious bureaucrats, approve of low salaries and high turnover of government officials. Abuse of power is worrisome, but adequately paid public servants do better, not worse, jobs. Poorly paid officials are tempted to cater to companies they're supposed to regulate in the hope of securing financial and other favors, including postgovernment employment.

The $100,000 a year that district and appellate federal judges receive is dwarfed by the earnings of successful lawyers. But that doesn't mean judges are underpaid. They have generous pensions, considerable prestige, and more power (along with more work) as the federal courts have become more important. Despite relatively low salaries, the quality of the federal bench may well have improved during the past decade with the appointment and retention of many outstanding appellate judges, including Stephen G. Breyer, Frank H. Easterbrook, and Richard A. Posner.

To help make its case for hefty pay increases to federal judges, the commission points out that 10 times as many federal judges resigned during 1974–1988 as had resigned during the previous 15 years. Much of that exodus, however, may be the result of the overall expansion in the number of judges in recent years and the larger proportion of younger judges, who tend to change jobs more often than their older colleagues.

POWER TIE. While the commission's evidence is not persuasive, a large pay increase for judges seems warranted. Precisely because the federal judiciary has become so powerful, the able and energetic lawyers in private practice who could be attracted to the bench by better pay are needed more than ever.

Criticisms of the commission's recommendations have focused on the proposed $46,000-a-year increase in salary for members of Congress. But the net improvement in income will not be large if the commission's recommendation to ban honoraria is implemented, too. Surely, supplements to congressional incomes by interest groups looking for government favors should not be permitted. No ethically managed corporation allows employees to accept large gifts from suppliers or customers.

Is the present salary of $89,000 high enough to attract suitable candidates to run for Congress in light of the high incomes earned by talented people in private employment and the sizable costs of being in Congress? The commission may be right that congressional pay is too low, yet congressional seats are highly prized even at the current pay. Fewer than 20 of the 535 members of Congress voluntarily quit prior to the recent election, and 95% of those who ran were reelected.

The commission's proposals, on their own, would boost federal spending just as Congress is struggling to cut the deficit. But full reform of the sort I suggest would shave spending. As the preponderance of federal jobs that are overpaid are brought in line with comparable private employment, both the deficit and the quality of our federal work force will eventually benefit.

LET'S NOT USE MIRRORS
TO BALANCE THE BUDGET

The Oct. 19 stock market crash has led to a clamor for cuts in the budget deficit. A smaller deficit is a good cause, but I fear that misplaced pressure for a balanced budget will create more problems than it solves. Although there isn't a shred of evidence to link the crash to deficits, calls for a budget reduction are echoing from economists, businesspeople, and the media.

Even people familiar with the facts believe that bad arguments are useful in pursuing the good cause of deficit reduction. The deficit in the U.S. was no smaller during the bull market in 1986 than it has been in 1987. The budget had a slight surplus when the market crashed in 1929. And stocks fell more in countries, such as Britain, that have relatively smaller budget deficits than does the U.S.

Deficits are not the fault of incompetent politicians who must be moved onto the right path, but of successful efforts by special-interest groups to raise their handouts from the government without paying higher taxes. If the Gramm-Rudman Act and other limits on deficits succeed in restricting government spending, legislators will try to satisfy pressure from powerful groups through regulations and hidden taxes imposed on the private sector.

During the past few years, Congress already has responded in such a way to pressure. Increased spending on medical care has been provided by forcing companies to raise the number of workers covered by generous medical insurance plans. The growing political power of elderly and retired workers has led to excessive support for claims of discrimination by older workers and to legislated increases in the scale of private pension plans. And federal lawmakers have tried to satisfy the agitation for subsidized child care by drafting legislation that requires companies to provide leaves for pregnant women and parents of newborn children.

Such leaves are unpaid in the bills before Congress, but it's only a matter of time until advocates cite the examples set by Sweden and West Germany and push for paid leaves. If legislation requires paid leaves for child care, companies will be less willing to hire and give responsible positions to young married women because of the likelihood that they will become pregnant.

HIDDEN HURTS.   Should budgetary reductions cause military pay to fall in comparison with civilian alternatives, the resulting difficulty in obtaining volunteers will stimulate renewed calls for the draft on the grounds that a voluntary system cannot work. The draft forces some young people who would be much more productive as civilians into the military. Low military pay, which makes a draft necessary, discourages the people who would make better soldiers from volunteering.

A tempting way to make the budget look more balanced is to sell government assets. Because government accounts do not subtract the value of government capital from the debt outstanding, sales of such assets raise revenue without changing reported indebtedness. The excellent reasons for privatizing many government assets and activities, however, should not be polluted by bad reasons attributable to defective government accounting.

I favor privatization of many public activities and a requirement that government agencies, such as the postal system, charge enough to cover their costs. But I strongly object to lower government spending achieved through regulations and hidden taxes on private companies and individuals.

ILLUSIONS.   Such policies often greatly reduce the private sector's efficiency and cause many innocent people to suffer. Congressionally imposed increases in the generosity of health insurance and pension plans by private companies may raise the welfare of some older workers, for example, but they also make it harder for unemployed older people to find jobs. Companies do not want to hire workers who require large indirect outlays in the form of pension obligations and medical expenditures.

A smaller budget deficit accomplished by regulations and hidden taxes creates the illusion of reduced government involvement in the economy. It also distorts one's perception of the distribution of federal spending among categories, because only certain types of outlays are readily shifted to the private sector. Spending on medical care, pensions, child care, and affirmative action is more easily shifted than is spending on military hardware or aid to unmarried teenage mothers. As a result, government spending in the not-easily-shifted categories appears to grow in relative importance as spending in other categories is shifted to the private sector.

I do not share the opposition of some economists to smaller budget deficits. A deficit is a tax on future generations that may be less able to bear taxes than the present one. Unfortunately, none of the plans to reduce the budget deficit really controls the political powers of special-interest groups. Unless a balanced budget emerges from greater resistance to the pleas of special-interest groups for handouts and low taxes, the medicine is likely to do more damage than the illness.

CONTRARY TO POPULAR BELIEF, THE ECONOMIC BOOM DID TRICKLE DOWN

It is widely believed that the Reagan years have been good for the middle class and the rich but not for the poor. This perception probably reflects the influence of David Stockman's famous accusation in *The Atlantic* magazine that supply-side economics should be seen as a Trojan horse in which the rich's taxes are reduced with the hope that the effects "trickle down" to the poor.

But Bureau of Labor Statistics and Census Dept. data for employment and earnings of blacks, teenagers, and women in 1976 (the last year of Gerald Ford's Administration), 1980 (the last year of Jimmy Carter's), and 1987 show these impressions of the record of the past eight years are largely mistaken.

Young and unskilled workers and minorities suffer much more from unemployment than older and skilled white workers. Yet not only is the overall unemployment rate down, from 7% at the end of the Carter years to 5.4% in July, but unemployment rates among blacks and teenagers are much lower than they were at the end of the Carter Administration. For example, the unemployment rate for blacks, although still much too high, has declined to 11.4% from 14.3% in 1980.

FAST RISE.   The trend in earnings of employed blacks has been less favorable. After rising sharply during the 1970s, wage rates of black males in the early 1980s fell compared with those of whites. However, earnings of black men have been rising faster during the past three years along with the sharp decline in black unemployment.

Unemployment rates could have declined because some of the unemployed withdrew from the labor force after becoming discouraged by the difficulty of finding jobs.

But the record shows the contrary: Employment rose while unemployment fell. From 1980 to July, 1988, 15 million more people got jobs, and the black employment-rate increase of 4.5 percentage points exceeds the 3.1 percentage point increase for all workers.

Is the decline in unemployment and the growth in employment due to a fall in real wages over this period, encouraging employers to hire cheaper workers? No, real hourly earnings rose slightly from 1980 to 1987. The connection between falling real earnings and a decline in unemployment is, in any event, hard to prove. From 1976 to 1980 unemployment remained high even though real earnings fell by more than 5%.

The Reagan Administration has been criticized by many women's groups, partly because it opposes the Equal Rights Amendment and comparable-worth laws. Paradoxically, female workers did very well during the past eight years. Unemployment rates of both white and black women declined, and the differential between the median earnings of full-time employed men and women fell, from 39 percentage points in 1980 to 32 points in 1987.

This strong improvement in the position of women is all the more remarkable since the gender wage gap remained fixed at about 40 percentage points from the late 1950s to the end of the 1970s, and many people believed the gap would never shrink without extensive government help.

Yet it did become a great deal smaller—under a government opposed to affirmative action. The full employment environment, the shift toward service economy, increased training, and higher labor-force participation all contributed to women's economic advancement.

Some critics of the Reagan Administration concede the great expansion of jobs, but contend that the new jobs generally require little skill and pay badly. We are becoming a nation of hamburger grillers, the argument goes.

However, in an article in the winter issue of *The Public Interest,* Marvin Kosters of the American Enterprise Institute closely examines job creation in recent years and finds the distribution of jobs between high-, low-, and middle-paying levels remained approximately the same during the 1980s as it was in the decade before.

CONTENTIOUS.   Indeed, the economic growth of the Reagan years favored educated and skilled workers, not the less educated and unskilled. Current Population Survey data show that the gain in earnings from going to college has been much higher in recent years than during the 1970s.

Professors Kevin Murphy of the University of Chicago and Finis Welch of the University of California at Los Angeles show that a college education is worth more now than at any time in the past 30 years.

These findings indicate that for the most part, blacks, women, teenagers, and other less advantaged workers have participated fully in the economic boom of the past six years. This conclusion is based on the facts, and stands apart from the contentious and politically loaded issue of whether the boom was caused by tax cuts, budget deficits, the declining dollar, or whether Murphy and Welch are correct in their assessment that the changing importance and structure of exports and imports during the 1980s greatly affected the wages of women, blacks, college graduates, and young people.

SHORT-TERM FIXES
COULD CAUSE TROUBLE DOWN THE ROAD

Public policies and private actions that help at first often have dreadful consequences later. Governments are especially prone to yield to the siren call of short-run benefits, yet their policies can dramatically change the long-term behavior of individuals and businesses.

One example is the new immigration law, which gives amnesty to illegal immigrants who have been in the U.S. since 1982. The law will improve the well-being of these immigrants at the cost of encouraging other illegal immigrants to expect additional amnesty decrees in the future. Another example is the inflation of the 1970s, which reduced the real value of the public debt and the burden of past deficits. Higher interest rates on long-term loans are the price we've paid for that inflationary episode. Lenders now demand higher rates because they anticipate future efforts to use inflation to reduce the burden of the deficits financed during the past few years.

Government efforts to protect borrowers provide another example. Many families accumulate more debt than they can repay because they overestimate their future incomes or they underestimate their expenditures. It is easy to sympathize with a desire to alleviate the plight of those in financial difficulty. The bankruptcy laws are particularly attractive, since they offer people the chance of a fresh start free of the burden of debt accumulated through past mistakes.

THANKSGIVING GIFT. A major revision of bankruptcy laws in 1978 greatly raised the value of personal debt that is dischargeable through bankruptcy. Further, to ease the plight of farmers, an addition to the Bankruptcy Code that took effect on Thanksgiving Day sharply increases the amount of debt that farmers can write off through bankruptcy. In recent years the incomes of farm operators have been low while they are burdened with heavy debt accumulated during the prosperous 1970s. As a result, the number of farmers filing for bankruptcy has risen significantly.

More liberal bankruptcy provisions would seem to reduce further the shadow of past mistakes. The evidence does indicate that a more liberal code raises the likelihood of debtors opting for bankruptcy as a solution to their problems. Professors William J. Boyes and Roger L. Faith of Arizona State University show in the April, 1986, issue of the *Journal of Law and Economics* that the 1978 act increased the number of personal bankruptcies, especially from 1978 to 1980. The latest revision of the code surely will raise the number of farmers who file for bankruptcy.

But these short-run gains to borrowers from a liberal bankruptcy code also bring major long-run costs. To protect themselves, banks and other lenders are changing the terms available for more risky loans and for borrowers with few assets and low income. They're raising interest rates, shortening the duration of loans, and, more often than before the liberalization in 1978, turning down requests for funds. Therefore, in the long run, these liberal bankruptcy laws may hurt the very people who benefit the most in the short run—the marginal borrowers who are more likely to encounter financial distress. It will be more difficult for them to get credit, and the terms of the credit available will be more stringent.

REDUCED LENDING.   The study by Boyes and Faith finds that the ratio of debt that is secured by collateral to unsecured debt of people who went bankrupt declined after passage of the 1978 revision. A plausible interpretation of this decline is that the new rules reduced the fraction of loans that are secured by more risky borrowers since lenders require less collateral from high-income and other creditworthy borrowers.

Similar long-run consequences will follow the recent success of many Third World countries in effectively repudiating part of the large debt owed to creditors in the West. This repudiation helps these countries now, but it will reduce the credit available to poor countries. It will also raise interest rates and shorten the maturity of the amount of credit that is forthcoming.

Some people have suggested that the restitution obligations imposed on criminals be dischargeable through bankruptcy in order to help give bankrupt criminals a fresh start. The U.S. Court of Appeals for the Second Circuit upheld this view in a 1985 decision. Fortunately, the Supreme Court in November reaffirmed the principle that restitution as well as fines imposed on criminals cannot be wiped out by filing for bankruptcy. If this were not the case, financial penalties would be a weak deterrent to crime, and the courts would have to rely more on imprisonment.

Politicians are subject to enormous temptations to harvest the short-run benefits from an amnesty program, from inflation, and from a liberal bankruptcy code. Unfortunately, since private behavior responds to public policies, these short-term benefits have long-term costs. Policymakers should therefore be encouraged to resist these temptations. It is far wiser to commit the political process to a long-term perspective that avoids both the initial gains and the eventual suffering.

TAXES

A Flatter Tax Just Might Keep Fickle Teams at Home

The bitter controversy over the plan of the Cleveland Browns pro football team to move to Baltimore — after several decades on the shores of Lake Erie — reveals the fierce competition in the bidding for major league sports franchises. This competition is of concern to more than just the residents of the cities involved in the bidding wars, because taxpayers elsewhere help pay the bill.

Other taxpayers have a financial interest since part of the cost of stadiums, new roads, and other facilities is financed with municipal bonds that are exempt from federal income taxes. My colleague at the University of Chicago, Casey Mulligan, has calculated the expected cost of the fight going on between Chicago and the nearby city of Gary, Ind., for the Chicago Bears — one of the most prestigious sports franchises. Although it is unlikely that the Bears will decamp for Gary, the threat has forced Chicago Mayor Richard M. Daley to promise to spend almost $200 million to upgrade the stadium where the Bears have been playing, city-owned Soldier Field. Gary, for its part, has offered to spend much more to build a new stadium and roads and other facilities.

Both sides plan to raise some of their funds from tax-exempt municipal bonds. Long-term, top-quality tax-exempt munis now carry an interest rate well under 6%. If the Bears had to finance a new stadium or improvements themselves, they would have to pay much higher interest rates. Therefore, the victorious city saves millions of dollars in annual interest payments because a local government, rather than the Bears, owns the stadium where the team plays.

MULTIPLE OCCUPANCY. Mayor Daley claims that the upgrade of Soldier Field would not cost Chicago taxpayers anything. He says higher revenue to the city from rental payments by the Bears and greater spending by the public would cover interest payments on the additional city bonds. Whether or not he turns out to be right — and such forecasts are usually too rosy — remodeling by the city rather than by the Bears means less income-tax revenue for the U.S. Treasury, because munis are involved.

When baseball's Brooklyn Dodgers moved to Los Angeles in 1958 to begin the musical-chairs contest among local governments for sports franchises, almost all stadiums used by major league sports teams were privately owned. Often the football and baseball teams shared premises: The Chicago Bears, for example, then used the still-private Wrigley Field, home of the Chicago Cubs. Now almost all major football and baseball teams, and a majority of basketball and hockey teams, play in publicly owned stadiums.

The National Football League and Major League Baseball especially have taken advantage of the intense competition among local governments for their teams to demand separate stadiums funded with public money. These plush centers are usually bad investments. They are too large, too luxurious—and vacant practically all the time: Even big-league baseball teams play only 81 games at home. Private indoor arenas, such as the United Center in Chicago, keep down their costs by obtaining several teams, preferably major league hockey and basketball teams.

HOME LOYALTY.   Franchises that own their stadiums and other specialized facilities also are less inclined to pick up and go to another city. That's because specialized sports facilities have little market value without a major league team playing there. The growth in government-owned stadiums is contrary to the trend toward privatizing garbage collection and other government services. Even Indianapolis, which has probably done more privatizing than any other city, continues to own the RCA Dome, home to the Indianapolis Colts football team.

Expansion of the market for lower-interest municipal bonds, especially tax-free munis, has made it possible for cities to compete for franchises by building uneconomic government-owned stadiums. The gap between interest rates on tax-free munis and comparable taxable bonds depends on the level of taxation and the degree of progressivity in the income-tax structure. People in high tax brackets, who have the most incentive to own tax-free bonds, bid down interest rates on munis so that their returns are comparable to yields on taxable bonds.

If Congress and President Clinton can agree on tax reform that has a much flatter income-tax schedule, the market for tax-free assets will decline. This will reduce the incentives of local governments to compete for sports franchises by offering to build new stadiums, and it will help return stadiums to private hands—where they belong.

WARNING: A HIGHER CIGARETTE TAX
MAY BE HAZARDOUS TO HEALTH FINANCING

Some members of Congress advocate a massive federal tax hike on cigarettes to help defray the costs of a health-care bill. The medical profession and other opponents of smoking agree on a large tax increase, though their goal is not to raise revenue but to cut down smoking. Recent research, however, indicates that a sizable cigarette tax would not generate much tax revenue, although it would cut smoking by a lot.

These findings appear in the June issue of *The American Economic Review*, in an article by Michael Grossman, Kevin M. Murphy, and me. In it, we estimate the response of cigarette smoking in the U.S. to changes in retail price, income level, and other variables. The research can be used to obtain reliable calculations of the effects of increases in the federal cigarette excise tax on government revenue.

These calculations assume that each 25¢ increase in the tax raises retail prices by the same amount—even though various studies indicate that prices may rise by a little more than the tax increase. Higher retail prices reduce smoking mainly by discouraging some people from beginning and by encouraging others to quit earlier than they otherwise would have, although higher prices also reduce the number of packs smoked by those who continue to smoke. Teenage smoking is especially sensitive to the cost of cigarettes.

Initially, a higher price for a pack of cigarettes does not cut smoking by a lot, since many smokers cannot quickly break the habit. But the impact is cumulative as each reduction in smoking further weakens the habit and encourages additional reductions. Indeed, our article estimates that the impact of a rise in price is about twice as large after the price has been in effect for a year: After one year, a 10% increase in price cuts smoking by about 4%, but after three years the reduction doubles to about 8%.

HOOKED POLITICIANS. The present 24¢ federal tax on a pack of cigarettes yields about $6 billion annually in federal revenue. The estimates of demand in our article imply that to reach maximum revenue in the long run would require a tax revenue of about 95¢ a pack and would raise only $6 billion annually more than the present tax. Note that somewhat larger tax revenues would be raised during the years it takes smokers to fully adjust to the higher price.

This estimate of tax revenue is much lower than that of the Congressional Budget Office because, in sharp contrast to our estimate of an 8% reduction in smoking per 10% increase in price, the CBO assumes that smoking falls at a constant rate, by about 4% for each 10% increase in the cost of a pack.

Some members of Congress are proposing a still larger increase of $1 a pack to raise the total federal tax to $1.24. That tax, in the long run, would raise only $9 billion in annual revenue—a mere $3 billion more than at present—but would cut smoking by more than 70%. Tax revenue rises and smoking falls as the total federal tax is increased to 95¢, according to our estimates, but both smoking and tax revenue fall as the tax is made larger.

The conflict between tax revenue and consumption reduction may seriously affect government policies toward smoking. If the feds get hooked on the revenue generated by smoking taxes, Congress may hesitate to impose severe regulatory restrictions on smoking. State lotteries provide a telling warning of how this pressure works: Despite the still considerable moral and other opposition to gambling and even though lotteries are actuarially very bad bets, many states advertise extensively to the poor and others to encourage the purchase of lottery tickets.

BOOTLEGGERS'S BOOTY.   Smuggling of cigarettes from neighbor nations would reduce still further the federal revenue generated by a tax hike. Canada recently was forced to reduce its draconian $2.69-per-pack cigarette tax by $1.82 because of massive smuggling from the U.S. A large U.S. tax hike would spur smuggling from Mexico and other Latin American nations with much lower taxes and would illegally divert some cigarettes meant for export to domestic use.

Cigarette taxes fall largely on the poor, since the heaviest smokers are in the lowest income and education brackets. Some smokers would be discouraged from starting if the cost of a pack rose from $1.80 to $2.80 with a $1-per-pack tax increase. But those who couldn't break the habit and continued to smoke, say, 1½ packs a day would pay $1,533 a year in cigarette taxes, a large amount for people on welfare and those with modest incomes. It makes little sense to help finance the increased cost of the President's health plan partly with a tax that falls mainly on the poor and less educated—groups that are supposed to be helped by his health reforms.

The case for much higher cigarette taxes is very shaky in light of the regressive nature of the tax, the limited amount of revenue that would be generated, the encouragement of cross-border smuggling, and the temptation that it would pose to the federal government to encourage smoking in order to raise tax revenue.

Your Tax Dollars Are at Work
—On the Wrong Jobs

The surprisingly narrow victories of Senator Bill Bradley (D-N.J.) and many other incumbents in the recent elections dramatically show how fed up taxpayers are with politics as usual. American voters have lost faith in those they have come to consider agents of special interest groups.

People looking for money from the government had an easy time during the 1960s and 1970s. The share of gross national product spent by federal, state, and local governments rose from 27% in 1960 to 37% in 1982. Nonmilitary spending rose even faster. The big winners were Social Security, medicare, food stamps, welfare, and other entitlements, which climbed to almost half of federal spending, while defense outlays declined from more than two-fifths of the federal budget in 1960 to just a little over a quarter in 1982.

OUTRAGE AND OUTPUT. Most voters may not be aware that they work nearly 40% of the time for the government. But they have realized that, whatever the amount, they do not get enough in return to justify the burden. The problem is that the thousands of interest groups competing for government handouts do not have to consider the cost, because the burden is imposed on others. As a result, the social benefits of government spending are often less than the social costs of the taxes and regulations that help pay for them.

Equally disturbing, the effort of catering to the demands of so many special interests diverts government attention and expenditures away from what it should be doing: activities that cannot be handled efficiently by the private sector. These include financing roads, airports, schools, and other forms of infrastructure; providing a safety net for those who cannot make it on their own; protecting against crime and foreign aggression; and managing government budgets responsibly so that outlays and revenues balance.

It is hard to judge the military, but governments in the U.S. are failing at nearly everything else. Roads are obstacle courses, airports are crowded, and bridges often seem on their last legs. Fear of crime dominates life in cities far more than in the early 1960s. Despite large increases in spending on schools, most students are poorly educated, especially minority members in big cities. Even with the enormous amounts spent on the poor, holes in the safety net are not getting smaller—and may be getting larger. The federal budget deficits of the 1980s and the fiscal problems of Philadelphia and New York and in Massachusetts and New Jersey—among other cities and states—indicate clearly that governments at all levels are not keeping their houses in order.

With taxes taking such a large share of GNP, the perception in Congress and the media that the budget "crisis" is attributable to insufficient taxation is hardly credible. Rather, government revenues are misallocated, with too much spent on bad programs and not enough attention paid to designing essential ones. Efforts to improve the lot of the poor or to repair the rotting infrastructure get sidetracked by spending on such things as agricultural price supports and by investigations into price "gouging" by the gasoline industry. Is it any surprise that governments are so ineffective at what they should be doing when they are doing so many other things too?

In trying to reduce the deficit, Congress and the President should have concentrated on cutting spending—and spending more wisely—instead of raising taxes on the rich and others. Prime candidates for cuts include farm and urban subsidies, defense, assistance to various industries, and benefits that go to the middle and upper classes. President Bush made a major policy error as well as a political blunder by reneging on his promise of no new taxes.

POWER TO THE PEOPLE. Yet there is a faint ray of hope that we are beginning to develop greater control over government spending. Taxpayers are getting better organized and are offering more resistance. This started with

Proposition 13 and the California rebellion in the late 1970s. Taxpayer opposition then spread to other states, to cities, and to the federal government with the Tax Reform Act of 1986 and the Gramm-Rudman Act. Although some ballot proposals to limit spending were defeated last week, nearly every initiative to issue new bonds was rejected.

Even the persistent budget deficits of the 1980s are a sign of the greater political power of taxpayers. Interest-group pressure for more spending was as strong during the 1980s as in earlier decades, but taxpayer opposition meant that greater spending could no longer be so readily financed with higher taxes.

Taxpayer resistance may also have forced the expansion of government spending to slow down. The fact is that the share of GNP absorbed by governmental programs, including Social Security and other transfer payments, has hardly grown since 1982.

It is too early to be confident that the growth of government has been permanently curtailed. But only if that is true can one reasonably expect to see more balanced budgets, sizable improvements in schools or the infrastructure, significant progress in fighting poverty and crime, and generally a better record on what should be the principal concerns of government.

IF IT SMELLS LIKE A TAX AND BITES LIKE A TAX...

A rapidly growing number of federal, state, and city laws mandate specific expenditures by companies. The Clean Air Act, for example, requires electric utilities and other industrial users of coal to install stack-gas scrubbers to reduce sulphur-oxide emissions. Many cities will not franchise cable television companies unless they subsidize installations in poor areas. A bill introduced in Congress requires employers to provide leaves to workers after the birth or adoption of a child. And at the urging of Governor Michael Dukakis, Massachusetts recently passed a law requiring companies to contribute up to $1,680 a year per employee to a state fund that subsidizes health insurance for workers.

The tax revolt has made politicians unwilling to call openly for new taxes. Even liberal think tanks preparing blueprints for the next Democratic Administration shrink from outright calls for much higher taxes, masking their spending plans with proposals to require additional spending on social programs by private business.

There are no free lunches, though. Ultimately, taxes must be raised to pay for all government expenditures, but sometimes taxes can be delayed, hidden, or given other names. For example, the large budget deficits of recent years will have to be financed with higher taxes in the future. And mandated business expenditures are hidden taxes that raise the cost of doing business in the same way as explicit taxes.

REDUCED DEMAND. Consider the frequent proposal to require child-care facilities at work for mothers of young children. This would raise the cost of employing women with children for companies that have not installed such facilities voluntarily. Essentially the same effect would be achieved by requiring these companies to pay a tax that is proportional to the number of small children under the care of their female employees. The government would spend the proceeds on constructing and maintaining child-care facilities at these companies.

The higher cost of employing women with children because of mandated facilities or such an explicit tax would discourage companies from hiring them, despite laws against discrimination in hiring. After a while, the reduced demand for such women would force them to accept lower wages, so that they themselves would ultimately foot part, if not most, of the child-care bill. This is one reason why the women's movement has had an ambivalent attitude toward such proposals.

Suppose that younger women did pay through lower wages for most of the cost of mandated child-care facilities. Is this appropriate, or should society subsidize such arrangements from general tax revenues, or should parents have to make their own? The answer depends on whether better child care at the workplace benefits mainly parents with young children or society as a whole by improving the mental and physical health of children.

DIRECT APPROACH. A related analysis applies to the state fund in Massachusetts to provide health insurance. Since companies can reduce their contribution to the fund by the cost of any health insurance they provide employees, this law will have little direct effect on larger companies that already have generous health insurance plans. But it raises costs for smaller companies with modest plans or none at all. The law then is equivalent to a tax on smaller employers, with the proceeds spent on health insurance for their workers. As such, it reduces the ability of smaller companies to compete against larger rivals. That's why large companies in Massachusetts generally supported the law, while small companies opposed it.

If Massachusetts wants to provide health insurance to state residents, why not do so directly instead of through employer contributions to a state fund? A direct approach could apply to all residents, not just to employees. Moreover, it would avoid the current favoring of large businesses at the expense of smaller ones.

The Clean Air Act requires scrubbers even when low-sulphur coal is used. These scrubbers reduce sulphur emissions, but the act forces utilities and other industries in low-sulphur coal areas of the country to use scrubbers even though they would have low emission levels without the devices. A more sensible law would directly tax sulphur-oxide emissions, letting companies decide whether to install scrubbers to reduce their emissions—and taxes. However, many companies in the Northeast that use high-sulphur coal would probably prefer the present law because it forces costs on their competitors in low-sulphur regions, thus removing what might have been an advantage in the marketplace.

To politicians, required business outlays are a boon, but even the well-informed have difficulty determining their complicated effects on labor and product markets. Mandatory expenditures are disturbing and dangerous because they hide taxes and help to avoid the difficult questions that such issues as child care, health insurance, and pollution control pose for society.

A Higher Cost of Giving
Is No Cause for Low Spirits

The U.S. is among the few countries that use their tax systems to encourage charitable contributions. The Senate and House tax reform bills being reconciled in a congressional conference committee both maintain the deductibility of charitable and philanthropic contributions. That deduction is likely to remain in the final tax reform bill. Yet the amount of charitable giving will surely decline once a new tax law takes effect. My position is that this should not provoke undue concern.

The principal reason for the expected decline in giving is that the new law will greatly reduce the marginal tax rate for higher-income taxpayers. A high tax bracket substantially lowers the cost of giving. For example, the 50% top tax rate in the current tax system means that a wealthy taxpayer who itemizes deductions pays only $50 for each $100 he gives to charity. Other taxpayers, in effect, contribute the remaining $50. In the Senate bill the top rate is reduced from 50% to 27%, so that an itemizer would be paying $73 of each $100 given. The increase from $50 to $73 raises the cost of giving for higher-income taxpayers by more than 40%.

CHURCH AND STATE.   Several studies have estimated the impact of changes in the cost of giving on philanthropic contributions. The growing consensus is that changes in tax rates have big effects on contributions. A recent book, *Federal Tax Policy and Charitable Giving,* by Professor Charles T. Clotfelter of Duke University, surveys the evidence. A 10% increase in the cost of giving by individual taxpayers apparently reduces their contributions by almost 10%. Since individuals give about 80% of all private contributions that philanthropic organizations receive, the provisions in the Senate bill would be likely to reduce total contributions substantially. Bequests make up about 10% of charitable contributions, business contributes only 5%, and foundations provide the rest.

Would a large decline in philanthropic contributions be undesirable? The answer would be obvious if contributions went mainly to the needy, since they deserve financial support from taxpayers. Actually, little of so-called charitable contributions goes to poor people. Almost 50% of all giving helps support churches, synagogues, and other religious bodies, despite a tradition in this country that frowns on government support of religion, which is what government subsidies through the tax system clearly amount to. An additional 15% of giving goes to higher education. The case for encouraging taxpayer contributions to higher education is questionable, since most college graduates and faculty members have incomes that are well above average. Similarly, wealthy people are the major beneficiaries of the 10% of giving that goes to museums, symphonies, and other artistic and civic groups. People who patronize such organizations hardly require government-supported charity. And there is no reason that the general taxpayers should, in effect, subsidize such groups.

There is a different and less dubious case for taxpayer support of giving to philanthropic organizations. This argument depends not on the needs of recipients but on inadequate private incentives to contribute. Many people want particular colleges, churches, museums, and hospitals to flourish. But they might not help because they expect other people to carry the burden. This creates a tendency for each concerned person to try to take a "free ride" on the contributions made by other concerned persons. A tax system that lowers the price of giving works to offset this tendency.

Still, while the free-ride argument has merit, the 50% tax rate in the present law may create an excessive incentive for charitable giving among the wealthy. Perhaps the most telling argument against the current generous tax deductions for charitable contributions is that they force all taxpayers to contribute, say, to the University of Chicago and Princeton University—to mention my alma maters—as well as to the Catholic Church, the Metropolitan Museum of Art, and other nonprofit organizations. Obviously, most taxpayers are not at all concerned about the welfare of these organizations.

COMPETITION. True, the U.S. system of indirect support through the tax system is preferable to the European model, where governments operate universities and hospitals and make grants to private artistic and philanthropic organizations. The U.S. approach encourages competition among private providers of philanthropy. It also decentralizes giving because contributions are the results of millions of individual and corporate decisions. The advantages of competition and decentralization are as compelling in the field of philanthropy as they are in markets for goods and services.

Although the U.S. system of using tax incentives to encourage private contributions is better than direct government subsidies, its high marginal rates may encourage too much giving by the wealthy. Further, it may also encourage such misdirected contributions as giving to nonprofit organizations with rich clienteles.

For these reasons, I see no cause for alarm over the large reduction in charitable contributions that tax reform may bring about.

DON'T RAISE THE DRINKING AGE, RAISE TAXES

Last year, Congress passed a law that will reduce federal highway funds to states that do not raise their minimum drinking age to 21 by 1986. Many states have already complied, and others plan to do so. But the law raises an important question of fairness: Is it proper to discriminate against young adults by denying them legal access to alcoholic beverages when they are old enough to vote and when most of them drink in moderation?

Proponents of the 1984 law point out that young drunk drivers are involved in many of the most serious auto accidents. However, young adults are involved in only a small share of on-the-job accidents due to drinking. Almost all bus drivers, pilots, air traffic controllers, and other people who hold jobs where drinking can cause serious harm to innocent individuals are older people. Yet Congress has not passed a law curtailing the access to alcohol of people who hold the safety of many others in their hands.

No one denies that drunk driving and drinking on the job are serious offenses that should be discouraged. But they can be reduced without legislation that places restrictions on young people or other adults. The first step is to replace the 1984 drinking-age law with higher federal excise taxes on alcoholic beverages. Then, arrest and severely punish drunk individuals who cause serious auto and industrial accidents.

Except for a small boost in the liquor tax in October, federal excise taxes on liquor, beer, and wine have been unchanged since 1951. Inflation during the past 15 years has greatly eroded the real value of these excises, which helped to hold down the prices of alcoholic beverages compared with other consumer goods. Doubling federal excise taxes on alcoholic beverages would restore their real values to only half of the 1951 level. If that happened, taxes on liquor would rise from $2.50 a bottle (a fifth) to about $5 a bottle. Taxes on beer and wine would also increase significantly.

CONSUMPTION CUTBACK.   There is considerable evidence that raising the prices of alcoholic beverages reduces consumption. Studies by Professor Michael Grossman and his associates at the National Bureau of Economic Research indicate that higher prices cause a cutback in drinking by young adults especially. This evidence suggests that raising taxes would be as effective as raising age limits in curtailing drinking by young adults. A 10¢ rise in the price of a bottle of beer would reduce their drinking by as much as a one-year increase in the minimum drinking age.

Not only moderate drinking, but also the heavy drinking that contributes to accidents is reduced by higher taxes. The studies by Grossman and associates also show that higher prices of beer and other alcoholic beverages reduce heavy drinking by teenagers, as well as young adults. Furthermore, Professors Philip J. Cook and George Tauchen of Duke University have shown that higher taxes on alcoholic beverages reduce the death rate from cirrhosis of the liver, a disease mainly caused by heavy drinking. Their evidence indicates, for example, that a $1 increase in the tax on liquor would eventually lower the death rate from this disease by more than 5%. This happens for two reasons: higher prices lead heavy drinkers to reduce their consumption, and fewer people become heavy drinkers.

Higher excise taxes obviously also provide revenues. Currently, federal excise taxes on alcohol raise about $6 billion annually. Even though higher taxes would reduce the consumption of alcohol, doubling these taxes might raise an additional $4 billion a year. This would make a modest dent in the enormous federal budget deficit.

A SICKNESS. Although higher excise taxes would reduce heavy drinking and raise additional revenues, they would also raise the cost of drinking to light and moderate drinkers. To avoid taxing these people unduly, we should limit the increase in excise taxes. Moreover, higher taxes should not be the only weapon to combat the harm inflicted by drunk individuals. We should also increase the certainty and severity of punishment for drinkers who cause serious auto and other accidents. The U.S. has been slow to introduce severe punishment partly because of the belief that alcoholism, since it is a sickness, cannot be deterred by punishment.

One can accept that alcoholism is a sickness and also accept that drunk driving and drinking on the job would be reduced if dealt with by arrest and punishment. Professor H. Laurence Ross of the University of New Mexico has compiled evidence from many countries that clearly shows that drunk driving is greatly reduced when the certainty of punishment is sufficiently high. My impression from visits to Norway and Sweden, two countries with stiff penalties for drunk drivers, is that heavy drinkers there often avoid driving for fear of the punishment.

An old and attractive principle of justice is to let the punishment fit the crime, without unduly punishing innocent people. Higher excise taxes on alcohol, combined with more certain and severe punishment of drinkers who cause serious accidents, would serve this principle well.

COURTS

THE HIGH COURT DEBATE
ISN'T HIGH—OR BROAD—ENOUGH

President Bush has stated that Clarence Thomas, his nominee to the Supreme Court, is the best person for the job. Yet everyone knows that not only Thomas' race but also his views on affirmative action, abortion, and other politically sensitive questions were decisive considerations for Bush.

The Senate Judiciary Committee will subject Thomas to a close and partisan examination, although the proceedings will be cloaked in highfalutin language: Does the candidate respect precedent? Does he believe in privacy and fairness? Such questions will generate prolonged hearings that may seem tedious to many people and will certainly prompt objections from the White House that the Senate is badgering the witness. Indeed, extensive hearings prior to confirmation were not expected by the Founding Fathers, who anticipated that the highest court would simply interpret the Constitution. But the impact the court has come to have on Americans has made the modern confirmation process inevitable.

The Supreme Court was much less important in the 19th century and the first two decades of this one—when governments were much smaller. With the vast expansion of federal and state legislation, issues touching on all aspects of our lives are now brought before the court. Since the Constitution is vague on many subjects—such as due process—and since federal and state legislation is often ambiguous, it was unavoidable that the highest court would emerge as a de facto legislative and regulatory body with enormous influence. Constitutional law itself became an important subject in law schools only during the 1930s.

To reduce the capacity of what is, in effect, an unelected upper chamber to deviate for prolonged periods from the wishes of the majority of voters, I proposed a constitutional amendment that would substitute a fixed term—possibly renewable—for the present lifetime tenure of judges (BW—Sept. 3, 1990). Such a change would help weed out senile and incompetent judges and those who get out of touch with public opinion.

FAULTY FORUM? Obviously, such a radical step is not likely to be taken soon. The confirmation hearings will continue to provide the only public forum to consider the qualifications, record, and philosophy of nominees such as Clarence Thomas who, if approved, will sit on the bench for a long time. Since 1950, the Senate has rejected several nominees: not only Robert H. Bork but also Nixon's nominees Harold Carswell and Clement Haynsworth. The Senate also defeated Lyndon B. Johnson's attempt to elevate Abe Fortas to Chief Justice.

Presidential nominations are greatly influenced by expectations about who can get confirmed. The intellectual caliber of certain recent appointments to the Supreme Court has been rightly criticized, but it is clear that some professors and judges who have made impressive contributions to legal thought, such as Richard A. Posner and Frank H. Easterbrook of the U.S. Court of Appeals in Chicago as well as Robert Bork, do not have a good chance of gaining approval from the present Senate. They are deemed too conservative. Similarly, liberals such as Laurence H. Tribe of Harvard University probably would not be approved by a conservative Senate.

Unfortunately, the political nature of the hearings means that the issues dear to well-organized interest groups with good access to the media are overemphasized relative to questions of greater significance. Pressure from vocal groups is a major reason why views on abortion are considered a litmus test of a candidate's qualifications to serve on the court. Such emotional controversies get attention, but they have less impact on most people than crime—which accounts for over one-quarter of all cases decided by the court—the regulation of business, employee rights, and other matters decided by the court.

LIP SERVICE. One important business issue concerns when federal legislation should preempt local laws. The chemical industry is unhappy with a June ruling by the court that federal regulations governing pesticide use do not preclude additional local controls. The explosion in large punitive-damage awards has led the insurance industry and trade groups to seek court protection with the claim that they have been deprived of due process. But the top court has not yet discovered constitutional constraints on the size of damages.

Liberal groups question whether Thomas and other recent nominees have sufficient respect for legal precedent. This lip service to precedent sounds like political sour grapes caused by unhappiness over recent reversals of court rulings on criminal procedure from the 1960s and early 1970s. Yet the Warren Court overthrew precedents that had guided criminal procedures for over a century. The present court has not been inclined to overthrow earlier decisions on business and labor issues, where precedent does help plan for the future by stabilizing the legal environment.

The Supreme Court will continue to exercise a powerful influence on economic and social issues as long as governments affect all aspects of life. It is only proper that confirmation hearings probe a nominee's views on many questions far removed from legal training and legal doctrine.

LIFE TENURE FOR JUDGES IS
AN IDEA WHOSE TIME HAS GONE

Is it wise to continue to give indefinite tenure to judges who are under enormous pressure to help make laws through creative readings of precedents, statutes, and constitutional provisions?

One of our founding fathers, Alexander Hamilton, warned in the *Federalist Papers* that if courts were "disposed to exercise Will instead of Judgement, the consequence would equally be the substitution of their pleasure to that of the legislative body." He felt that lifetime tenure gives judges the independence from politics that would encourage them to interpret the Constitution rather than exercise "will." During the 19th century, Hamilton appeared to be right, because judges generally took a rather limited view of their purpose.

But the behavior of judges changed radically in the wake of the enormous expansion of the federal government during this century. In modern times, thousands of groups look to the government for help in solving their economic and social problems. The legislative and executive branches have responded with massive growth in spending, taxes, and regulations that has created endless litigation in the federal courts.

How can judges, especially justices of the U.S. Supreme Court, take a narrow view of their responsibilities when they are asked to rule on abortion, civil rights, worker discharge, taking of property, AIDS testing, and untold other issues on which important segments of the American people have passionately held views? To expect judges to resist such pressure and adopt a limited interpretation of their power assumes an unrealistic view of human nature.

POPULARITY CONTEST? In his recent, provocative *The Tempting of America*, Robert H. Bork exhorts federal judges to "consider themselves bound by law that is independent of their own views of the desirable...and not make or apply any policy not fairly found in the Constitution or a statute." While he argues persuasively against both liberal and conservative thinkers who want judges to be guided by contemporary beliefs about what is fair, the appropriate economic system, and other principles that can be found in the Constitution only by straining, he does not examine whether judges are likely to follow his advice under present circumstances.

The answer is clearly no, because, like other professionals, judges are influenced by a desire to be popular with friends and the media, by prevailing views of what is fair and the proper role of governments, and by other ideas they have been exposed to as students and practicing attorneys. The mood among all outspoken groups is to immediately look to the government, including the judiciary, to remedy ills and resolve controversial issues. Judges inevitably try to respond to this mood, and lifetime tenure permits them to do so without having to worry about reappointment or forced retirement.

Judicial decisions have a major impact on all segments of the population, so it is certainly proper for the Senate to closely question nominees for the U.S. Supreme Court and other federal courts about their opinions on controversial subjects. That this was seldom done in the past is not a valid reason for the Senate to refrain now when courts are more influential and judges are under pressure to issue decisions that may express only their personal opinions.

That is why Supreme Court nominee David H. Souter should be pressed hard to state his general philosophy and his thinking on important public issues.

RADICAL REFORM. But close questioning of nominees is not enough. I believe that much more radical reform is needed. The resignation of U.S. Supreme Court Justice William J. Brennan Jr. and the anticipated departures of other octogenarian justices make it timely to reconsider the constitutionally stipulated lifetime tenure of federal judges. I say this because the judiciary has, in effect, become a second legislative body. It is time to begin to think about amending the Constitution to give federal judges fixed terms that could be renewed — or not — when they expire.

Hamilton's discussion in the *Federalist Papers* suggests that many of the founding fathers would have supported fixed terms subject to renewal rather than lifetime tenure if they expected judges to exercise "will" rather than "judgement."

The details of such a major reform would have to be worked out carefully, but federal judges' terms might run for 12 to 16 years — perhaps the latter for Supreme Court justices. Even 12 to 16 years extends well beyond even a two-term President's ability to make appointments and often beyond the period of the subsequent President. An appointment needs to be long enough to insulate judges against momentary whims of the electorate, yet it also needs to give Presidents the opportunity not to reappoint judges who are ill or incompetent, who issue outrageous opinions, or who use unreasonable interpretations of statutes and the Constitution to oppose consistently popular views of the vast majority of the people.

It is necessary to control the enormous power exercised by a small group of men and women over the lives of the American people.

THE COURTS SHOULDN'T
BECOME PINK-SLIP POLICE

The Montana Supreme Court recently upheld a state act, the only one in the nation, that forbids companies to fire workers without showing what's termed "good cause." Whether a business can do so is determined in court when suits are brought by discharged workers.

Although the Montana statute greatly limits damages and excludes recovery for emotional distress, the statute as a whole is a mistake. Discharge of employees should continue to be at the discretion of employers—in legal jargon, "at will" or "no fault"—unless it's limited by explicit union and nonunion contracts and procedures. After all, workers are able to quit without proving their employers engaged in wrongful behavior, except when contracts stipulate the length of service.

U.S. companies and workers in most industries are facing severe competition from goods produced elsewhere. It's an especially bad time to saddle such businesses with inefficient employment practices that raise costs and lower profits in the short run but mainly harm workers in the long run.

Economic efficiency requires that management retain most of the power to determine which workers are best-suited to a company's needs and to fire workers who don't get along with others or produce enough to justify their salary. The result is usually appropriate levels of employment and pay if employers have to compete for workers. With competition, employees can move to other companies if they're not earning as much as they're worth. And businesses with a reputation for fair treatment are able to attract a higher-quality and more loyal work force.

RARE CASES.   Some workers are laid off when the economy is depressed or their companies run into trouble. Others are fired for unsatisfactory performance soon after they start working. Studies show that the great majority of workers who lose their jobs find new ones quickly at comparable pay and seldom litigate their discharges.

Wrongful-discharge suits are more likely to be brought when new supervisors fire workers with whom they don't get along and who have seniority, when management decides to restructure employment, or when new bosses conclude that some workers are overpaid. The bringers of such suits typically are discharged workers who remain unemployed for a long time and have to take substantial cuts in pay to get new jobs. They tend to be older employees with seniority. Many of these suits appear to be brought in hopes of getting an out-of-court settlement from a management that fears a jury will be sympathetic toward a discharged older worker.

In the Montana case, the company, a nursing-home operator, claimed the plaintiff was discharged because of a corporate restructuring, while the 46-year-old employee who brought the suit alleged that his firing violated an implied understanding that he could remain at the company for the rest of his working life. The worker's claim appears unlikely, for how many smaller companies in highly competitive businesses with uncertain futures would make such long-term employment commitments?

But behind the Montana case is a rather typical situation: Many wrongful-firing suits are based on the worker's assertion that there was an implicit agreement for a continuation of employment. A court, however, is a poor place to determine when an implicit understanding is expected to give way to the demands of the competitive and rapidly changing conditions that are found in most industries.

POOR SUBSTITUTES. The main role of the judiciary in labor relations should be to preserve competition among employers and to enforce labor contracts. The courtroom is a good place to discover when contracts have been violated or to pinpoint obvious examples of discrimination by race, gender, or religion. But juries and judges are poor substitutes for competitive employer evaluations of worker productivity. Why waste considerable resources on litigation that makes little economic sense and introduces further uncertainty into employee-employer relations?

Rather than laws requiring employers to prove employee "fault," workers need to have clearly stated rules about severance conditions, especially pay, in the event that they're fired. Such rules are now explicit in most larger companies, and it might be useful to require all businesses to have them. But some congressmen and state legislators have been eager to go much further and pass politically appealing and vague laws about wrongful discharge. Legislation in some European countries is even more extreme and flatly denies the employer's right to fire workers, except for the most blatant behavior.

Wrongful-discharge laws illustrate a tendency in the U.S. for legislatures to pass the buck to the judiciary, which must then interpret and implement policies that have little economic justification and are ill suited to courtroom adjudication. Communist countries are learning the value of relying on competition rather than rules to regulate economic affairs. Why are capitalist countries forgetting this rudiment?

PART 11

Capitalism and Other Economic Systems

The collapse of communism is the most significant political and economic event of the past half century. It is unassailable proof that capitalism with free markets is the most effective system yet devised for raising both economic well-being and political freedom. "Chicago" economics argued this for many decades, but it took the dramatic end of communism to show that what is true in theory and in the past also holds in the modern world.

We use Argentina's experiences during the past 100 years as one of the most instructive examples of the advantages of free markets over centralized government control. That nation thrived for several decades at the end of the nineteenth century and beginning of the twentieth century through open trade and other free-market policies. But then its government began extensive interventions in the foreign trade and domestic markets that resulted in the decline in the ranking of Argentinean per capita income from among the top ten nations to below the top 50. Fortunately, in 1989 the Menem government began a return to the earlier free-market policies. Argentina's performance since then has been excellent, aside from the difficulties caused by the "Tequila effect" from Mexico's devaluation.

In the late 1950s Cuba and Taiwan were both small agricultural export-oriented islands with reasonably high per capita incomes by world standards at that time. Cuba then began its experiment with communism, while Taiwan moved toward much freer markets. The results speak for themselves. Cuba remained agricultural-based and incomes rose rather slowly, while Taiwan became industrial-based, rich, and a major exporter in world markets. Is better evidence needed on the superiority of markets over central planning? Unfortunately, an unrepentant Fidel Castro continues to force communism down the throats of a frustrated Cuban population.

During the early days of the rebellion against communism in Eastern Europe, many persons looked toward Sweden as a role model for a "middle way," as we discovered on a trip there in the early 1980s. We decided to write a column to dispel the mistaken impression that Sweden had found a successful middle way, for its economy performed very badly since 1970 mainly due to rapid expansion of taxes and government spending. This essay was widely distributed in Sweden by free-market groups.

Sweden has continued to flounder economically during the half-dozen years since that was written. Nevertheless, many voters in central and eastern European countries apparently still long for a "middle way" since they returned to power only partially repentant ex-communists.

CAPITALISM

DEMOCRACY IS THE SOIL
WHERE CAPITALISM FLOURISHES BEST

Some advocates of free markets in the Soviet Union, Poland, and other Eastern European countries are calling for strong central authority under Gorbachev, Walesa, or others to drive their nations toward market economies. They fear that ethnic rivalries, endless debates, and special interests could prevent elected democratic governments from making the necessary changes. But market systems are far more likely to flourish in a democracy.

I believe authoritarian measures to impose the free-market system contain the seeds of their own failure. The case for them is based partly on the experiences of Chile, Hong Kong, South Korea, and Taiwan. General Augusto Pinochet force-fed Chile drastic free-market reforms that eventually transformed that country into the most vibrant economy in South America. Authoritarian leaders in Taiwan and South Korea radically altered their economies from dependence on protected domestic markets toward active exports in the world market. The Hong Kong government, appointed by Britain, used free-market principles to convert a minor group of islands into an economic powerhouse.

These examples, however, are special cases. Strongman regimes that centrally directed their economies into poverty are far more common. In Argentina, the disastrous policies of Juan Perón and the military rulers who followed him reduced that once wealthy country to Third World status. Castro in Cuba, Mao with his great leap backward, Burmese generals, Khomeini's Moslem fundamentalists in Iran, Nasser in Egypt, and dictators in most of Africa have firmly guided controlled economies toward ruin.

INTENSIVE CONTACTS. Quantitative evidence on the economic growth since 1960 of more than 60 countries confirms that authoritarian regimes usually perform worse, not better, than democratic ones. My own calculations show that democratic countries grew more rapidly in per capita incomes in the three decades, even when compared with other countries that started with similar per capita incomes and education levels.

Clearly, central political authority and dictatorial power don't add up to a sure-fire remedy for an ailing regulated economy. English historian Lord Acton's famous remark that "power tends to corrupt, and absolute power corrupts absolutely" says in a nutshell why dictators do not like the decentralized economic power found in a competitive market economy. It takes away some of their own power.

Given the technological base and interdependence of the modern economic world, when authoritarian regimes promote competition and markets, they encourage political opposition. A vibrant economy nowadays is built on strong education, advanced technologies, exports, joint ventures, domestic subsidiaries of multinational corporations, and frequent contacts with people in other nations. Students must be sent abroad to study engineering, science, business, and economics. Executives have to travel to arrange sales and financing, while technicians and executives from other countries must visit to buy goods for export and to sell imports. These intensive contacts with other countries through trade and training help undermine support for totalitarian political leadership.

'FIFTH COLUMN.'   The educated classes who are so important to an advanced economy want to be able to say and read what they desire and to vote for whom they wish. Otherwise, many engineers and other skilled personnel who go abroad for training do not return, partly out of dissatisfaction with the restrictions on freedom at home.

Dictators may try to hold on to power by quarantining their economies and citizens against contacts with rich countries. Stalin and Mao kept their countries isolated, while Albania, Cuba, Iraq, and North Korea allow their citizens few opportunities to study or interact with Westerners. Nevertheless, information about what is going on elsewhere gets through by way of the Voice of America, the BBC, smuggled videotapes, and other channels. Even Albania is beginning to experience the uprisings that have transformed the rest of Eastern Europe.

It would appear that the very process of becoming a modern economy that is integrated into world commerce generates a kind of "fifth column" opposed to authoritarian rule. Consequently, it is no accident that Pinochet and South Korea's Chun Doo Hwan stepped down, or that Chile, South Korea, and Taiwan have taken serious strides toward democratic government. Nor is it surprising that opposition to the Shah was led by Iranians studying, working, or exiled in the U.S. and Western Europe, and that the international boycott that cut off foreign capital and export markets has begun to bring an end to apartheid in South Africa.

It's clear, then, that when authoritarian regimes promote economic progress, they are likely to lose their authority, because students, intellectuals, and executives will demand greater civil and political freedom. No wonder the KGB, military members of the Communist Party, and bureaucracy of the Soviet Union are so fearful of market-oriented reforms.

MEMO TO MANDELA:
DON'T EQUATE APARTHEID WITH CAPITALISM

It is an ominous sign that Nelson Mandela and the African National Congress have reaffirmed their commitment to nationalize South African mines, banks, and many other industries and to expand government control over the private economy.

When they took that position a few years before the party was banned in 1960, capitalism was seen as passé. Leftwing ideology was riding high in the world, and many nations embraced socialism and central planning. Communist economies were growing rapidly and appeared to point the way to the future. Almost all the newly independent nations of Africa followed the examples set by China and the Soviet Union, rather than Japan and the U.S., and chose public ownership of vital industries and detailed regulation of the economy.

South African black leaders should ponder the miserable performance of these controlled economies on their continent. During the past 30 years, annual growth in per capita incomes has averaged no more than one-third of 1% for the 27 sub-Saharan African countries with national income data (South Africa is excluded). In more than half of these countries, per capita income actually fell.

Civil wars, tribal and ethnic conflicts, and changes in world prices, as well as mismanagement, contributed to this abysmal record. But even countries such as Nigeria did badly, despite abundant supplies of oil and other natural resources that rose steeply in price during the 1970s. Nigeria's heavy government involvement in the economy exacerbated conflicts among groups, as taxes, regulations, and other political actions were used to discriminate against Chinese and Indian traders, and various minority black ethnic groups.

COMPETITIVE EDGE.   The ANC has equated the repressive policies of the South African government with its capitalist system. But capitalism usually expands opportunities for unpopular minorities—be they black, Chinese, or others—through competition among employers for their labor and by giving minorities freedom to start their own businesses. Even in South Africa, business groups commonly opposed apartheid and many other forms of discrimination; the main support for separatism came from white workers, unions, and consumers. In recent years, many leading businessmen have come out in favor of granting the ANC its major requests, such as universal franchise and the end to discriminatory legislation.

White businessmen in South Africa are no fairer-minded than white workers, but the workers have feared competition for jobs from blacks and an end to their privileges. Businessmen have preferred less regulation because profits decline when employers are not allowed to hire cheaper black labor and when shopkeepers must turn away blacks.

The history of discrimination against blacks in South African mining, an industry the ANC still wants to nationalize, is revealing about the economic and political alignment of different groups under capitalism. The late distinguished South African economist, William H. Hutt, showed in *The Economics of the Colour Bar*, published in 1964, that diamond and gold mines rapidly increased their employment of blacks and other minorities in the latter part of the 19th century and the beginning of this one. Blacks even began to advance into supervisory positions.

LEGAL CHEATING.   White miners disliked the competition and turned to the political process for help. They succeeded in getting passed a series of laws that discriminated against nonwhite workers. The Colour Bar Act of 1911 reserved many mining occupations for whites and limited the number of blacks in mining to a fixed multiple of the number of white foremen. The second Colour Bar Act in 1926 and other legislation went beyond mining and prevented blacks from accepting lower wages to gain a foothold in various white-dominated occupations and industries.

After World War II, South Africa officially adopted its policy of apartheid, or separate development of the races. However, this policy has never been successfully implemented because many more blacks have continued to work in white areas than are allowed under apartheid. Profit incentives help explain why. Smaller businesses in cities and other areas reserved mainly for whites have been especially willing to hire blacks without asking questions about whether they were legally permitted to live and work there. Blacks have preferred to work in white areas because wages are much higher than in black territories.

The evidence from many countries shows that private enterprise and the quest for profits not only promote economic growth but also open up opportunities to unpopular minorities. By contrast, socialism and laws that discriminate in favor of politically powerful groups have retarded the economic progress of most blacks in Africa, possibly even more than the nasty discriminatory legislation of South Africa. To exact revenge for the damage inflicted by decades of apartheid and other vicious forms of government discrimination, the ANC leadership is considering socialist policies that would probably worsen the economic position of most blacks.

SURPRISES IN A WORLD
ACCORDING TO ADAM SMITH

The privatization revolution sweeping the world surely ranks among the remarkable economic developments of the past few decades. What started in the 1970s and early 1980s as right-wing Thatcher and "Chicago boys" policies in Britain and Chile has spread to most countries, and it has caught on no matter what the economic views of the parties in power. The motivation is similar everywhere: the large deficits and inefficient employment and investment practices of state-run enterprises.

Privatization reverses the trend toward state ownership that began at the turn of the century in Britain, France, Germany, and other advanced industrial nations. At first, mainly railroads and local transport were nationalized, but eventually states took over companies in the electric-power and other sectors. It is easy to forget that the British renationalized the steel industry a mere 25 years ago and Mexico expropriated its banks in the early 1980s.

During most of this century, public-enterprise orthodoxy held that the state should run many industries because their presumed economies of scale make them "natural" monopolies. The evidence until the mid-1970s did not clearly show the inferiority of public management. For example, per-capita incomes in communist countries with pervasive state enterprises appeared to grow as rapidly as in other economies.

WORLD LAB.   But the past couple of decades have provided decisive results. The apparently good communist record has turned out to be built with mirrors, and the collapse of communist governments has revealed their basket-case economies. West German taxpayers have discovered to their dismay that most factories in East Germany, the supposed industrial powerhouse of the communist bloc, are worthless in the modern economic world.

The privatization movement itself has become a rich source of data, for it is now possible to compare companies before and after they become private in various parts of the world, in countries with different cultures and stages of economic development. The World Bank recently issued preliminary reports by its economists on the effects of a dozen privatizations in Britain, Chile, Malaysia, and Mexico. They studied three telecommunications companies, four airlines, a gambling company, and four others.

In 11 of the 12 cases, privatization raised the sum of the welfares of workers, consumers, investors, and the government sector. Improvements in productivity and better investments led to large gains in nine cases. Profits expanded in each episode, and although consumers were sometimes hurt by price increases, they also benefited in other cases from price reductions. Since few of the companies in this study had serious competition, private ownership appears to perform better than public management—even without the pressure from strong competition.

Sharp cutbacks in employment generally contributed to the growth in productivity, which supports the common belief that public enterprises usually have too many employees. Yet, surprisingly, workers as a group generally benefited from the privatizations through higher wages for those who remained employed, generous severance pay, and employee participation in stock-ownership plans.

ROADBLOCKS. Despite the snowballing privatization programs, political pressure from unions and other special interests has prevented the sale of many companies still run by government. For instance, all countries maintain a state monopoly of regular mail delivery. This never made much sense, and makes none at all in view of the World Bank study: The report implies that productivity is likely to be higher with a privatized mail service, even if it has considerable monopoly power. And the growth of electronic- and express-mail rivals means that private mail delivery will have much competition. A second example: The school system is everywhere a fully subsidized, government-run organization. The voucher movement in the U.S. aims to privatize schools, but neither President Bush nor Governor Clinton is advocating school vouchers or other forms of privatization.

In Italy, the inefficient industrial giant Instituto per la Ricostruzione Industriale remains a public enterprise, overseeing a number of state holdings. Many insurance companies, banks, and energy companies have also stayed public. France badly runs its major computing and car companies, Groupe Bull and Renault, along with its coal industry, banks, and other companies. Czechoslovakia is the lone regime of the former East bloc that is moving rapidly to privatize its bloated state sector. Britain sold off over 1 million housing units, but the government still owns one-quarter of the housing stock. Oil production is a state monopoly in Mexico, Norway, Venezuela, all the Middle East countries, and elsewhere.

Adam Smith persuasively argued more than two centuries ago that private ownership is essential to promote the wealth of nations. The evidence fully demonstrating this point has finally become so powerful that only dyed-in-the-wool socialists continue to believe that extensive government ownership of industry is a prelude to anything but economic disaster.

ECONOMIC SYSTEMS

ARGENTINA'S WELCOME TURN
TOWARD THE OPEN ROAD

In trying to console a young man who feared that England was ruined by its defeat at Saratoga in 1777, Adam Smith said: "There is a great deal of ruin in a nation." During the past 60 years, Argentina has severely tested this assertion with disastrous economic policies promoted by governments of all political stripes. At the invitation of a private Argentinian foundation, I recently traveled to Buenos Aires to better understand the lessons of the Argentine experience.

At the beginning of this century, Argentina attracted large-scale immigration from Italy, Spain, and Eastern Europe because its per capita income ranked among the 10 highest in the world. But after its unparalleled fall in economic standing, more than 70 countries now have higher incomes.

In the 1930s, driven by populist sentiment and the advice of prominent Latin American economists, Argentina began to abandon the open economy and free-market policies that were responsible for its prosperity. High tariff walls were erected to shield domestic companies from international competition. The state nationalized most heavy industry, regulations and price controls became pervasive, and unions dictated policy on labor issues. Successive governments resorted to the printing press rather than taxation to finance growing public expenditures, so hyperinflation began to destroy the economy in the 1980s.

DOLLAR DAYS. When Carlos Saúl Menem of the Peronist party was elected President in 1989, Argentines and the international business community prepared for the worst. Instead, Menem firmly supported the efforts of Domingo Cavallo and other economic ministers to control inflation and dismantle state management of the Argentine economy. To open the economy to global competition, tariffs have been drastically cut. In a little over three years, most state-owned enterprises have been privatized, including telephone, gas, and airline companies. And the government recently proposed selling 50% of the giant state oil company. Price controls over most products have been eliminated, and regulations have been sharply reduced. To allay fears about inflation, the number of pesos that can be issued has been tied to dollar reserves. Transactions no longer have to be in the Argentine peso, and dollars freely circulate among businesses and consumers.

In a private meeting, President Menem told me that he will continue to back free-market policies. Despite his Peronist protectionist background, he proudly said the speed of reform was unprecedented.

In my view, Menem's support is explained by the shadow cast over all of Latin America by the free-market reforms of Argentina's small neighbor, Chile. Under the authoritarian rule of General Augusto Pinochet, Chile dismantled controls that had been similar to Argentina's. Domestic companies were forced to compete on the international market through steady reductions in tariffs, which have now reached a uniform 11%—among the lowest anywhere. Chile sold off many state enterprises, including airline and bus systems, electric power and telephone companies, and large quantities of state land. Here I must declare a personal interest: Many of these reforms were carried out by former economics students at the University of Chicago.

GROWING FAST. These and other free-market reforms under Pinochet have been maintained by the government that was elected democratically in 1989. As a result, Chile's growth in the past 10 years has surpassed that of all other Latin American countries. The reforms also helped diversify the economy so that the importance of copper in total exports is now far below its 80% share in the early 1970s.

There is a sharp rivalry between Chile and Argentina, and Argentines tend to regard themselves as culturally superior. Thus, many Argentines concluded that if Chile could succeed by adopting market solutions, they could, too—and do a better job. Paradoxically, Chilean businessmen and companies have become major participants in Argentina's newly privatized economy.

Although Argentina's economy has begun to grow, it is not yet out of the woods. To increase the value of the state-owned companies up for sale, many of them were given protected monopoly markets. Social Security and other employment taxes and regulations are still much too expensive. Stiff quotas on imported cars and other goods still shelter some domestic producers from competition. A higher rate of inflation than in developed countries has caused the Argentine peso to be overvalued compared with the dollar and other world currencies. Yet a devaluation risks destroying investors' fragile confidence that Argentina will no longer print its way to hyperinflation.

Crucial decisions lie ahead for the Menem government, complicated by congressional elections in October. But most people seem willing to endure hard times to make the future brighter. Reform there, as in the rest of Latin America, now means privatization, freer markets, and democracy. If Argentines continue to follow the trail blazed by Chile, their nation will have a chance to recover the economic standing it had when this century began.

WHEN THE GOING GETS TOUGH, IDEOLOGY GETS FLEXIBLE

The headlong retreat throughout the world from central planning, state ownership of capital, and detailed regulation of economic life is truly remarkable because it is largely being led by parties that have historically abhorred the market economy.

Although the changes in the communist world are grabbing the headlines, similar moves are taking place elsewhere. New Zealand's Labor government has pushed extremely radical free-market reforms. Michael Manley of Jamaica, a pro-Cuba, anti-American socialist during his disastrous first term back in the 1970s, has followed policies sympathetic to privatization and deregulation since the voters returned him to power a couple of years ago. The new President of Argentina, Carlos Menem of the interventionist Peronista party, initially used an economic plan drafted by conservative businessmen.

Nothing shows the flexibility of ideology more than a statement made to me by the director of the department of ideology of the Polish Communist Party. The party was not sure, he said, whether public ownership is an essential part of socialism. When asked about the difference between capitalism and socialism, he said that they were still working on that. What remains of communist ideology if it abandons the belief in the inevitable exploitation of workers under a system of private enterprise? Without that basic principle, socialism would hardly be distinguishable from capitalism.

WRONG BEFORE.   There is not much merit to the claim that the communist world would have given up central planning and state ownership long ago were it not for the influence of Marxist thought. For it did not become clear until recently that communist economies were lagging behind market ones. Indeed, many Sovietologists in the West agreed with Khrushchev's boast that the Soviet Union would bury the U.S. in the race for economic supremacy. There was even serious debate over whether China or Russia would become the dominant economic power. Japan was ignored, and other capitalist economies were considered too weak.

According to the best Western estimates, up to the mid-1970s, Eastern European economies grew more rapidly than did most others and every bit as rapidly as Western European economies. Then, the complexities of centrally planning a modern, high-tech economy apparently slowed down performance. During the past 15 years, growth in the communist world lagged seriously behind growth in the West. The result was that support for central planning and state ownership completely collapsed after little more than a decade of clear evidence of sub-par growth.

True, bureaucrats and workers in cushy positions in the many state-owned companies in communist countries may still resist change out of fear that they will lose their jobs and power. But very little of this resistance depends on ideology. I doubt if more than a handful of people who have lived under communism are intellectually committed to central planning and Marxist economies.

However, many professors and intellectuals in the West continue to parrot Marxist slogans about the exploitation of workers under capitalism. They ignore the obvious fact that workers have done better in material terms under capitalism than under communism, which is precisely the reason for the ferment in Eastern Europe today.

BEWARE SMUGNESS.   Socialism is not the only economic system that must deliver the goods if it expects to receive popular support. For example, if the Iranian and other economies in the forefront of the Islamic fundamentalist revolution continue to stagnate, as I believe they will, blame will be placed on Islamic precepts such as opposition to payment of interest on loans and to managerial positions for women. Before long, these precepts will be replaced by those found in the West, which could culminate in a counterrevolution against fundamentalism itself. Iran already has started to relax its attitude toward the economic activities of women.

By the same token, advocates of markets and private enterprise should not be too smug and self-satisfied, because the present worldwide love affair with free economies is fragile. Remember that the Depression of the 1930s and economic destruction during World War II brought about a seemingly unstoppable movement toward socialism during the 1950s and 1960s. The new attachment to private enterprise will also crumble should another global depression usher in an extended period of economic stagnation.

The lesson is that while economic ideologies may exercise an excessively rigid influence on public policies when decisive evidence on economic growth is unavailable, they are quite flexible and will change when the evidence changes. As the rejection of capitalism after the Great Depression illustrates, sometimes there is excessive reaction against economic systems that are experiencing only short-term difficulties. By and large, the world is much better off because the organization of economic activities depends a lot more on results than on preconceived philosophies.

Capitalism vs. Communism:
Why It's Still No Contest

A jest current during the 1960s in the West had it that an optimist was someone who learned Russian, while a pessimist was someone who learned Chinese. This quip was a reaction to the cold war, to the rapid economic growth of the Soviet Union during the 1950s and 1960s, and to a belief that communism in China was producing even more impressive economic miracles. Nikita Khrushchev boasted that Russian output would catch up with America's before long. Many defenders of the West conceded the growth race to communism, but they averred that freedom was worth the sacrifice in output.

However, in a 1962 book for the National Bureau of Economic Research, *The Growth of Industrial Production in the Soviet Union*, the late Professor G. Warren Nutter swam against the current by arguing that Soviet economic growth would slow down soon after the Soviet Union rebuilt following World War II and introduced modern Western technology. Sovietologists attacked Nutter's study as politically motivated and flawed by ignorance—he was a conservative and an amateur in Soviet studies who did not even read Russian. But he turned out to be right.

At the end of May, Ronald Reagan will become the first President to go to Moscow since Richard Nixon in 1972. The Soviet Union he will visit is still poor, with a per capita income that is well below half that of America's, and the gap is widening. Although U.S. per capita income has grown by 2% per year in the 1980s, some recent Soviet estimates indicate that per capita income for the period has not increased. The available evidence also shows that the West greatly overstated China's growth. Per capita consumption in China barely increased from 1957 to 1977. Few other communist regimes bested Russia and China, and several did much worse.

CHINESE FLAVOR. Perhaps because of the very poor and erratic performance under Mao, China was the first large communist country to implement radical economic reforms. It eliminated collective farming in the late 1970s and early 1980s in the largest of all privatization programs. Reform of its industrial sector came more slowly, but here too China has decentralized and now allows greater scope for private enterprise.

Gorbachev's *perestroika* (economic restructuring) and the current ferment in the Soviet Union are partly inspired by China's successful reforms. They are also inspired by the remarkable economic growth achieved by Japan, Taiwan, Korea, Singapore, and Hong Kong with few natural resources. The success of these decentralized free-enterprise economies has done more to discredit central planning and state ownership in Third World countries than have the billions spent by the U.S. on influencing world opinion.

Private-enterprise economies rely on competition to determine prices, wages, and profits. Competition gives consumers, workers, and owners of capital financial incentives to allocate their spending, labor, and capital to the sectors where they are valued the most. In a famous debate among economists in the 1920s and 1930s, some socialist theoreticians accepted the crucial importance of balancing supply and demand through competition. But they claimed that centrally planned economies can use supply and demand more effectively than capitalist economies to guide resources to their most productive uses.

MIXED ISSUES.   However, the record of communist countries indicates that centrally planned economies have inherent weaknesses that cannot be corrected by tinkering with the system to try to mimic or improve the competitive forces operating under capitalism. These countries have learned the hard way that the connection between capitalism and efficiency is not the utopian fancy of ivory-tower economists but a conclusion drawn from centuries of experience in all parts of the world.

One major problem with central planning is that political and economic issues get mixed together. For example, planners must sell food cheap to placate urban consumers, maintain oil and gas prices at less than world levels to satisfy the military's desire for low-cost fuel, and prevent managers from firing incompetent workers because that smacks of capitalism. In planned economies, political considerations are so powerful that they frequently overwhelm the dictates of supply and demand and cause serious mismanagement of labor, capital, and raw materials.

The rapid growth of political involvement in the economies of the U.S., Canada, and other Western countries since World War II also sharpened the conflict in the West between the pursuit of efficiency and the political appeasement of special interests. Fortunately for these countries, however, political control over economic decisions is still much weaker than in communist countries.

It seems unlikely that communist countries will be able to provide much leeway for the forces operating under capitalism without abandoning central planning. Meanwhile, few can doubt that communist economic philosophy is retreating throughout the world and that communism has lost Khrushchev's race between competing economic systems.

Too Much Government
Is What Ails the Third World

Why have only a few Third World countries managed to grow out of poverty? The welfare of the Third World depends far more on the answer to this question than on trade and budget deficits or the crash of stock markets. A prescription for growth would be a wonder drug for alleviating the economic misery in most countries.

World per capita income has grown more rapidly since the late 1950s than during any period of comparable length in modern history. However, the enormous variance in growth rates among countries is as disturbing as the rapid average growth is impressive. For every Taiwan, South Korea, or Japan with incomes that grew more than 6% a year, there is a Bangladesh, Bolivia, Ghana, Jamaica, or Poland that made little progress or even declined.

An example is Jamaica, a country I have recently visited. Thirty years ago Jamaica appeared to be a more promising candidate for growth than either Taiwan or South Korea. Taiwan feared invasion by China, and South Korea was recovering from a devastating war. By contrast, after independence in 1962, Jamaica became a vibrant democracy with competing parties and peaceful elections, and initially it had a small and efficient government sector. Jamaica has wonderful beaches and is close to a large tourist market. It has natural advantages for growing sugar, coffee, and many fruits and vegetables; has good reserves of bauxite; possesses an energetic and reasonably well-educated labor force. Per capita income probably did grow more rapidly in Jamaica than in Korea and Taiwan during the 1950s and early 1960s. But since then Jamaica and many other promising countries have dismal records.

WORK ETHIC. The economic failure of many countries is sometimes attributed to easygoing Caribbean, African, Latin, or other temperaments unconcerned with material aspects of life. I believe that any national or ethnic "temperament," if it exists, is vastly overrated as a factor in economic development. Economic incentives in the form of higher wages and promotions for superior work do wonders in converting apparently lethargic people into hardworking, ambitious ones. The same Jamaicans and Poles who do not seem ambitious when in Jamaica and Poland work hard and do very well if they migrate to the U.S. Even some Chinese, whose appetite for hard work is legendary, were lazy and apathetic in mainland China during the Cultural Revolution.

The great success of several Asian countries is sometimes credited to a culture that encourages frugality and saving for the future. But Taiwan saved little until financial reforms around 1960 released interest rates and provided additional incentives to save. Other countries, too, would become good savers with a stable economic environment and with capital markets that pay and charge competitive rates of interest.

The pervasiveness of government and opportunities for private initiative are far more important than temperament and culture. Some countries have grown with large government sectors, but extensive state ownership of business and widespread controls over wages, prices, and other economic activities generally do act as a brake on economic progress.

Unfortunately, Third World countries accepted the ideology prevalent among many intellectuals during the 1950s and 1960s: that growth is best promoted by state ownership, controls, and policies to encourage import substitution. Many newly independent countries took over failing private businesses, nationalized banks, protected domestic companies against imports, ran up large foreign debts, and heavily regulated the private sector. In Jamaica, the ratio of government spending to gross domestic product ballooned from 25% in 1970 to almost 50% in 1980, while regulations became pervasive.

ABOUT-FACE. At first, South Korea and Taiwan adopted this ideology, but they quickly did an about-face and began to encourage exports and the growth of private companies. Other Third World countries are finally rejecting earlier policies and are trying to stimulate the private sector and individual initiative.

The slow progress in countries that are reforming their economies—this includes such giants as China, India, and the Soviet Union as well as small nations such as Jamaica—illustrates that it is far easier to regulate and extend the state's reach than to deregulate and retrench. When the state becomes heavily involved in the economy, many special interests from the bureaucracy, business, labor, and consumer groups come to rely on state benefits. Of course, they actively oppose reforms that curtail their subsidies.

After a shift toward freer markets, economies often do worse before they do better, partly because of the need to circumvent opposition. Although reforms began in 1980, Jamaica's income started to rise rapidly only recently. It remains to be seen whether electorates in Third World democracies and governments in totalitarian states will have the patience to persist in freeing their economies in the face of initial hardships and opposition from entrenched interests.

THE LESSONS OF CUBA AND TAIWAN

Social scientists are at a serious disadvantage when it comes to testing theories. Unlike physicists, they can't perform large experiments that isolate some variables while holding others constant. Instead, they are forced to rely on the natural experiments generated as a byproduct of historical change, experiments that may span many decades.

Over the past quarter century, Cuba and Taiwan have provided an excellent "experiment" on the effectiveness of different systems in promoting economic growth and social progress. The governments of these two islands have pursued widely divergent policies—with very different effects. Cuba has been an enthusiastic proponent of Marxism and centralized direction of economic affairs, while Taiwan adopted a decentralized private-enterprise system.

Despite some obvious differences, Cuba and Taiwan were surprisingly similar in the late 1950s. Both were densely populated islands with hostile giant neighbors that threatened invasion and cut off trade. Taiwan became home to the Nationalist Chiang Kai-shek government after the Communists won the civil war in China in 1949. Fidel Castro led the revolution that ousted the Batista government in 1959. In those days, both islands had relatively high per capita incomes.

Cuba's main exports were sugar and tobacco, while Taiwan's were sugar and rice. Both went through massive economic and social upheavals as Taiwan absorbed almost 2 million refugees from mainland China and Cuba lost several hundred thousand, mainly skilled, emigrants.

FREE TO TRAVEL.   The results of this test are now in. By virtually every economic and social measure, Taiwan has either greatly surpassed Cuba or done at least as well. The stellar economic record of Taiwan is well-known. It became a world-class industrial power after per capita gross national product grew by a remarkable 6.4% annually from the late 1950s through the early 1980s.

Taiwan has relatively little income inequality, and the health and educational levels of its population have risen rapidly. Admittedly, Taiwan has only one major political party—and it's hardly a political democracy. Yet its citizens are free to go abroad and can move at will within the island—freedoms not available to much of the world's population. There is also considerable freedom to criticize economic and social policies.

The economic situation in Cuba is harder to gauge, partly because prices are not closely related to production costs, and embarrassing data are sometimes withheld or published late. As a result, published estimates of Cuba's economic growth differ enormously. The study *Revolutionary Cuba* by Claes Brundenius of Sweden, offers the most credible, optimistic assessment. He concludes that during the past 20 years income inequality has been reduced substantially, and large improvements have been made in health and education. He estimates that real per capita GNP grew by 2.7% per year from 1961 to 1980, roughly equal to the average rate of growth for the rest of Latin America.

Jorge Perez-Lopez of the Labor Dept. questions these estimates. In a forthcoming book, Perez-Lopez argues that from 1966 to 1980, Cuba's economic growth rate averaged only half as much as Brundenius suggests.

HEAVY SOVIET AID.   No matter who is correct, Cuba's performance pales by comparison with Taiwan's. Even if we accept Brundenius' numbers, from 1960 to 1980 per capita income in Cuba grew less than half as fast as per capita income in Taiwan. Sugar still accounts for more than 70% of Cuban exports, and the Soviet Union buys much of Cuba's sugar at many times the world price. Indeed, the Cuban economy continues to be supported by heavy Soviet aid, whereas U.S. economic assistance to Taiwan ended in 1965. Unlike the Taiwanese, Cubans cannot easily leave, nor can they readily criticize the economic and social policies of their government.

What can we learn from this tale of two islands? One important lesson is that a decentralized private-enterprise system is a far more powerful engine of progress than a centralized Marxist system is. Comparisons of the artificially partitioned countries, West and East Germany or South and North Korea, teach the same lesson.

A second lesson is more readily provided by Taiwan and Cuba. Form and substance often get confused when people evaluate economic systems. Fidel Castro is a charismatic leader who is popular throughout the world. He overthrew a dictatorship, thumbs his nose at the U.S., and speaks eloquently about the plight of the oppressed. By contrast, the leaders of Taiwan have been dour and lacking in personality. Most countries deny Taiwan official political recognition. And many also restrict imports from the island.

Castro's personal appeal leads to sympathetic evaluations of Cuba's performance. Certainly, there are legitimate grounds for arguing over Cuba's economic performance under Castro. But there is no room to doubt that Cuba's record is less impressive than the rhetoric of its leader and that it is also far inferior to Taiwan's.

TRANSITION OUT OF COMMUNISM

RULE No. 1 IN SWITCHING TO CAPITALISM: MOVE FAST

The very different paths taken toward market economies by the ex-communist nations provide a remarkable laboratory on how to transform centrally planned economies. The evidence from these experiments is loud and clear: It's best to introduce large changes rapidly without waiting to discover the "right" sequence of reforms. Moving quickly allows the transformation to be guided mainly by the spontaneity of innovative market forces rather than by government planners or technocrats.

Still, many economists advocate a slow, systematic pace. They believe that the ordering of reforms toward a market economy makes an enormous difference to the long-term success of the process. Yet history offers little guidance on what the proper sequence might be, simply because of the unprecedented scale of transformation required by the collapse of communism. Nor does economic theory provide an adequate blueprint. Markets have their own dynamics that are often impossible to anticipate.

Prime Minister Vaclav Klaus of the Czech Republic has led the highly successful transformation of that nation. In a recent book of essays, he emphasizes that an overhaul should be done rapidly and with a "mixture of intentions and spontaneity." Similarly, Adam Smith more than 200 years ago in his *Theory of Moral Sentiments* argued that important public policy changes cannot be planned the way a master chess player moves pieces around on a chess board.

FOOT-DRAGGING. Rapid reform can also prevent interest groups who thrived under communism from organizing effectively to slow and even derail the transition to a market economy. These groups were on the defensive for a while after the old regimes toppled. But now, most of the current leaders in the ex-communist countries are former communists, and these politicians are slowing the pace of change by appealing to the elderly and others hurt by the capitalist upheaval.

Telling evidence that foot-dragging on the road to the free market hurts is not hard to find in Eastern European nations. Take their experience in privatizing state-run companies. Hungary, Poland, Romania, and most other ex-communist nations have held off privatizing thousands of midsize and large enterprises until government "restructures" employment, overhauls accounting practices, and changes the product mix at the various concerns. Since getting companies "ready" takes time and runs into opposition from management and workers, government-directed privatizations have been slow and inefficient. In Poland, despite its quick shift toward sensible fiscal and monetary policies, almost half of its large enterprises remain in government hands. Unemployment is well over 10%, and only a few companies are traded on its stock exchange.

BRILLIANT IDEA.   In sharp contrast, the Czech Republic acted before political opposition could organize and relied on market forces. Klaus and a small team of associates came up with the brilliant idea of selling vouchers at a nominal price to the general public that they could use to bid for stock in different companies. In just three years, the Czechs used vouchers to privatize over 2,000 enterprises, and they have essentially completed this stage of the transformation process.

Despite a few scandals and other problems, the Czechs succeeded beyond even the most optimistic expectations. Many mutual funds and other financial intermediaries formed to buy vouchers and bid for shares. These investors gained a voice in guiding the newly privatized enterprises. A sophisticated stock market developed where shares in hundreds of companies are traded every day, not the few dozen traded on other exchanges in central Europe. The Czech Republic has the lowest unemployment rate in Europe, even though most of its privatized companies have been restructured by their new owners.

The success of the Czech approach encouraged the Russian Republic to introduce a slightly modified version of the voucher plan in 1992. It took Russia only two years to privatize some 14,000 midsize and large companies, and by June, 1994, more than 85% of the country's industrial labor force was working in the private sector. Russia has not yet achieved macroeconomic stability or a stable currency, but it has managed to quickly shift an economy dominated by state-owned companies to a system of private ownership.

Abundant evidence from the ex-communist countries indicates that it is a mistake for government bureaucrats to attempt to fine-tune the transformation to market economies. It is much better to unleash the spontaneous creativity of businesspeople, workers, and markets.

THE LAST THING THE SOVIETS NEED
IS A FOREIGN-AID PACKAGE

Western Europe, the U.S., and Japan should not cave in to pressure to provide economic assistance to the Soviet Union and countries in Eastern Europe. Also, they should stop making loans and grants to other countries, too, aside from those for humanitarian purposes.

Economic aid gives governments breathing room to postpone the crises—such as occurred in Argentina, Mexico, and the Communist countries—that force reluctant governments to take unpopular remedial measures. Thus foreign grants delay privatization programs, reduction of subsidies, cuts of import barriers, and cutbacks in other excessive and misguided controls that are largely responsible for bad economic performance.

A Soviet aid package would go to the central government, or to the governments of the Russian and other republics, not to the fledgling private sector and would-be entrepreneurs. Economic aid is usually channeled through other governments because it is far easier to negotiate with them than to help companies and families directly.

SHORT-TERM FIX. Since too much government is typically the problem, not the solution, economic aid is counterproductive. Governments use it as a short-term fix to keep economic pressure on longer. This prolongs problems and does little to solve long-term woes. Any country that institutes significant reforms and creates a healthy economic environment will have scant trouble attracting loans and investments from Western companies and banks.

Some economists recommend that grants and loans to the Soviet Union be tied to reductions in their spending on nuclear and conventional weapons. But the country's dismal economic performance is already forcing large military cutbacks. In spite of any such link to arms cuts, if aid from abroad reduces the economic pressure to reform, spending on arms could be greater than would have occurred without the assistance.

The harmful effects of economic aid are not confined to formerly Communist countries, as can be seen from the experiences of Egypt and Israel, the two biggest recipients of assistance from the U.S. during the 1980s. Egypt is a miserably poor country that has taken only a few steps to throw off the socialist shackles imposed by Gamal Abdel Nasser during the 1950s and 1960s. It continues to have a huge and corrupt government sector, enormous subsidies of food and other goods, a weak private sector, and subsidized, state-run companies that are sheltered from competition with better products made elsewhere.

Although Israel grew very well until the 1970s, since then it has been bogged down with unemployment, much slower growth, and periods of hyperinflation.

Relative to the size of its economy, Israel probably has the largest public sector in the free world, with government-run companies dominating many industries, extensive wage controls, and restraints on foreign competition. Israel would have gone much further toward reducing the government's stranglehold were it not for continued generous economic assistance from the West, especially the U.S. Some Israelis have been so exasperated that they are calling for greatly reduced dependence on foreign aid.

ROADS AND BRIDGES.   The stories are similar for India, Pakistan, and the African countries that have enjoyed—if that is the word—easy access to Western largess. Their bad economic performance also is traceable to large subsidies to favored interest groups and too many controls over the private sector.

The U.S. alone provides more than $1.5 billion of aid annually through such international organizations as the African Development Fund, the International Development Assn., and the World Bank. These agencies usually lend or give money to governments, not to the private sector. Obviously, some grants and loans from countries and international organizations have been spent on socially useful infrastructure, such as roads, bridges, airports, and sewage systems. But these account for a small share of all assistance. And since spending on infrastructure is only a minor part of the budgets of recipient countries, they could easily spend more without foreign help if they had the will to do so.

Economic assistance is supposed to do for Eastern Europe and the Soviet Union what the Marshall Plan did for Western Europe after World War II. But the problems then were very different. Europe was prostrate from the war and needed time to restore the basically private enterprise systems of the prewar era.

What Eastern Europe needs is just the opposite: constant pressure for a radical shift away from government control and toward freer markets. Just as the Marshall Plan helped restore the old system to Western Europe, similar assistance to the East would help maintain the excessive government direction and management of their economies.

The truth that a child's initiative is weakened when parental help is too readily available applies to economies as well. They are more likely to prosper when they are forced to put their own houses in order and have to bear the economic burden of the transition toward productive market economies.

WHY COLD-TURKEY CAPITALISM
WOULD BE BEST FOR THE SOVIETS

I recently was invited to Moscow to explain the principles of market economics to government officials, young economists, executives of state enterprises, and private entrepreneurs. I stressed that market systems rely not on edicts and regulations, but on the people themselves looking out for their interests. The bedrock of the market system—that shopkeepers and consumers, workers and management, or suppliers and customers do not voluntarily make a deal unless both sides expect to benefit—rubs against the Soviet grain. Most Soviet edicts against "speculation" apply to ordinary business transactions.

So far, despite all the talk about *perestroika,* government officials haven't done much in the Soviet Union. To move quickly in the right direction, Moscow's control of wages, working conditions, and consumer and producer prices, including the currency-exchange rates, must be replaced by thousands of voluntary transactions in labor, product, and foreign-exchange markets.

Soviet leaders can learn from the Polish reforms that began in January of this year (1990). The government boldly abolished regulations over practically all prices, including the exchange rate. Unfortunately, Warsaw made a major mistake by freezing wages. This wage policy had much to do with Poland's subsequent decline in industrial output and with the recent defeat of the government. The Polish reformers apparently forgot that wages, like prices, need to be freely set by market forces in order to allocate efficiently a country's most precious resource, human capital.

A major problem for Moscow is the prevalence of state ownership. No system can provide proper economic incentives unless people have the right to buy, own, and sell property as they see fit. Self-interest and voluntary transactions cannot be successful motivators when most property is owned by the state. But private property has been the bogeyman of socialist theorists, and many Soviet leaders cannot easily set aside what they regard as the evils of private ownership.

SIMPLE GIFTS. Yet rapid progress is impossible unless the Kremlin's enormous assets are privatized quickly. Land, housing, retail establishments, and many services can become private property right away. They can simply be given to the present occupants: farmers, tenants, or employees. It would even be technically possible to privatize many large factories quickly. The workers or the population at large can be given ownership vouchers, or shares, which could be bought and sold. The initial distribution of shares is not so important: Before long, controlling interests will be bought by groups that are able to run the factories efficiently.

Political considerations explain why privatization programs usually take so long. Resistance comes from managers and employees who fear for their jobs, bureaucrats who worry about loss of power, and consumers who believe that assets will be given away cheaply to political cronies or foreign companies.

Soviet officials told me that people have been slow to buy farms and other businesses in recent experimental programs, because seven decades of communist rule have weakened their desire or capacity to own property. Can a few decades of communism have changed the age-old desire to own land?

A more likely explanation: skepticism that ownership might not last. The Soviet people have not forgotten how Stalin seized peasants' land. In addition, price controls and central allocation of materials still hamper the operation of most businesses. I am sure that when prices are determined by market forces, when businesses can bid for supplies, and when confidence grows that ownership is secure, interest in private property will pick up.

SAFETY NET.   Many in the Soviet Union and elsewhere in Europe fear that monopoly price-gouging will be common if prices and wages are set free. The monopoly problem can be diminished by encouraging competition in product and labor markets. Any person should have the right to start a business and produce whenever he or she wishes without going through endless red tape. Workers must be able to move anywhere and take any jobs they can get without a bureaucrat's permission. And if the government follows an open trade policy and allows ruble earnings to be converted into hard currencies at market rates, foreign companies would also compete against domestic companies by exporting to the Soviet Union, and through joint ventures there.

To help break the inflationary pressure resulting from printing too many rubles, the government must stop financing deficits of state enterprises: These should be forced to make it on their own until they are privatized. Some of the funds should be spent instead on a safety net for workers and retirees who suffer drastic cuts in their standard of living during the transition period.

There is no way to transform the Soviet command system painlessly into an efficient economy, or to transform it overnight. But the duration of the pain can be reduced and the benefits increased if the essentials of a market system are quickly put into place. During the crucial next 12 months, we will learn whether the Soviet government and people have the will to do what is necessary.

AS ROLE MODELS GO,
SWEDEN IS SUSPECT

As the newly emerging democracies in Central Europe prepare to throw off state ownership and central planning, some reform-minded leaders are casting about for a "third way." They are looking for an alternative to what they see as the excessive materialism of market-based economies. The potential role model usually invoked is Sweden.

I believe this would be a serious mistake. True, Sweden has long been seen as a wealthy market economy that nevertheless has little inequality and a network of government programs to protect the weak and poor. I can remember being greatly impressed as a teenager by journalist Marquis Child's popular 1936 book

Sweden: The Middle Way, which made Sweden sound like paradise. Unfortunately, if it ever was a paradise, it seems to have fallen from grace.

The good habits and deep respect for the work ethic slowly built up in Sweden during the previous century have been gradually eroded by the adverse effect on incentives of 25 years of expanded taxes and regulations. Unfortunately, the new governments in Eastern Europe don't have such a cushion, for 45 years of Communist mismanagement have already eroded habits of work discipline in those countries.

In the century preceding 1960, Sweden's performance was exceptional for a country with fewer than 9 million people. It had one of the fastest-expanding economies and relatively little inequality. Swedish companies such as Asea, Volvo, and Ericsson became major players in international business.

QUICK FINNISH.   But during the past 15 years, Sweden's growth in per capita income has been far less than the Organization for Economic Cooperation & Development average. Twenty years ago, many Finnish workers were drawn to Sweden by its much-higher incomes. Now, most of them have returned home, since Finland's per capita income has been growing fast and may well surpass Sweden's before the century is over.

I believe that Sweden's performance has deteriorated mainly because of the rapid expansion in regulations and in the share of national income spent by central and local governments. This share rose from about 45% during the early 1960s—only moderately above the average in other market economies—to 67% in 1986, which is the highest in the Western world. By contrast, the Finnish government continues to spend little more than 40% of its national income.

The huge government sector in Sweden imposes an enormous burden on taxpayers. Until a couple of years ago, the marginal income tax rate exceeded 60% for most middle-class families, and it was over 80% for many of them. Swedish voters have begun to recognize that tax rates are too high: Political pressure forced the government to support legislation that reduces the top marginal income tax rate to 50% by 1991, and has lowered the share of income spent by the government to about 60%.

During the 1970s and 1980s, Sweden introduced very generous retirement and health benefits, lengthy paid leaves after workers became parents, liberal rules on taking days off when one is too sick to come to work, and many other types of transfer payments. In addition, union and government policies sharply lowered differences in pay by education level, job experience, and other measures of worker productivity.

LOTS OF LEAVE.   Under these conditions, work effort and investments in human capital are bound to suffer. The average Swedish worker was out sick for almost a month in 1988—and received full salary for all sick days. On a typical day, almost one in four employees is absent from work because of reported illness, parental responsibilities, study leave, or any of the many other reasons that entitle a worker to stay home. Swedish women are much less likely than American women to work full time, and Swedish men work many fewer hours per year than American men. Why put in a lot of effort at work when it is possible to get paid for staying home, when better jobs don't have much higher wages, and when taxes absorb practically all of any increase in pay?

On a recent trip to Sweden, I encountered a good example of these effects on incentives. Graduate students in economics take an average of 8 to 10 years to finish their doctoral studies, compared with 4 to 5 years in the U.S. The reason: The Swedish equivalent of an assistant professor earns only a little more after taxes than graduate students do with their generous government fellowships. In the U.S., once economics students receive a doctorate and take a full-time job, their incomes more than triple.

The Swedish government taxes new businesses heavily, but it provides many loopholes for large companies. This explains why some large companies continue to do well in the international market. But Sweden can't get back on the road to rapid economic growth as long as taxes take more than half of national income and the country retains the many regulations and programs that discourage hard work and acquisition of skills.

Present-day Sweden is not a good role model for countries that want to greatly improve the living standard of their average citizens.

WHY SOLIDARITY MUST PLAY POINT MAN FOR ECONOMIC REFORM

Few people in Eastern Europe still believe in a socialism that requires state ownership of most property. Many of the Solidarity leaders I met on a trip to Poland in June want an economic system based largely on private initiative. Even a high-ranking member of the Ideology Dept. of the Polish Communist Party made the remarkable statement to me that "public property is not the essence of socialism." Therefore, with enough determination, Solidarity can substantially free Poland's economy during the honeymoon period of the new Parliament. Hungary has already taken several steps to extend greatly its private sector.

Without freer foreign-trade sectors, domestic reform cannot succeed in small countries such as Poland and Hungary, which are heavily dependent on exports and imports. The Polish zloty is obviously greatly overvalued at the official rate of about 800 to the dollar, and I urge the new government to abolish the official rate and float the zloty freely. The unofficial rate, to some extent already a de facto floating rate, has risen recently to more than 4,500 zlotys—a measure of how unrealistic the official rate is.

Floating rates, when combined with moderate tariffs and quotas, force internal prices of tradable goods to conform to world prices. In particular, competition from imports would allay the fears of some Polish economists that freeing internal prices would give too much monopoly power to state enterprises in such heavy industries as steel.

The U.S. and other countries should help Poland and Hungary reduce their large hard-currency debt, but President Bush and Alliance leaders are right to ask the Poles to solve most of the debt problem through their own actions. The fall in the unofficial zloty rate over the past couple of years has already greatly stimulated Polish exports. Floating rates, combined with much greater reliance on private enterprise, would boost exports from both countries a lot more. The resulting current-account surpluses would cut their foreign debt in a way that encourages rather than discourages future commercial loans.

GRIM OPTIONS. State-enterprise deficits in Poland and Hungary must be reduced quickly to help bring public spending and inflation under control—especially in Poland, where the annual inflation rate recently exceeded 100%. These enterprises can be forced to do better by cutting their subsidies and giving them greater control over prices and employment, though eventually many state enterprises will have to be privatized or shut down.

In Poland, private companies are limited to a few sectors, mainly agriculture and repairs, and to a small scale. But they should be allowed to enter most industries, issue publicly traded stock, and hire as many workers as they wish. Competition would determine the form and the scale appropriate for different activities.

Many advantages of private enterprise can be realized only if the state reduces its regulation of prices and production methods. Market forces of supply and demand, rather than state regulation, should determine the prices of most goods and materials, wages, and employment. Explicit subsidies, when politically necessary, should replace the present wasteful system of queues, rationing, and large hidden subsidies to state enterprises in the form of free rents and low interest rates.

RIOT FEARS. Almost all economists in Poland and Hungary recognize that radical reforms are desirable in the long run, but many believe they're neither politically nor economically feasible in the near future. They fear protests and riots if many people lose their jobs, if food prices and rents rise rapidly, and if other privileges under the present system are quickly abolished. They may be right, but I agree with those leaders of Solidarity who are convinced that only dramatic steps toward a freer economy have a decent chance of succeeding and that gradual change gives the opposition too much time to sabotage reform.

Slow progress gives groups who would lose special privileges more time to mobilize opposition. Hungary and Poland, the Eastern bloc countries in the most favorable position politically to radically change their economies, have their best shot at a successful transition away from state socialism with quick and forceful reform toward private enterprise and open foreign trade.

Some Solidarity leaders argue that workers and consumers will accept substantial unemployment and other hardships in the short run if they are convinced that state socialism is being replaced by a system that rewards honest effort and initiative. It's a sad commentary on socialist economies that the most ambitious men and women of Poland leave to work in West Berlin, in the U.S., and elsewhere because their own manufacturing and service sectors provide so few incentives for hard work.

Reasonable people can disagree about the precise sequence and timing of steps to free the Polish and Hungarian economies. But no one can doubt that their success in shifting from state-directed to free economics will influence greatly what happens in other Eastern bloc countries, including the Soviet Union.

PART 12

International Trade and International Agreements

The rapid expansion of international trade during the past several decades not only promoted economic growth, but it greatly reduced the disadvantages of being a small nation since the huge international market is now an excellent substitute for large domestic markets. This has meant that ethnically diverse groups with a history of political and economic conflict are no longer forced to coexist in the same country in order to gain the economic advantages of a larger scale.

We show that many very small countries have been doing extremely well by taking advantage of the international market for their goods. These examples encouraged the splintering of several nations where ethnic groups had coexisted in an uneasy truce, such as Czechoslovakia into the Czech Republic and Slovakia, and Yugoslavia into Bosnia, Croatia, and Serbia. It also fueled demands for greater autonomy and even independence by many ethnic groups in other countries, including French Canadians, Catalonians, and Kurds.

An essay in this part criticizes the plan of the European Union to replace the German mark, French franc, and other member currencies with the ECU, a common currency for all member nations. Since the international market in capital has made possible effective competition between currencies of different nations, we propose to go in the opposite direction and increase rather than eliminate the competition among European currencies.

A necessary first step to encourage greater competition is to allow all member currencies to be acceptable as legal tender within each country. Then greater competition would help control the inflationary issue of money by reducing government revenue from erratic or rapid expansion in their money supply. If monies competed, governments that badly handled their control over currency would find that they no longer have a protected monopoly. Families and businesses will shift out of their "own" currency and into competing ones when their "own" begins to depreciate significantly in value. This proposal was reprinted by newspapers all over Western Europe and elicited many letters both pro and con.

A series of international conferences in recent years, some under United Nations sponsorship, discussed how to protect world resources against population growth and environmental damage. But despite the reckless alarm sounded by the biologist Paul Ehrlich and others, no one has shown that population growth has major harmful effects. After all, even though world population grew rapidly and doubled during the past 50 years, per capita incomes in poor as well as rich countries expanded at their most rapid rate in many centuries. Moreover, we show that continuing economic growth and improved education rapidly bring down birth rates without compulsory sterilization and the other draconian measures advocated by scare-mongers.

Environmental disasters such as Chernobyl do have major international consequences. However, the environmental movement has reduced its credibility by relying on very weak evidence to forecast calamities that have not happened, such as Ehrlich's forecast of mass starving in the 1970s from population growth.

Another example of environmental oversell is the repeated allegation that carbon dioxide pollution of the world's atmosphere is creating a disastrous greenhouse effect. Despite the success of international conferences in having controls placed over the industrial production of CO_2, the scientific evidence of a forthcoming calamity is not convincing. We argue that there is no reason to do much yet; the best policy is continued monitoring of global temperatures and other possible evidence of significant warming.

INTERNATIONAL TRADE

FORGET MONETARY UNION—
LET EUROPE'S CURRENCIES COMPETE

On a recent trip to Spain, I was frequently asked by journalists and the business community about the plans to introduce in January, 1999, a common European currency, probably to be called the Euro. Although not an expert on monetary matters, I took a strong stand against this plan. I believe that a much better approach would be to increase, not eliminate, competition among European currencies.

Monetary union would be supported by a majority of the populations of all 15 member nations if they were confident that the future European central bank will behave like the German central bank. However, they fear that monetary policies of the European Monetary Union (EMU) will emerge from compromises and political infighting among members with different monetary and fiscal needs. A recent poll found that 73% of Germans "don't think" that a common currency could be as stable as the German mark, which probably explains why German Chancellor Helmut Kohl did not risk a referendum on the EMU among the German people. Under pressure from Euroskeptics within the Tory party, Britain appears to have decided to delay its entry in the EMU until after 2002.

SHARING POWER. Some Germans have already voted against the monetary union with their assets: The Swiss franc has been rising in value relative to the mark because Germans have shifted assets into Swiss franc-denominated assets, even though these pay lower returns than German assets. The franc will remain an independent currency because the Swiss have chosen to stay out of the European Union. German government bonds that mature after 1999 now command an interest premium as a result of the uncertainty about monetary union.

Plans for the EMU are most popular in Greece, Italy, Spain, and other countries that have had greater inflation and more erratic monetary and fiscal policies. Fortunately, there is a way to help the populations of these nations without punishing Germans and others with strong monetary policies. Rather than centralize power in the hands of a single central bank, a much better approach is to decentralize monetary power further by encouraging competition among monies.

An important step in this direction would be for each member nation of the EMU to permit the taxes it collects to be paid either in its own currency or in the mark, British pound, French franc, and possibly several others. Shopkeepers, employees, and suppliers would also be allowed to accept payment for their goods and labor in any of these monies. Market forces of supply and demand would determine the exchange rates between the currencies, so that the unpopular ones would lose value.

DEFICIT CHECK. Competition among currencies helps discipline irresponsible governments by reducing their incentive to increase their money supplies and to finance budget deficits arising from dubious expenditures, such as inefficient state enterprises. Currencies will fall in value if governments try to inflate their way out of fiscal difficulties, since individuals and businesses will shift transactions into stabler monies.

Presumably the population of each nation will continue to prefer its own money. But as they gain familiarity with the new system, consumers, workers, and businesspeople will make greater use of the monies with more stable purchasing power. This approach allows Germans and others to rely mainly on their own currencies as long as they continue to perform well.

After an adjustment period, the transaction costs of dealing in several currencies is likely to amount to only a minor inconvenience. After all, many shops at international airports now accept over a dozen monies, and they find that only slightly more inconvenient than taking American Express, Eurocard, and other credit cards. Moreover, businesses can economize on these costs if they wish by choosing to deal only in one or two monies. A dominant currency could emerge from the free choices of the different populations as they concentrate their transactions in the stablest currency, be it the mark, pound, or even the lira, if it is well-managed.

Nations from all over the globe have discovered the enormous advantages of competition over monopoly in the production of steel, telecommunications, air travel, and other goods and services. The European Union has completely ignored this lesson in its plan for a common money. But it may not be too late to reverse direction and thereby encourage greater competition between European currencies in order to penalize and discourage irresponsible government-based monetary and fiscal policies.

THE COMMONWEALTH'S BEST CHANCE
IS COMPETITION

Competition among the member republics of the Commonwealth of Independent States offers a great opportunity for economic progress and political freedom. The most significant and lasting gain from the collapse of the Soviet Union could be competition among different policies and institutions that were not possible before. The competition would exert pressure on each republic to put its house in order as it tries to attract domestic and foreign investment and the allegiance of its citizens.

Just as consumers benefit when companies vie for their patronage with different goods and services, so too would the various ethnic groups in the CIS be better off if they could choose among different governments, each with its own policies and programs.

Competition among the republics' economic and political policies would be especially effective, of course, if the CIS allowed free movement of goods, capital, and people among member states. If that were possible, and if economic growth were lagging in parts of the CIS—possibly because of foolish policies—both people and capital would leave for better conditions in economically successful republics. Migration would also be unusually heavy out of states that oppressively restricted individual liberty: Thus, freedom to migrate would help protect minorities against the most outrageous forms of discrimination. For example, if Azerbaijan discriminated against its Armenian minority, some of them might well migrate to Armenia or another republic.

OPEN BORDERS? It was no accident that essentially all communist countries sharply limited the right to emigrate, especially for younger skilled workers. These governments were well aware of the power exercised by those who can vote with their feet. When it first became possible to leave the German Democratic Republic less than two years ago, a mad exodus by tens of thousands of young people precipitated the government's collapse.

Although the republics may agree, however, on free trade in goods and capital, free migration of people throughout the Commonwealth and coordination of many other policies is not likely in the near future. The republics fear domination by the Russians, and there is intense hostility among other ethnic groups. Such frictions were exacerbated by Stalinist policies of moving large populations forcibly in and out of different regions. But the example of growing cooperation among formerly unfriendly countries of Western Europe suggests that cooperation among the former Soviet republics may grow over time.

Some economists point to the European Community's agreement to have a common currency by the end of the century and lament that ethnic rivalries and fears will prevent the Commonwealth from replacing the old ruble with a new ruble. But I believe that a common money should be allowed to evolve and should not be imposed at the beginning. Supporters of a uniform currency usually-ly assume that it will be well-managed, with a low rate of inflation and with easy convertibility into hard currencies. But what if it were badly controlled, like the Argentinean peso or the ruble in recent years? The fact is that poor management of money has been far more common than good management.

MINTING IT.   It is better to let republics issue their own currencies, if they want to, and reap the benefits of competition among different currencies. Thus, if the Russian ruble were strong and the Ukrainian money were not, companies and households in Ukraine would naturally use Russian rubles in some of their transactions.

Flight from their money puts pressure on governments to behave more respon-sibly, while the advantages of having a currency widely used encourage more sensible monetary policies. A republic might even control the amount of its money by linking it to hard currencies, the way the Hong Kong dollar has been pegged to the U.S. dollar.

Obviously, competition among the republics in nuclear weapons would not be a good thing. It is essential that the new Commonwealth establish controls and safeguards over the thousands of nuclear warheads in its territory. The West would like to see many of these destroyed and could offer disarmament and other inducements to the republics with nuclear weapons.

It may seem unlikely that small republics, such as Moldova and Armenia, can compete effectively in the world economy if the CIS does not guarantee free trade among its members. But countries with relatively small populations, often domi-nated by a single ethnic group and with their own languages and currencies, have done well on average. Their per capita incomes have grown faster than average in recent decades. International trade and flows of capital give producers and consumers in small economies access to large markets and products from elsewhere.

The economic viability of small-fry nations helps explain why Yugoslavia and other countries with strong ethnic rivalries will also dissolve into loose confed-eracies or completely separate nations. They too will gain from competition among different states, as people choose with their wallets and their feet.

LET THE CHEAP DOLLAR
CURE THE TRADE DEFICIT

A popular view in recent years is that traditional remedies such as a falling dollar can no longer remedy the U.S. trade imbalance. The large budget deficit, high wage rates, and a hollow manufacturing base, plus the trade barriers of other countries, have supposedly sapped the curative powers of a cheaper dollar.

In response to an earlier column of mine advocating free trade (BW—July 20), even sophisticated executives challenged me to name domestic companies that would benefit from a weaker dollar. Fortunately, the economic world has not turned upside down. Producers and consumers, including foreign consumers, still respond to incentives. The evidence strongly supports the old view that many U.S. companies increase their sales abroad when the dollar is much cheaper.

Skepticism about the efficacy of the dollar's devaluation grew when the American trade deficit increased from $80 billion in 1984 to about $150 billion in 1986 and 1987 despite a sharp fall by the dollar against the yen, mark, and other currencies. However, the deficit has finally begun to fall in recent months and should continue to recede now that American companies have had time to develop the marketing skills and other knowhow to sell abroad.

FALSE PERCEPTION.   Manufactured exports from the U.S. reversed the decline of previous years and are 60% higher than their low point in 1983. Imports have stopped rising, and the January figures indicate they have started to fall. Even the Japanese trade surplus has narrowed for 10 consecutive months as imports from the U.S. and elsewhere have climbed.

The perception that manufacturing in the U.S. is incurably sick stems from the 25% drop in manufactured exports during the early 1980s and the rapid growth in imports of cars, steel, and other goods. But the 40% rise in the value of the dollar from 1980 through 1984 greatly raised U.S. costs of production compared with costs in Japan and other countries. The dollar's fall during the past two years has offset the previous rise, and now many domestic companies are quite able to compete with the strongest companies abroad.

Protectionists who support the Gephardt amendment to the trade bill and other restrictive measures claim that much of the trade deficit is due to low wages and the exploitation of labor in foreign countries, dumping by foreign companies, and restrictions on imports of American goods. U.S. wages are now much lower than West Germany's and about the same as Japan's, yet Germany has one of the largest surpluses with the U.S., and Japan has the biggest. Although workers do get much lower wages in Taiwan and South Korea, the U.S. trade deficit with those countries grew rapidly during the past few years, despite the fact that their wages increased much faster during the same period.

DUMPING CHARGES.   Why should Americans complain if foreign companies want to give "aid" by dumping—selling goods in the U.S. below cost? One answer is that the companies will raise prices sharply once domestic competition is forced out of business. Yet documented cases of such predatory pricing are rare, despite the charges of dumping whenever foreign competitors offer better prices and quality.

For a decade, Zenith Electronics Corp. persisted in an unsuccessful suit that charged Japanese television manufacturers with dumping. Although practically all domestic manufacturers of TVs were driven out of business by cheap imports, prices of imported televisions did not go up. Strong competition between foreign producers and potential competition from domestic companies invariably prevents predatory price increases. To curb the alleged dumping of computer memory chips by Japanese manufacturers, the Reagan Administration reached an agreement with Japan in 1986 that helped Japanese producers reduce output. As a result, prices of memory chips to American companies have more than doubled.

Japan, Korea, Taiwan, Germany, and most other countries that trade with the U.S. do use tariffs, subsidies, and quotas to restrict imports and stimulate exports. These harm their consumers as well as American businesses. Yet the trade barriers of Japan or Germany may be no greater than those of the U.S., with its quotas on cars, steel, textiles, sugar, and other imports, and its subsidies to exports through the Export-Import Bank and programs to sell accumulated agricultural surpluses. Nor can the trade barriers abroad fully explain American deficits. Japan, for example, reduced trade barriers during the past few years while its surplus with the U.S. was rising.

Consumers in all countries gained access to a rich variety of goods at reasonable prices during the past 30 years as international trade expanded rapidly. The growth of world trade is the outstanding example of international cooperation during the period since World War II. Will Congress jeopardize these achievements with additional legislation to punish countries that produce goods wanted by American consumers?

SEEING THROUGH THE RHETORIC ON "FAIR" TRADE

Many people objected to my recent column (BW—May 25) in which I advocated an open-trade policy for the U.S. and opposed punitive measures against such countries as South Korea and Taiwan that have trade surpluses with America. Critics differed with me in part because these countries impose tariffs and other import restrictions. Korea and Taiwan use quotas and more subtle devices to keep out many imported goods and to encourage exports. Korea, for example, still does not import cars, and Taiwan severely limits rice imports.

Consumers in other countries, along with exporting industries in the U.S., would gain, no doubt, if America's threats to retaliate against Korea and Taiwan forced them to reduce their trade barriers. Unfortunately, however, a policy of retaliation against "unfair" trading practices usually makes matters worse, because it becomes an excuse to protect domestic producers against stiff foreign competition.

Companies and workers camouflage their desire to raise profits and earnings with calls for retaliation against alleged dumping and exploitation of cheap labor by foreign producers. The results are higher prices to domestic consumers and protected, less efficient domestic industries that do not need to compete against the new products and improved efficiency of foreign producers.

Consider the long litigation by Zenith Radio Corp. against Japanese companies selling TV sets and other electronic goods in the U.S. Zenith contended that the Japanese conspired to sell these products below cost. Such a policy seems to benefit American consumers, but Zenith claimed that eventually U.S. companies would be driven out and the Japanese would raise prices to monopoly levels. The Supreme Court in 1986 rejected this implausible story. It concluded in effect that the Japanese produce these goods more efficiently. Most claims by domestic companies that foreign producers are dumping goods or are using predatory pricing policies are no more valid than the one by Zenith. Unfortunately, some of these claims have induced America to restrict imports.

SLIGHTED INTERESTS.   We also can presume that "fair" trade is hardly the goal of Representative Richard A. Gephardt's (D-Mo.) proposal to ignore the multilateral nature of trade among countries and seek bilateral trade balances with individual countries. Nor can it be called fair trade to put pressure on Korea, Taiwan, and other Asian countries to shift purchases of such goods as industrial chemicals, trucks, and capital equipment from Japanese to U.S. companies—especially when Japanese products are cheaper and of better quality.

It is a commonplace that political decisions in economic matters usually slight the interests of consumers and cater to specific groups of workers and producers. The reason is clear: The typical consumer is harmed only a little by higher prices of particular goods, but companies and their employees benefit greatly from much higher prices for their products. Trade policy is especially likely to ignore consumer interests since foreign producers have only a small voice in domestic politics. The political power of American industries is evident from the stiff quotas on cars, steel, TV sets, clothing, and many other imports—quotas that significantly raise the prices of these goods to U.S. consumers.

For centuries domestic producers in many countries have exaggerated the unfair practices of other nations to obtain protectionist legislation that helps them prosper at the expense of consumers. More than 200 years ago, Adam Smith criticized trade retaliation in his *The Wealth of Nations:* "It seems a bad method of compensating the injury done to certain classes of our people [because of import duties by other countries] to do another injury to ourselves, not only to those classes, but to almost all the other classes...."

HISTORY LESSON.   In an excellent essay on reciprocity and fairness in trade, Professor Jagdish Bhagwati of Columbia University notes a fascinating parallel between Britain at the end of the 19th century and the U.S. today.

Protectionists attacked Britain's free-trade policy with the same arguments now used to justify the campaign for retaliation. The great Prime Minister William Gladstone defended free trade with telling attacks on the motives behind demands for retaliation. But even his oratory and prestige could only delay the collapse of Britain's free-trade policy. Eventually many British industries succeeded in getting tariffs and other barriers imposed on competing imports.

Free trade helped Britain become the premier industrial nation during the second half of the 19th century. Although many factors contributed to its decline as an economic power in the 20th century, surely part of the blame goes to workers and owners who hid their desire for protection behind demands for retaliation. The U.S. should learn from Britain's experience and reject the seductive calls for a level playing field and fair trade. The gain to American consumers and to the efficiency of the U.S. economy are reasons enough for following an open-trade policy—even when other countries do not.

TAIWAN AND KOREA SHOULD BE PRAISED, NOT PUNISHED

If it were to become law, the Gephardt amendment to the House of Representatives' trade bill would put pressure on countries running trade surpluses with the U.S. to reduce their exports and increase their imports. While the amendment obviously would affect Japan, it would probably hurt South Korea and Taiwan the most. On a recent trip to these two countries, I found much unhappiness at this kind of pressure from the U.S. Forcing Korea and Taiwan to reduce exports to this country would not solve America's balance-of-payments problem, but it could seriously harm their economies. Almost 50% of Taiwan's exports and 40% of Korea's go to the U.S. In 1986 the U.S. merchandise trade deficits with Korea and Taiwan came to $7 billion and $15 billion, respectively. Although these figures are large compared with trade with those countries, they are a small fraction of the total U.S. 1986 trade deficit of $150 billion.

There were no complaints about unfair trade practices of Korean business before 1982, when Korea regularly ran trade deficits with the U.S. Surely, Korea and Taiwan did not discover only in the past few years how to dump goods or exploit cheap labor in order to undersell U.S. companies. Indeed, since 1980 real wages have grown by more than 35% in both Korea and Taiwan, compared with little change in this country.

No, the growth in exports from Korea and Taiwan is not the result of exploitation of cheap labor, dumping, or other unfair competition. It is due to the outstanding performance of their economies, which are still surging ahead. In both countries the annual rate of growth in real per capita income during the past 25 years exceeded 6%. Even though they import essentially all their oil and other sources of energy, both Korea and Taiwan weathered the enormous rise in energy prices during the 1970s remarkably well. Taiwan's per capita income now ranks among the highest in the world, and Korea has grown from a very poor country to one of the richer ones. Yet Taiwan's income inequality is among the lowest in the world, and Korea's is modest by the standards of other developing countries.

These outstanding records underscore the power of a private economy and the potential of judicious foreign aid. In the early 1950s, South Korea was prostrate from the Korean War, and Taiwan had to absorb 2 million soldiers and officials from mainland China. After receiving much aid from the U.S., both governments wisely shifted in the late 1950s from tight control over protected domestic markets to export-led private-enterprise systems. At that time, this shift was unprecedented in Third World countries, where the prevailing ideology was socialism and government management. Reliance on the private sector permitted their businessmen and labor forces to take advantage of the enormous opportunities in the world marketplace.

Of course, the Chinese and Korean cultures emphasize hard work and stoicism, but these qualities do not explain their success completely. North and South Korea have the same culture, and the North was richer and more industrialized before the war. The North, however, made the grave error of borrowing a centrally directed economic system from its Soviet and Chinese Communist allies. This mistake provides a rare and decisive "natural" experiment in the social sciences. The contrasting results in North and South Korea leave no room for doubt about the important role of private enterprise in South Korea's development: Per capita incomes were about the same in 1960, but now they are some two to three times larger in the South. Although South Korea's hesitant steps toward free elections and greater democracy are well publicized, its political climate is like a breath of freedom compared with the oppression in the North.

PUNISHING CONSUMERS. No country worries about the so-called excessive exports and unfair trade practices of North Korea, Cuba, India, and many other countries that use cheap labor. And surely the U.S. does not prefer the mismanaged economies of such dependent states as North Korea and Cuba, which require frequent bailouts from Russian and Chinese allies. By contrast, South Korea and Taiwan grew into strong economies and are able to stand on their own feet. Moreover, why should American consumers be punished along with Korea and Taiwan because the Hyundai is the most popular new car to be imported in recent years or because Taiwan manufactures cheap and popular vcRs and clothing?

The remarkable economic success of South Korea, Taiwan, and the other newly industrialized countries of Asia has done far more to spread the virtues of private enterprise in the developing world than have the preachings of the U.S.

and all the economic theories. Congress and the President should certainly reject the Gephardt amendment and ease the pressure that has forced Korea and Taiwan to agree to hold down exports to the U.S. Otherwise, such pressure may disrupt the economies of these remarkable examples of success through reliance on private enterprise and the world marketplace.

SMALL NATIONS

WHY SO MANY MICE ARE ROARING

The number of nations has almost doubled in the past 50 years, to 191 independent states. The usual explanations for this multiplication, which invoke nationalism and ethnic conflicts, overlook a major reason: The economic cost of independence has been sharply lowered by the rapid growth in post-World War II international trade.

Since 1950, world imports and exports have grown at the remarkable rate of about 10% a year. Even during the economic slowdown of the 1980s, international trade continued to expand at 5% a year. The result has been that prosperity no longer depends on a large domestic economy—even tiny nations can hawk their wears in the world market.

In fact, small nations now have advantages in the competition for international markets. Economic efficiency requires them to concentrate on only a few products and services, so they often specialize in niches that are too small for large nations to fill. Because small economies are more homogeneous, they tend to suffer less from internal clashes among special interests. Their goods and services tend to be less exposed to trade quotas and other restrictions, since they don't amount to enough to affect producers in large countries. Similarly, economic alliances such as the European Union are usually willing to accept a smaller nation as a member since its production would not pose much of a competitive threat.

There are many examples showing that smallness is no handicap. Mauritius, a 720-square-mile island nation in the Indian Ocean, has prospered by concentrating on clothing exports and tourism. Hong Kong and Singapore began their striking economic development by specializing in importing goods from all over the world and distributing them to other parts of Asia. The volume of imports and exports in both still greatly exceeds their gross domestic product because so many of their combined 7.3 million inhabitants are active in trading goods and financial instruments.

The tiny principality of Monaco has 5,000 citizens and about 30,000 residents squeezed into 368 acres. It has carved out several specialized niches of international trade, becoming a gambling center and tax haven for tennis stars, businesspeople, and others with high incomes who move there to escape income and estate taxes. Outsiders have bid up land values to more than six times comparable property on French soil only a few years away.

Hong Kong, Singapore, Monaco, and Mauritius are not just isolated examples of the advantages of being small. Since 1950, real per capita GDP has risen somewhat faster in smaller nations than it has in bigger ones. I believe that the economic success of many small economic entities has contributed to bringing into the open some of the festering ethnic conflicts that already existed around the world—between Kurds, Serbs, and Croats, as well as English- and French-speaking Canadians. Many of these groups concluded that they can do better economically by becoming separate nations and concentrating on producing specialized goods and services for the world economy.

SUCCESS STORY.   Less than two years ago, the former state of Czechoslovakia split into the Czech Republic and Slovakia. Both have had problems adjusting to independence—they had been closely linked by a common currency, trade, and interrelated production networks. But the Czech Republic is already booming: It has low unemployment, rapid growth, and a reorientation of exports toward Western nations. Many Czechs opposed the breakup, but their economy became stronger when it was separated from a poorer Slovakia. That new nation will also thrive after privatization forces its entrepreneurs to learn how to compete in world markets.

The Czech experience can be duplicated in many other nations with ethnic and cultural differences. For example, it is commonly believed that French-speaking Quebec will decline economically if it separates from the rest of Canada. That view ignores the role international trade plays in economic success. After perhaps a severe adjustment period, Quebec could find a prosperous place in the world economy by trading with Canada, the U.S., and Mexico as well as the rest of Latin America. That separation could also help the economies of English-speaking Canada because it would reduce cultural battles and eliminate the confrontations with Quebec over the allocation of tax revenues and government expenditures.

Smallness can be an asset in the division of labor in the modern world, where economies are linked through international transactions. Nationalism is merely riding the crest of world trade to forge new nations.

As Nations Splinter,
Global Markets Are Merging

Antagonistic nationalities pitted against each other in the Soviet Union, Yugoslavia, Iraq, and elsewhere are creating an uproar. Soon, the turmoil may force some of these nations to split into separate states or to form confederations of quasi-independent republics. Yet next year, the economies of 12 Western European states with a long history of political conflict will be merged into a large free-trade area. These divergent movements—toward political fission and toward economic integration—reflect two trends: declining advantages of the large nation-state and increasing gains from access to bigger markets.

Large, centrally run countries have traditionally been better able to deal with foreign aggression, to raise taxes to pay for government services, and to provide open internal markets for trade in goods and movements of people. In *The Federalist Papers*, those were the main reasons cited by Alexander Hamilton in support of replacing the Articles of Confederation, then guiding the newly created United States, with a constitution giving greater authority to the federal government.

But all of Hamilton's considerations have weakened with the passage of time. The military advantages of nations with big populations have been eroded during the past half-century by advances in weapons and the policing powers exercised by the U.S. and the U.N. Economies of scale of larger countries in raising taxes and dispensing subsidies are sometimes used to exploit weaker ethnic and national groups.

ONE WORLD.   The advantages of large internal markets have been offset by trade pacts among independent states and growing trade among all states. International trade has boomed since 1960 as a response, in part, to much lower costs of transporting goods and people, cheap and fast methods of communication, and the multilateral reductions in tariffs that have been negotiated since 1977 through the General Agreement on Tariffs & Trade. These developments have encouraged companies to look for markets and supplies beyond the borders of any single country. Even the huge U.S. market is no longer sufficient to sustain economic growth, which explains why the ratio of U.S. exports to gross national product has tripled since the 1950s.

More than 70 new nations, most of them quite small, have been created since the end of World War II. Despite their size and limited natural resources, growing opportunities to trade with other countries have brought prosperity to some that have promoted exports and imports rather than relying on limited domestic markets.

Singapore's population is less than 3 million, yet its real per capita income has grown by more than 7% annually since the early 1960s—surely some sort of record. Exports of textiles, electronics, financial services, and other goods and services exceed, in value, 150% of the nation's GNP. Taiwan has also achieved extraordinary economic success by exporting more than half its output.

Still, international trade is not a perfect substitute for a free-trade area, since exports must surmount sizable quotas and other obstacles in gaining access to world markets. Free-trade agreements among independent states that are only loosely confederated can overcome these obstacles and give sovereign nations access to much wider markets. Such agreements are easier to reach than political integration: They don't arouse such strong fears of exploitation by powerful nationalities and other interests.

OLD TENSIONS.   By the end of 1994, Argentina, Brazil, Paraguay, and Uruguay are to form a common market that will contain 190 million people and account for more than half the output of Latin America and the Caribbean. The U.S. has concluded a free-trade agreement with Canada and wants to negotiate similar arrangements with Mexico and Chile, although those proposals have encountered strong opposition. Agreements such as these eliminate barriers to trade in almost all goods and services, but they do not address other policies of the countries involved. U.S. negotiations with Mexico won't—and politically couldn't—discuss the clamps by the U.S. on immigration from Mexico.

The European Community will soon have free trade in nearly all nonagricultural goods, unrestricted movement of labor within the 12 participating countries, and limited harmonization of taxes and subsidies. But it is unlikely anytime soon that the EC will achieve a single currency, a single central bank, or common defense and foreign policies, which are the aims of many proponents. The gulf crisis exposed serious differences among members, with Britain and France sending troops while Germany and others stayed on the sidelines. Age-old national tensions between the French and British or between the Germans and their neighbors are too ingrained to be ended by a few decades of good will.

I can't see the pressure for autonomy by ethnic groups in Yugoslavia, Czechoslovakia, the Soviet Union, Canada, Ethiopia, Iraq, or elsewhere slackening. On the contrary, the divergent trends toward greater political autonomy and wider economic alignments seem sure to continue into the next century.

Actually, Small-Fry Nations Can Do Just Fine

When separatists in Quebec, Lithuania, Ethiopia, Sri Lanka, Spain, and elsewhere demand secession and independence, they are often accused of encouraging the formation of states that are too small to be economically viable. But it is not at all clear that on balance large countries have decisive economic advantages.

The average annual growth in per capita income from 1960 to the mid-1980s in the top 50% of countries as measured by population size was no larger than the average growth in the bottom half, and countries with relatively few square miles even grew a little faster than countries with larger areas. Differences in per capita growth rates were also negligible between large and small countries that in 1960 had comparable educational levels and per capita incomes.

These surprising conclusions are based on data compiled by University of Pennsylvania economist Robert Summers and his associates. Not only are growth rates similar, but per capita incomes are also no higher in larger countries. Indeed, countries with either bigger populations or larger areas tend to have slightly lower per capita incomes than smaller countries.

Why should this be? Obviously, small countries are limited by the size of their domestic markets. These are not big enough to permit economies of scale in production of cars, steel, planes, or many other products. Even so, nations can increase their markets through international trade, something that has become easier in recent decades with the rapid growth in world commerce. And small countries do rely more on the world economy—exports are a larger fraction of the incomes of smaller countries than of larger ones.

LONG FOCUS. Yet the large international market does not entirely substitute for small domestic markets, since trade between nations is limited by tariffs and quotas. The international movement of people is even more tightly regulated. Both goods and people usually can flow much more freely between regions and other sectors within an economy than across national borders.

For example, Quebec residents are able to move to Toronto or sell goods to Vancouver without worrying about the tariffs, immigration quotas, and other factors that impede flows into the U.S. or Mexico. Goods from the Ukraine have better access to markets in the Soviet Union than in Western Europe. Smaller countries tend to specialize in products that do not require large domestic markets. Instead of cars or planes, Chile exports fruits and vegetables, Israel sells small arms, the tiny island of Mauritius produces textiles to ship abroad, and, of course, Kuwait produces oil.

But big countries also have various economic problems that offset the advantages of large internal markets. One of the more important arises from the harm caused by the jockeying of interest groups for subsidies and favorable regulations. The many different sectors of large economies get political favors that raise taxes and the cost of goods and labor to other sectors. In this way, government aid to grain producers in Canada's West raises wheat prices in Quebec and other Eastern provinces, while oil and gas subsidies to the East are at the expense of Western producers.

KING COTTON. Conflict between interest groups in large countries even leads to serious civil disturbances. Without doubt the clash over slavery in the U.S. was the clear and immediate cause of the Civil War. However, the South's desire to have low tariffs on manufactured goods from Europe and to widen world markets for its cotton was also a major source of friction, for its interests conflicted with those of New England manufacturers. They wanted tariff protection for their goods to avoid competition from Europe, and also low prices for Southern cotton, which was a raw material in the North's textile industry.

By contrast, there are fewer opportunities to promote policies that impose cost on other sectors in the more homogeneous economies of small countries. It's not surprising that countries with fewer economic regulations tend to be small. Examples are Taiwan, Singapore, and Chile.

I doubt that the integration of East and West Germany will yield greater economic advantages than they would have enjoyed as two separate market-oriented countries permitting free movement of people and goods across their borders. The main problem with the East German economy has not been its small size but the centralized direction and state ownership of industry. Indeed, integration is causing a conflict between groups in East and West Germany that will slow down needed reforms in the East. That region wants its affluent cousins in the West to subsidize the continuation of inefficient uses of labor and capital, and several wildcat strikes have broken out in the East to demand slower changes and bigger handouts.

To be sure, nationalism and ethnic conflicts and loyalties, not economic calculations, are usually the inspiration to secede from larger states. But whatever the motives, the statistics on actual performance show that dire warnings about the economic price suffered by small nations are not at all warranted.

ENVIRONMENT

LET'S DEFUSE THE POPULATION BOMB
—WITH FREE MARKETS

Parson Thomas Malthus is alive and well and living at the U.N. Rising population is on a collision course with limited growth in food supplies and other life-sustaining resources. That may sound like a sentence from the 1798 Malthus classic, *An Essay on the Principles of Population*, but it was in fact one of the themes at a recently concluded U.N. conference that paves the way for a massive meeting on population next September in Cairo.

One hotly debated proposal at the conference calls for quadrupling—to more than $4 billion—the amount the U.N. gives to poor nations for family planning programs. But a study by Lant Pritchett of the World Bank in the March, 1994, issue of *Population and Development Review* makes a persuasive case that people in poor countries have lots of children because they want large families, not because they don't know about birth control.

Families in Third World countries still typically have more than six births because children are put to work at an early age. But even poor parents have fewer children, however, when they have the right incentives. As nations develop, attitudes change: Families come to prefer having fewer and better-educated children who can prosper in modern economies. Economic development and the education of women, not family planning programs, are the most effective contraceptives.

BETTER OFF TODAY. But many biologists, ecologists, and others who disagree envision disaster unless the population surge is contained by more radical means. They are concerned because the world's population since 1950 has more than doubled—to 5.5 billion people—and is projected to double again, to 11 billion, by the year 2055. That compares dramatically with the more than 100 years it took for the world's population to double after 1850, and more than 150 years to double that of 1700. They also worry that population growth since 1950 has been especially steep in the poorest Third World countries. The African population increased from 200 million people to almost 700 million, whereas Asia's total (even excluding Japan) increased from 1.3 billion to just over 3 billion.

Staggering increases. Yet I do not believe they are necessarily cause for alarm. Population density in Africa is still far below that in Japan, the Netherlands, Taiwan, and many other affluent countries. Moreover, the neo-Malthusians don't seem to understand that the typical Third World family is now much better off than 40 years ago. Per capita incomes in most of these nations have grown at good rates, although incomes in some African countries did decline during the 1980s or even earlier. Third World populations expanded rapidly because children and adults live much longer than they did even a few decades ago, not because families there are having more babies. They are having fewer babies. How can one lament population growth due to dramatically fewer deaths from malnutrition and contagious diseases?

Despite some terrible famines, nutrition has greatly improved in most Third World countries. Food is cheaper and more abundant despite fewer acres in the world devoted to farming. Rapid technological progress in agriculture and in the extraction of energy resources has greatly increased availability of food, oil, gas, and other natural resources.

EDUCATION PUSH.   The pessimists respond that what happened in the past cannot continue, and that production of food and fossil fuels will be unable to keep up with the much larger populations that are forecast for the next century. Population growth may pose some potential long-run problems for the supply of food and natural resources, but those problems have been greatly exaggerated by scaremongers. In the past, countless projections about food supplies and natural resources turned out to be far too pessimistic. For example, unforeseen technological improvements reduced the cost of food and natural resources during this century despite rapid growth in both populations and industrial output that was expected by neo-Malthusians to sharply raise these prices.

Population forecasts have proved similarly unreliable and have often simply extrapolated past trends. Birth rates fell far more rapidly since 1950 than had been expected in Colombia, Hong Kong, Mexico, Taiwan, and other poor countries that had rapid economic development, which greatly increased the education and workforce participation of women. The population of African and other Third World countries will grow more slowly than is being predicted if these nations adopt the market-, education-, and export-oriented policies that succeeded for the Asian tigers, Chile, and other countries that grew out of poverty.

The U.N. can best contribute to reducing population growth and misery in the Third World by offering sensible economic advice to poor nations. The advantages of free markets and basic schooling for everyone in reducing the desire for large families should be the major theme in the Cairo population conference next fall.

On Global Warming,
Let the Coolest Heads Prevail

International agreements are needed when one nation's industrial activity damages the environment in other countries. This is why President Bush has been severely criticized for being the only leader at the Rio summit to oppose a stringent accord on controlling global warming caused by the greenhouse effect. But the U.S. has taken the correct stand: The jury is still out on the effects on atmospheric temperature of carbon dioxide (CO_2), chlorofluorocarbons, and emissions of other gases, mainly from the burning of fossil fuels.

These gases are trapped in the atmosphere and reflect back heat that warms up the earth's land surface and oceans. Since it isn't possible to use ordinary scientific procedures to determine whether this has a major impact on the earth's temperature, claims about global warming caused by such a greenhouse effect are based on theoretical models of the atmosphere. The models are complex, but even scientists who are strong advocates of greenhouse theories admit that the analyses are oversimplified. For example, the models typically pay little attention to how the gases alter cloud cover.

DIRE CLAIMS.   In the global-warming field, physical scientists are like economists: They can test their theories only by using historical events. But the historical evidence on the earth's climate offers no support for the dire predictions of more extreme greenhouse-effect devotees. The output of CO_2 and other alleged culprits has been growing far more rapidly during the past 50 years than previously. Yet, while the earth has warmed up since the beginning of the century, practically all the warming happened prior to 1940, and it could thus have been caused by other factors. If the large increase in the supply of these gases has so far not had a discernible effect on the world's temperatures, can one have much confidence in claims that the earth will heat up a lot unless production of these gases is sharply cut back?

Of course, public policy on economic and scientific matters cannot always wait until fully persuasive evidence is available. Proponents of major controls on carbon emissions believe that the consequences of global warming are sufficiently worrisome to justify moderate steps now. Running the risk involved in waiting for more decisive evidence, they argue, may result in having to take much more drastic action later.

But many scientists are still far from convinced by warming theories. I believe the U.S. and other countries should heed these skeptics and wait before implementing major restrictions on carbon emissions. In the next couple of decades, new information about crucial parameters of warming models will become available. This should resolve much of the uncertainty, making it clear whether or not these gases will do much damage. It is certainly possible that the global effects have been exaggerated and that large reductions in coal output and the burning of fossil fuels are not necessary.

For example, there is still considerable uncertainty over the fate of the CO_2 and other greenhouse gases that enter the atmosphere. Each year, some of them get absorbed in soil, trees, water, and other natural materials without causing harm. This absorption rate is generally assumed to range from about 0.5% to 2% per year. If the true rate is at the high end of this range, much of the industrial output during the next couple of decades should not contribute to future warming, since the gases would be absorbed in natural materials over this period of time.

EASING DOWN. No one can predict the future development of technologies that will cut back the industrial demand for coal and other fuels. But modest expenditures, through prizes and other inducements by the nations that gathered at Rio, could speed up progress for the discovery of methods and techniques that reduce the emission of harmful gases. Even if greenhouse theories are right, heavy carbon taxes will not be required if technology improves fast enough.

How bad will the situation be if no action is taken now and if global warming does turn out to be a serious problem? A study by Ian Parry at the University of Chicago compares the effects on the world economy of sharp reductions in future fuel use with the consequences of moderate reductions over a much longer period. The difference between these economic effects depends on the cost of shifting capital from heavy fuel-using sectors, the damage to crops from warmer temperature, and related considerations.

Although Parry's study ignores new technologies, he still concludes that the cost of delaying action for a couple of decades is probably not large—even if the greenhouse problem is important. The harm from waiting becomes substantial only with what appear to be highly unlikely economic scenarios, such as vast flooding of coastal areas caused by catastrophic climate changes. Global warming is potentially an urgent issue, but the present evidence does not justify panic-induced actions. While there should be research and development on reducing emissions of greenhouse gases, with efforts spurred by financial and other inducements, drastic steps should be avoided until much more is known about the validity of warming theories.

THE HOT AIR INFLATING
THE GREENHOUSE EFFECT

The expansion of the world's economy is a potentially serious threat to the environment, but some advocacy groups and scientists have tried to frighten people into action with grossly exaggerated claims about the seriousness of certain risks.

A prime example is the pile of books and articles published during the past decade envisioning the most dreadful consequences from global warming caused by the greenhouse effect. That refers to an increase in the atmospheric concentrations of carbon dioxide (CO_2), chlorofluorocarbons (CFCs), and other heat-trapping gases. The buildup of these gases during the past 150 years is claimed to be responsible for most of the 0.3C to 0.6C rise in surface temperature during this century.

These studies of the greenhouse effect expect temperatures to rise a lot more — their estimates range from 2C to 5C — by the time atmospheric concentrations of greenhouse gases reach double their 1860 levels, sometime during the first half of the next century. Worried by such predictions, the 1988 Toronto Conference on the Changing Atmosphere, attended by 48 countries, recommended cutting CO_2 emissions by 2005 to 80% of their 1988 level — requiring a major reduction in world economic output. Senator Timothy E. Wirth (D-Colo.) has proposed a tax on the carbon emitted from fuels that would rise to $100 a ton by 2000 — raising the cost of a ton of coal or oil by several hundred percent.

MINOR EFFECTS. Such extreme proposals to cut back carbon emissions are responses to forecasts of global warming that are highly questionable. One difficulty with the greenhouse explanation is that when the rapid buildup of these gases began 50 years ago, most of the temperature rise had already occurred. And a recent survey of the evidence issued by the National Academy of Sciences (NAS), *Policy Implications of Greenhouse Warming*, concludes that the increased concentration of greenhouse gases since the end of the 19th century need not necessarily have been the primary cause of the rise in global temperature in those years.

As to the future, even if the continuing growth of CO_2 and other gases in the atmosphere raises global temperatures, it's anyone's guess how that would affect the world's economy and ordinary living. Any likely amount of warming will probably have minor effects on manufacturing, mining, transportation, finance, and most other services. However, some crops would suffer from too much heat and dryness, countries with warm climates would get less comfortable, and in extreme cases, some coastal regions would be flooded by melting glaciers. On the other hand, warming would presumably benefit cold climates such as Canada's and encourage farming in high-latitude regions.

Thus, it appears that the consequences of such warming may be serious but probably would not be so bad. How should public policy respond to a possible, but far from certain, greenhouse warming? A recent study by William Nordhaus of Yale University and the NAS report support the Montreal Protocol that calls for the phasing out of chlorofluorocarbons, which are used in refrigeration and to clean electronic components, by 2000. CFCs are not a major source of global warming, but they damage the earth's protective ozone layer and can be phased out at what appears to be a modest cost.

EDUCATED GUESSES. However, Nordhaus' study and the NAS report are skeptical about the advisability of drastic action to reduce CO_2 emissions. Nordhaus cautions that estimates of damages are no better than educated guesses, and he suggests only modest taxes on coal and other fuels, for he concludes that even large increases in CO_2 emissions during the next 50 years are unlikely to have a major adverse impact. The NAS report proposes a few general policies to improve energy use, further research on the likelihood and effects of warming, and preparation to take more drastic steps should they become necessary.

A study at the University of Chicago conducted by Ian Parry is examining the consequences of the enormous uncertainty about the magnitude of and damages from any greenhouse effect. His work supports the conclusion of Nordhaus and the NAS: Only extreme and unlikely circumstances justify high fuel taxes to cut down drastically the CO_2 emitted into the atmosphere.

The greenhouse effect is just one important illustration of the misleading claims about many environmental risks. Population growth, a perennial source of environmental fears, is another. To take one familiar example, Paul R. Ehrlich warned in his popular 1968 book *The Population Bomb* that hundreds of millions would starve to death in the 1970s and 1980s because the world's population was growing so rapidly. Although this widely reported forecast proved to be ludicrously wide of the mark, Ehrlich and other published doomsdayers continue to be taken seriously.

So little is known about global warming and other potential environmental risks that it is hard to generate effective policies even when the evidence is presented accurately. It becomes almost impossible when advocates bombard the public with worst-case scenarios.

THE PROPHETS OF DOOM
HAVE A DISMAL RECORD

The crisis virus invades even the best minds. In 1865 one of the world's greatest economists, William S. Jevons, wrote *The Coal Question* to express his fear that British industrial growth would halt because the country's coal reserves were running out. Yet Britain still has enough coal to protect the industry and the jobs of more than 100,000 miners against competition from imports. Jevons also forecast that the price of coal would rise as it became scarcer. Instead, the real price of coal in Britain rose hardly at all between the 1870s and the early 1970s. Jevons failed to anticipate fully the development of substitutes for coal, of new engines, and of other technologies that made more economical use of fuel.

The dire population forecasts of the parson Thomas Malthus are well known. In 1803 he warned that population would always continue to increase sufficiently to hold real wages at low levels unless young men and women delayed marriage and had fewer children. Yet for most of the following 150 years, real wages in Britain increased, despite a rapid growth in population and a lowering of the average age at marriage. Malthus failed to foresee the continuous advances in technology after the Industrial Revolution as well as the desire for small families in modern economies.

SOBER JUDGMENTS.   The crisis mentality is not confined to the 19th century or found only in economists with dismal outlooks. In their useful book *The Doomsday Myth*, Professors Charles Maurice and Charles W. Smithson of Texas A&M University consider various forecasts of economic doom in the past. The shortage of wood in 17th century England, for example, was expected to cripple the British navy and raise the cost of heating homes beyond the means of most families. Instead, a century-long rise in the price of wood hastened the development of coal as a superior fuel.

The fact that outstanding thinkers like Jevons and Malthus could not foresee future developments should have taught would-be soothsayers a lesson. But sober judgments seldom compete successfully for attention with crisis-mongering, and the 1960s and 1970s were vintage decades for the gloom-and-doomers. The spirit of Malthus spoke again in numerous forecasts of runaway world population growth that would destroy the environment and hobble economic development. The ghost of Jevons presided over the fear that the world would run out of fossil fuels. Many voices warned also of an environmental crisis, a nuclear crisis, and an urban crisis.

The available evidence is not kind to these forecasts. Estimates made in the 1960s of future world population growth have already been revised downward substantially as China, India, and other developing countries have reduced their birth rates. Developed countries have begun to worry about families that are too small and about birth rates that are below the level necessary to prevent declines in their population. The apparent shortage of fossil fuels merely reflected the high prices received by OPEC. These prices induced both economies in fuel use and discoveries of alternative supplies that have shattered the cartel and ended concerns about an energy crunch, at least for the moment.

LOSING MUSCLE.   While the 1980s have been more relaxed than the preceding two decades, they have seen some crisis-mongering. The sizable federal budget deficits of the past four years have engendered predictions of disaster. Moreover, both the U.S. and Europe are said to be in the process of losing their industrial muscle to the Pacific Basin. The U.S. inability to compete in the world market for manufactured goods allegedly has caused the recent large deficits in its foreign-trade balance.

But strong modern economies do not seem to require a dominant manufacturing sector. The U.S. economy performed very well from 1947 to 1975, yet during those years the share of manufacturing in total employment declined from 35% to only 23%. Indeed, even the absolute number of workers in manufacturing grew slowly during most of this period. Recent foreign-trade deficits apparently are related to the demand by foreigners for dollar assets rather than to the U.S. inability to compete in world markets. The dollar has actually risen in value relative to other currencies during much of the time that the trade deficit has been increasing.

Continued large budget deficits, unlike other supposed crises, will eventually cause serious problems. For example, future governments might be tempted to inflate away a much heavier debt burden. But how do the people who have worried about each large deficit in the last four years explain the buoyancy of the American economy and the mild inflation during this period?

We should be honest and admit that economics and other social sciences cannot predict the exact response to competition from a Japan or a South Korea or to apparently declining supplies of oil and other resources. Still, the evidence of hundreds of years indicates that individuals and organizations that are free to respond to clear signals on prices and other matters will find ingenious and often unexpected solutions to apparently insurmountable economic difficulties.

PART 13

Stock Markets and Recessions

Immediately after the crash of the United States stock market in 1987, we wrote the essay included in this short part predicting that it would not cause a major depression. This went against a cover story by *Business Week* entitled "How Bad" and other articles at that time which detailed similarities to 1929, and expressed fear that the market's crash would also bring the economy down.

Our contrarian forecast was based on a simple calculation: even the 24 percent fall in stock prices meant only a small drop in the total wealth of people that includes their human capital. The prediction based on this calculation turned out to be right on the money, for the economy hardly faltered, and the stock market returned to its previous high in a few months.

During the heydays of the 1980s when Japan had both a booming economy and a skyrocketing stock market, many in the West believed that Japanese bureaucrats had discovered how to pick promising new industries, which they supported through subsidies and in other ways. Westerners also believed that the Japanese government had actively intervened to maintain its stock market at artificially high levels. Both claims seemed to us to be highly unlikely since even intelligent bureaucrats elsewhere had failed miserably at either picking industrial "winners" or at preventing stocks from falling when confronted with bad news.

An essay in Part 9 attacks such romanticism about the success of Japanese industrial policy, and another essay in this part denies that the Japanese stock market is rigged either by the government or by large companies. Since the Nikkei Exchange fell by more than 60 percent from its peak in 1990 to a low in 1993, and since the government's repeated attempts to revive the market dismally failed, claims about rigged markets have faded away since we wrote our piece in 1990.

SO YOU THOUGHT
THE TOKYO STOCK MARKET WAS RIGGED?

The collapse in prices on the Japanese stock market over the past few months has been seen as a sign that Japan's economy is in trouble. But I don't believe it.

Prices on the Tokyo Stock Exchange grew by several hundred percent from 1985 to the end of 1989, while price-earnings ratios more than doubled. At the beginning of this year, shares were selling at almost 60 times reported earnings, compared with less than 15 times in the U.S. and most other industrial nations. The inflated p-e ratios suggest that stock prices in Japan were too high and were due for a correction.

My view is supported by the findings of a careful study by Kenneth R. French of the University of Chicago and James M. Poterba of the Massachusetts Institute of Technology. They show that p-e ratios in Japan are greatly exaggerated by accounting practices that understate earnings compared with the way they are reported elsewhere. For example, Japanese companies understate the earnings of subsidiaries and depreciate assets very generously. However, French and Poterba find that by the end of 1989 p-e ratios were much higher in Japan than in the West, even after accounting adjustments to ensure comparability and after a reasonable allowance for future growth in earnings.

TALL ORDER. The boom in Japanese stocks and the failure of prices there to fall much during the worldwide crash of October, 1987, convinced many Wall Street pundits that the Japanese government rigs its stock market. Would they claim that government rigging also caused the enormous boom in Japanese land prices during the past several years? The government cannot control stock prices for the same reason it cannot control land prices: There are too many buyers and sellers. Thousands of individuals in Japan and abroad own about 30% of all shares on the Tokyo Stock Exchange, while hundreds of companies own most of the rest. In any case, the talk about rigging waned after the 30% slump in stock values from early January to the end of March.

The prolonged rise in Japanese p-e ratios was a "bubble" that expanded as shareholders made huge paper profits. Knowing that all price balloons eventually burst and believing that the rigging talk was nonsense, I put some money where my pen was and bought a small number of American Stock Exchange puts on the Nikkei in early February and sold out at the end of March. Through luck—

which is essential since the timing of a bust is highly uncertain—I caught almost the whole fall and had a nice return on the investment.

Despite the collapse of its enormous stock price balloon, the fundamentals in Japan remain strong, and prospects for the economy are excellent.

Office of Economic Corporation & Development (OECD) data show Japanese men work longer than men in other OECD countries. Average annual hours of work exceed 2,200 in Japan, compared with 1,800 for workers in the U.S. and fewer still in Western Europe. Japanese workers also tend to take less free time while on the job than Americans and Europeans.

WORKING WOMEN. True, the Japanese labor force is aging faster than in other countries, but a much larger fraction of Japanese men over age 65 work (Economic Viewpoint, Mar. 19), and the labor-force participation of married women has started to grow rapidly from low levels. Companies in Japan are also beginning to give women better jobs and more opportunities for advancement.

Japanese workers are well-educated and trained. More than 90% finish high school, compared with less than 80% in the U.S. Japanese schools emphasize math, science, and other basic knowledge and give four times as much homework as American schools. As a result, Japanese students score near the top in international tests on mathematics and science; American students are near the bottom. Japanese companies also hire carefully and provide extensive on-the-job training.

The Japanese savings rate has fallen steeply since the early 1970s as the growth in per capita income slowed dramatically from the remarkable rates of the 1950s and 1960s. Yet Japan still saves and invests a larger fraction of its income than the U.S. and Western Europe, although differences in the definition of savings exaggerate the gap.

I give little credence to the view that much of Japan's economic success is the result of the allegedly brilliant guidance of the economy by the Ministry of International Trade & Industry and other government agencies. Government policies are determined by the same kinds of political pressures from special interests found elsewhere—one need look only at Japan's support of agriculture or the recurring corruption scandals. Japan does benefit from low crime levels, limited litigation, and a government that spends and taxes a smaller fraction of gross national product than those in the West.

The collapse of the Japanese stock market is a useful corrective to speculative excesses. It is also evidence, if any is needed, that this market obeys the usual laws of supply and demand. But the bust does not mean Japan will be a weakened competitor on world markets.

LASSOING HERD INSTINCTS
FOR THE GOOD OF THE MARKET

Large crashes or booms in financial markets often have little to do with real changes in the economy but are triggered by minor events—such as the collapse of the UAL Corp. buyout plan on Oct. 13. The reason for this is the well-known herd instinct, in which investors act on the basis of what they think other traders will be doing.

The bandwagon effect is an old story on Wall Street. As John Maynard Keynes put it many years ago, "the energies and skills of the professional investor and speculator [are devoted]...to anticipating what average opinion expects the average opinion to be." Yet I believe it still gets short shrift in modern theories of finance.

Investors have little confidence in any current level of stock prices because they are worrying about the intentions of other traders. Thus, even minuscule changes in prices can get highly leveraged as signals of the intentions of other traders. Instead of buying vigorously when stock prices are falling, or selling when they are rising, the majority may either remain on the sidelines or behave perversely. Then prices may have to fall a lot before enough bargain hunters begin to buy stock, or they may have to rise a lot before enough investors become willing to sell their shares.

A systematic analysis of stock-price movements along these lines was recently developed by Gerard Gennotte and Hayne E. Leland of the University of California at Berkeley. It is easy to stress the herd instinct when investors are assumed to be irrational and subject to whim, but it is far more challenging to combine bandwagon behavior with rational expectations and logical decisions. I do not know whether their approach or any other yet available captures the essence of stock price determination, but their study tills new ground in combining the bandwagon effect with rational investor behavior.

HEM ANGST. The herd instinct is not just confined to the stock market. Sociologists have long emphasized that interdependent behavior explains the rapid growth and decline in the consumption of many goods, especially those subject to fashions and fads. After fashion leaders shortened their skirts during the 1960s, many other women jumped on the bandwagon because they believed the trendsetters had better information about what was "in," and they did not want to appear old-fashioned.

Expectations about the behavior of other investors sometimes become self-fulfilling and generate large swings in stock prices that are not closely related to earnings, interest rates, or other fundamental determinants of value. This can be seen in the many big price swings that have taken place during the past 60 years. On 38 separate occasions, one-day changes in average prices on the New York

Stock Exchange exceeded 7%, and on 960 occasions, one-day swings exceeded 2%. One study shows that large price changes most often occur in September, October, and November, and very large price drops are preceded and followed by other drops. Large price movements are not mainly due to panic selling when prices begin to fall—a popular explanation of stock crashes. About half of the large price movements were upward.

Most of the large swings in stock prices were not followed by depressions or booms. A good example is the 20% meltdown in prices that took place on October 19, 1987. Some investors may have panicked during this crash. But surely the media and government officials panicked even more, as they compared it with the 1929 crash and expressed fears about a major depression similar to that of the early 1930s.

WEATHER REPORT. In a column published shortly after the 1987 crash (BW—Nov. 9), I predicted only mild consequences and no depression. The great strength at that time in employment, profits, prices, and other economic indicators were far better predictors of the future than the market crash. The continued boom in the economy during the past two years has made comparisons with 1929 look silly.

If booms and busts in stock prices are caused by limited information, stock performance could be improved by more of it. For example, advanced announcement of large institutional orders coming to market—sunshine trading—might give investors better information about the sources of price changes. And strong assurances by Federal Reserve Board and government officials during market crashes could help prevent any further deterioration in investor confidence.

Unfortunately, most of the current proposals—including sizable taxes on securities transactions, the banning of portfolio insurance, Securities & Exchange Commission Chairman Richard C. Breeden's suggestion to suspend program trading during volatile times, and Treasury Secretary Nicholas F. Brady's recommendation that the SEC have the power to close stock markets during periods of "crisis"—are likely to shake the fragile confidence of traders and may well increase rather than decrease the frequency of booms and busts in prices.

The strength of the economy in the face of very large swings in stock prices during the past several years provides a powerful case for not imposing new, unproven, and potentially damaging regulations on financial markets.

WHY A DEPRESSION ISN'T IN THE CARDS

Many people remember the depression that followed 1929's stock market crash and wonder if a similar catastrophe is now in store. I don't know what caused either crash, but I am confident that a major depression will not follow this time unless economic policy takes a radical turn for the worse. The market's violent gyrations are surely disturbing, yet that is no reason to exaggerate the consequences for employment, output, and inflation.

The 25% decline in share prices over the last two months lopped almost $1 trillion from the value of stocks. Although that's a huge number, the average person's total wealth took only a modest fall because most wealth is embodied in the skills and training that generate present and future earnings. Such "human wealth" constitutes 75% or more of the U.S.'s total wealth. The rest consists of corporate capital, capital in unincorporated businesses, housing, consumer durables, government capital, and cash.

The Commerce Dept. estimates nonhuman wealth at about $13 trillion. Thus a $1 trillion fall in the value of stocks reduces this wealth by less than 8%—and total wealth by less than 2%. Such a decline would have a noticeable effect on spending and a major effect on the demand for luxury homes and cars. But the decline in spending from a 2% fall in wealth cannot cause a major depression.

STILL STRONG. The change in expectations that clobbered stock prices may also discourage new capital investment. But the effect on business spending is also likely to be small given the economy's strength after the remarkable performance of the past five years—a strength that contrasts clearly with the situation in 1929. Output is growing at a good pace, with real gross national product expanding at a 3.8% annual rate during the third quarter, while inflation is modest, unemployment is at its lowest rate in years, excess capacity is minimal, and manufacturing is reviving.

Congress and the President are likely to agree soon on a partial solution to the budget deficit through a combination of higher taxes and a modest cut in federal spending. And a further decline in the dollar against foreign currencies, which seems inevitable, would help the economy by narrowing the trade deficit.

Even so, some disquieting discrepancies have surfaced between the movement of stock prices and "efficient market theory," which holds that the value of a company's stock fully reflects whatever information investors have about present and future earnings, interest rates, and other fundamental determinants of the company's worth. This idea, which is much celebrated in finance and economics and has provided many important insights into the pricing of options and other financial assets, asserts that prices change in response to changes in information about these fundamentals.

Disturbingly, stock prices, housing prices, and foreign exchange rates appear to fluctuate more violently than can be explained by changing information. The most dramatic example is the more than 20% decline in stock prices on Oct. 19, but equally perplexing is the steep rise in the stock market from the end of 1985 to its Aug. 25 peak this year.

These gigantic movements in stock prices are embarrassing to the efficient market theory because there was no new information about fundamentals that could justify such big and rapid changes. The budget deficit was as large during the time stock prices were rising as it was when they fell. Increases in the rate of inflation and in interest rates have been too gradual to explain the sharpness of Bloody Monday's drop. Nor does the prospect of increased U.S. involvement in the Iran-Iraq war appear to be the culprit, since few investors fear that a major conflict will erupt.

SELF-FULFILLING. The discrepancies seem to stem from the way investors form their expectations. Instead of relying on fundamentals, many investors try to figure out what others will do and then rush to do it first. John Maynard Keynes said that "the energies and skill of the professional investor and speculator [are devoted]...to anticipating what average opinion expects the average opinion to be." Some investors search for patterns in price movements or rely on other factors that have little to do with underlying fundamentals.

Unfortunately, expectations based on extraneous factors and on guesses about the behavior of others can become self-fulfilling, generating large swings in prices for a while. Self-fulfilling expectations are not irrational, but they do weaken the relationship between prices and fundamental determinants.

What to do? Reassurances by the President, the Federal Reserve Board chairman, and other top federal officials may help calm investors when prices swing sharply, especially during panic selling. Some economists even believe that the federal government should restrict the use of index options, program trading, and other new financial instruments and trading methods in order to help smooth out fluctuations in the stock market. However, in light of the damage done by most government regulation of financial markets, I believe it would be a serious mistake to implement major new regulations at this point.

HOW BAD WILL THE NEXT DOWNTURN BE?
FLIP A COIN

Some people believe that the expansion and contraction of business cycles in the U.S. are becoming tamer because of the length of the current expansion, now in its 76th month. Aside from one during the Vietnam War, this boom is the longest since the end of World War II. However, just as one swallow does not make a spring, one unusual boom doesn't say much about the future course of business cycles, and I doubt that the business cycle is becoming any gentler.

The sad fact is that economists, including the experts on business cycles, do not know why booms invariably come to an end. And they know little more about why recessions—be they severe or mild—draw to a close. This is true despite an enormous effort devoted to theoretical and statistical studies of cycles during the past hundred years.

Economists are not even sure whether business cycles are self-generating, continuing on their own steam because of the internal logic of markets and economies. It could well be that each cycle represents a unique response to external shocks, such as the sharp rise in oil prices during the early 1970s, or bad monetary and fiscal policies.

UNRULY BUNCH. The truth is that the term "business cycle" is itself a misnomer, for economies are subject to fluctuations, not repetitive cycles of similar lengths and amplitudes. Expansions and contractions vary greatly in length. For example, although the nine post-World War II expansions averaged only 48 months, two besides the current one exceeded 55 months, and two were shorter than 25 months.

The current boom followed the worst depression of the postwar period—from July, 1981, to November, 1982. There was a lot of slack in the economy when business began to improve—unemployment exceeded 10.5%, and industry had much unutilized capacity. It should be no surprise that the subsequent boom proved long and buoyant.

Many bankers and economists believe that the length of the boom is also the result of wise monetary policy by the Federal Reserve. Some even claim that it could continue more or less indefinitely if the Fed does not overreach in the fight against growing inflation. And there's no reason to doubt the Fed would pursue such a course. The problem is, it just doesn't know how.

Others explain this long expansion and their hopes for mild cycles in the future by various programs of the Reagan Administration. In particular, they cite greatly reduced personal tax rates and other supply-side policies, deregulation, a lower value of the dollar, and the budget deficits. Many of these programs have improved the economy's performance, but no one has shown that they have much relevance for the severity of business cycles.

In the past, unwarranted optimism or pessimism often followed one unusual episode. The Depression convinced many prominent economists in the 1930s that capitalist economies could no longer generate full employment without massive assistance from government spending. These economies were alleged to suffer from "secular stagnation," a term coined by Alvin Hansen, then a well-known professor at Harvard. The boom after World War II and throughout most of the 1950s and 1960s killed all talk of continued stagnation.

Decades after the Depression, in the latter half of the 1950s and first half of the 1960s, when prices in the U.S. stayed rather stable, some economists predicted an end to serious peacetime inflation. Yet the most severe bout of peacetime inflation in U.S. history occurred shortly afterwards, in the 1970s.

SCARE BEARS. A more recent example of such extrapolation from events was the widely shared—but erroneous—belief at the time that the stock market crash in October, 1987, would be followed by a depression propelled by a sharp drop in investments and consumer spending. A false analogy was drawn from the Depression, which followed not long on the heels of the 1929 crash. This pessimism about the economy has been forgotten by many as the present boom continues unabated after the crash.

A number of economists, myself included, went against popular opinion and forecast that the crash would not have a major effect on the U.S. economy. We were right not because we had profound insights into the causes of business cycles and the operation of stock markets—I certainly don't—but because we believed that the experience of 1929 held few lessons for 1987, since we doubted that the 1929 crash caused the subsequent depression. Moreover, the economy looked strong in October, 1987, and even the 25% decline in stock values only slightly reduced the total wealth of the vast majority of workers and consumers.

Given the business cycle experience of the past half-century, there isn't any reason to believe that the next contraction will be especially mild. The lesson is that the U.S. economy will continue to have serious recessions—and the length of the expansion that precedes them tells us little about how severe they will be. But I repeat my warning that we economists cannot predict business cycles very well.

PART 14

Economists

The first essay in this part has special significance to both of us. It discusses our reactions to learning on Tuesday, October 13th, 1992, that Gary had won the Nobel prize in economics. The news was especially sweet since we did not expect it.

To be sure, we knew that for at least a decade Gary's name had been high up on the list of Nobel candidates, despite the controversy that surrounded each new paper or book he published, including the column he wrote (included in Part 11) attacking Sweden's so-called "middle way." Many economists expressed the belief that he would soon win the Nobel prize, and for a few years he had been the number-one pick in a betting contest organized by some American economists.

So every October for a while we had anticipated the autumn with some trepidation: would he win that year? But in 1992 we did not feel any Nobel pressure. The major reason was that Gary's colleagues from the University of Chicago had won the previous two years, Ronald Coase in 1990 and Merton Miller had shared the Nobel prize in 1991. It seemed highly unlikely that they would choose a third consecutive economist from the University of Chicago. There was also a more serious reason why the Nobel prize was not on our minds: Gary had been sick with a nasty flu and high fever since the beginning of October. His doctor urged hospitalization, which we both resisted.

That Tuesday morning Guity woke up at 5:00 to finish correcting a stack of midterms. Fortunately, Gary slept soundly for the first time in a couple of weeks. Guity came down to the kitchen, had breakfast, and started working. At 5:30 the phone rang, and Guity rushed to answer to make sure that no second ring woke Gary up. She presumed a careless person had misdialed the number he wanted. After she picked up the phone she realized it sounded like a long distance call—

probably her mother calling from Iran. But a voice broke the silence and said in English, "May I speak to Professor Gary Becker? It is a call from Sweden." Guity told the caller he was sleeping. The voice said "It is important."

Guity began to believe that it must be connected to the Nobel deliberations, but we did not know that the economics prize was being announced that day. Perhaps they simply wanted additional information about someone else. "Gary, wake up; it is a call from Sweden" she repeated several times as she tried to overcome his resistance and wake him from a deep sleep. Finally, he got up, picked up the phone, and began to listen. His face remained impassive and gave no indication of what was being said. Eventually, with a faint smile he responded "Asser [Lindbeck], please thank the Committee on my behalf for the honor they have bestowed on me." Only then did Guity's growing suspicion turn to certainty: Gary had won the Nobel prize. Her reaction was a shriek of joy.

When the Wake-Up Call
Is from the Nobel Committee

At 5:30 in the morning of Tuesday, Oct. 13, I was awakened from a deep sleep by my wife. "There's a phone call from Sweden," she said. I mumbled that she should let me sleep, but she kept repeating the same phrase. Finally, I got up to take the call that changed my life. The Royal Swedish Academy of Sciences informed me that I had just been awarded the 1992 Nobel prize in economics.

Since then, I have had a constant barrage of congratulatory phone calls, telegrams, and faxes from relatives, friends, would-be friends, and former and present students. Although I'm not a person who easily expresses his feelings, I tried to tell them how overjoyed I was. In interviews with newspapers, magazines, and radio and television programs, I was asked to present my ideas in general terms: Often, the reaction was that they were either obvious or far out.

I have also been asked to comment on all kinds of questions. Suddenly, I am treated as an expert on everything. Although that is a tempting notion, I've tried—not always successfully—to stick to the areas where I have expertise.

I have been annoyed in the past when Nobel laureates in economics have used their honor as a pulpit from which they launched sermons against political candidates they opposed. If economics has any claim to be a science and to belong in the Nobel award structure—and I firmly believe that it does—then this should be an occasion to avoid political propaganda and to convey to the public some flavor of the scientific quality of economics.

CHICAGO LIGHTNING.   One of the questions most frequently put to me is whether I was surprised to receive this award. I knew that I was on the list of economists being considered. I also knew that in a poll of many U.S. economists, I had been favored to win for the past few years.

But this year, when the week for the selection rolled around, I didn't think I had the slightest chance. That was because last year the prize was won by a colleague from the University of Chicago, Ronald H. Coase; and the year before that, another Chicagoan, Merton H. Miller, shared the award with two others. Since it seemed inconceivable that the award would go to Chicago three years in a row, I was sleeping soundly when lightning struck.

I am constantly asked what we are going to do with the prize money—$1.2 million before Uncle Sam takes his very large bite. The answer to that is a simple lesson in economics. Wants always expand to take advantage of new opportunities, which explains why consumers in rich countries feel no more satiated than do those in poor countries. My wife and I won't have the slightest difficulty spending the prize money. We have already been inundated by suggestions from a host of stockbrokers, car salesmen, and others who are quite happy to help us resolve any uncertainty we may have.

I won the award for applying economic analysis to social problems, especially race and gender discrimination, investments in education and other human capital, crime and punishment, and the formation, structure, and dissolution of families. Everyone recognizes that most people respond to costs and benefits in deciding how much to buy of simple goods such as fruit, clothing, or a car. I claim that this common-sense idea applies to all human decisions.

CRIME AND MARRIAGE.   Yet, some of the implications are fiercely resisted. For example, this view implies that criminals also respond to incentives, so crime increases when potential miscreants believe they won't be punished much for robbery and other crimes. This is more than a law-and-order message, for the analysis also implies that crime increases when legal jobs are hard to get, perhaps because of extensive unemployment or because teenagers leave school with few skills.

According to my approach, people marry when they expect to get more pleasure from marriage than by remaining single and continuing to search for a better mate. The number of children a couple has depends on the costs and benefits of child rearing: Therefore, couples tend to have fewer children when the wife works and has a better-paying job, when subsidies from the government through child allowances and tax deductions for dependents are smaller, when the cost of educating and training children rises, and so forth.

By the same token, couples divorce when they no longer believe they are better off by staying married. In particular, divorce rates grow when women's earnings are higher compared with those of men; the gain to such women of remaining married is thus diminished. And the no-fault divorce laws that have become so common tend to worsen the plight of divorced women with children.

What I have tried to do in these columns during the past 6½ years is to apply the same kind of analysis to policy and social issues that are of general interest. I hope that my Nobel prize doesn't delude me into thinking I have all the answers, and I hope that my columns can continue to analyze the many social issues where the economic way of looking at life has something valuable to say.

A TRUSTBUSTER WHO SAW THE LIGHT

The death of George Stigler a few weeks ago at age 80 deprived the world of a still-active, highly creative Nobel prize-winning economist. A leader of the free-market Chicago School, his views and those of his colleagues on antitrust came to be known as the Chicago approach and enormously influenced government policies and court decisions since the early 1980s.

Early in his career, Stigler was a gung-ho activist on antitrust policy, calling for the bust-up of some monopolies and for extensive restrictions on mergers presumed to cut competition. But these positions were radically altered in the 1960s as he became convinced that antitrust enforcers often had misguided agendas. Instead of a single-minded devotion to improving competition, Stigler said, regulators respond to pressures to attack or defend "big" business, to protect small companies, and to appeals from political constituencies.

He began promoting a minimalist antitrust policy that essentially permitted all honest business practices except conspiracies to raise prices and divide markets. The way to prevent monopolistic practices, he believed, is to encourage domestic and foreign competition rather than through detailed regulation of business by the Justice Dept.

But his antitrust work was only one of many contributions to economic theory. He was the first to analyze systematically the unawareness of consumers and workers about wages and prices. His conclusions: Information about the types of jobs available and prices charged by different sellers of goods is not free; it takes time and effort to discover. He contributed to the theory of pricing by cartels such as OPEC and examined how companies adjust production methods to uncertainty about demand. Stigler also wrote about the increasing specialization of workers as the scale of production expands and why nutritional needs could be met on a pittance. The last paper demonstrated that practically all spending on food has little to do with satisfying nutritional requirements and caters instead to desire for variety and taste.

PROBING MIND. Stigler was no ivory-tower theorist who shunned policy and practical issues, although he did turn down several positions in Washington. The evolution of his thinking on antitrust policy shows an open and probing mind that lost confidence in the value of most regulation of economic activity, even when it could improve the economy.

Stigler's changing views on antitrust policy colored his approach to other regulatory agencies. In 1962, he wrote a classic paper with Chicago associate Claire Friedland on state regulation of electric utilities. It asked an absurdly simple question: Do the various state regulatory agencies achieve their intended objective of lowering the cost of electricity? After studying the evidence, Stigler and Friedland remarked on their "inability to find any significant effects of the regu-

lation of electrical utilities." Their study of the Securities & Exchange
Commission's regulations of new stock issues reached a similar conclusion.

Although subsequent research disputed some of their findings, most have
stood up well to close scrutiny. These studies stimulated a large literature that
examined whether the actual effects of civil rights legislation, welfare programs,
and countless other laws are close to their intended purposes.

Stigler asked a much deeper question: What do various regulations really aim
to achieve? His conclusion: Most agencies are "captured" by the companies
being regulated, which often are helped at the expense of the public.

LASTING LEGACY.   He and his students showed that the old Civil
Aeronautics Board prevented the introduction of any new interstate airlines; that
trucking regulation raised the cost of transporting goods; and that environmental
policies often discriminate against small businesses and against companies in the
Southwestern U.S. In essence, Stigler argued that regulations frequently make
matters worse by reducing competition.

Stigler's work contributed in a major way to the widespread disillusionment
with government-centralized direction and regulation of economic life. Socialism,
central planning, and other goals of the 1940s and 1950s sounded good on paper
but have not worked out well. This is not because of the sophomoric argument
that "true" socialism and planning have never been tried, for devastating defects
are intrinsic to systems that permit political considerations to dominate economic
ones. The decisive advantage of market systems is that they decentralize power
away from the Washingtons of the world and toward individual businessmen,
workers, and consumers.

George Stigler's lasting contributions to the analysis of public regulation and
economic theory were made with a grace, humor, a lively writing style, intellectual honesty, and a generosity that is rare. Few such intellectual giants come along
in any generation. I consider it an enormous privilege to have written several
articles with him and to number him among my closest friends. The economics
profession, the University of Chicago, and especially his friends already badly
miss this "unregulated economist"—the apt title of his memoirs.

WHY WE CAN'T LIVE
WITHOUT ECONOMISTS

Jokes about the shortcomings of economists are endless. The reason is simple.
Both business and government need guidance that only economists can provide,
especially forecasts of inflation, aggregate employment and output, and of the
effects of tax reform, the federal deficits, and other events that affect the future

of the economy. Yet—and this is the source of the jokes and criticism—such predictions are often unreliable. The fact is economists are poor at forecasting short-term changes in the economy.

The recent annual meeting of the American Economic Assn. in New Orleans spotlighted the current state of thinking about the profession's limitations, as well as its achievements. The 6,000 members in attendance could choose from over 100 sessions on many subjects. The meetings on macroeconomics, which deals with inflation and changes in aggregate output and employment in an economy, were the most popular, whether the speakers holding forth were Keynesians, monetarists, rational expectationists, or supply siders.

The extent of the disagreements at these sessions testifies to the conflicting views within macroeconomics. In one panel, four excellent economists analyzed the effects of federal deficits on the economy. Their conclusions ranged from predictions that there would be rather little effect to moderately adverse effects to sizable adverse effects. Sadly, the available evidence is too weak to permit a choice among these views. My own opinion, and I am not a specialist in macroeconomics, is that even large deficits do not damage an economy if they last for only a few years.

UNSUNG SPECIALTY. My field is microeconomics. This discipline studies how consumers, workers, and other participants in economic activities decide such economic issues as what to buy, how much to save, where to work, and how many hours to work at any given wage. Although microeconomics stirs its share of controversy, economists generally agree—and they have substantial evidence to support their view—about its basic assumption: that economic participants make rational choices. Microeconomics attracts less attention from the media than does macroeconomics, yet it has had stunning practical successes during the past decade.

Although these successes include the industry deregulation movement and several other issues, I will concentrate on two subjects popular at the recent AEA meeting: finance and law.

A revolution in thinking initiated during the 1950s replaced ad hoc precepts about financial issues with models of rational choice. One model, for example, explains how investors determine the type of securities to hold in their portfolios by analyzing the trade-offs between expected return and risk. Related models are used to analyze the effect of company debt on prices of common stock and to guide the use of options and arbitrage.

As a result of such applications, the intellectual foundations of finance have been recast into a microeconomic framework. This approach now dominates the teaching of finance. It also permeates mutual fund management and the behavior of commercial and investment banks and other financial intermediaries.

LEGAL INFLUENCE. The law and economics movement began with academic economists and lawyers who believed that economic analysis could greatly

improve antitrust policy. It has spread to all other legal fields and has also infil-
trated legal practice. Microeconomic analysis in legal decisions has grown rapidly partly because scholars of the law and economics, such as Robert H. Bork,
Frank H. Easterbrook, and Richard A. Posner, moved from academia to the
bench.

Microeconomics has also achieved great success in altering thinking about criminal
law. Claims that criminals cannot be deterred by punishment because they are mental-
ly sick or alienated from society dominated thinking about criminal justice in the
1950s and 1960s. The microeconomic approach assumes that, on the contrary, most
criminals make rational choices given their circumstances. This view has had an enormous influence on public policy and judicial decision-making during the past decade.
Hostile reaction to judges and legislators considered soft on crime and the revival of
capital punishment are part of the evidence that the microeconomic interpretation of
criminal behavior has won many followers.

This discussion explains why economists are prominent in public policy debate
and in analysis of business decisions. My attention to the important practical and
theoretical achievements of microeconomics should not suggest that macroeconomics remains stagnant. The large disagreements among macroeconomists
today is far healthier than the agreement in the 1940s and 1950s on an unrealistic
model of the economy.

Despite economics' accomplishments, the public demands more from it, especially from macroeconomics, than it can deliver at present. This conflict between
what the public wants and what economists can deliver explains why economists
continue to face ridicule at the same time they are courted by government, business, and the media.

INDEX

ABOUT THE AUTHORS

GARY S. BECKER won the Nobel Prize for Economics in 1992. Since 1985 he has written a monthly column for *Business Week*. He is also a frequent editorialist for *The Wall Street Journal* and a regular guest on such television programs as *The McNeil-Lehrer Report* and *Adam Smith's Money World*. Gary Becker is Professor of Economics and Sociology at the University of Chicago, a Fellow of the Hoover Institution, and an advisor to Presidential candidate Robert Dole.

GUITY NASHAT BECKER is Associate Professor of History at the University of Illinois at Chicago, a Fellow of the Hoover Institution, and a graduate of the Columbia University School of Journalism. She has written several books and appeared on many TV and radio programs. The Beckers live in Chicago.